Where Are All the Kids?

Teri Leonard Michaud

GREEN HEART
LIVING
— PRESS —

ISBN Paperback: 978-1-954493-70-4

Published by Green Heart Living Press

This is a work of creative nonfiction. The events are portrayed to the best of the author's memory. While all the stories in this book are true, some names and identifying details have been changed to protect the privacy of the people involved.

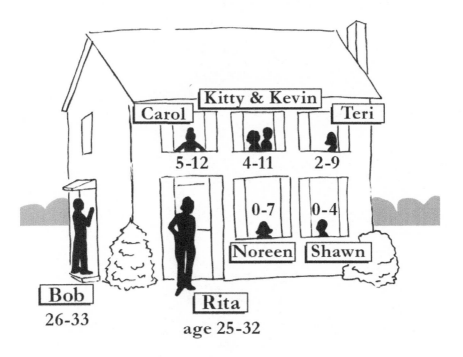

1

CASH

Kevin climbed onto the bathroom radiator, looking for bad guys, shooting his squirt gun out the open window. *"Pow. Pow. Pow.* Hey Mommy, why is Daddy lying in the bushes, smiling, and singing?"

"Get down, you crazy monkey." Rita kept her tone light, hiding her anger. Bob was two stories down, in a pool of streetlight, like a turtle on its back beside the porch steps. She scanned for new damage on his truck in the driveway.

Carol, ever Daddy's best friend, interrupted her bath to pull a towel around her skinny torso. "Daddy's hurt? Go help him, Mommy."

She nudged Rita to the side of the window, but it was too high for Carol to see below.

"He's fine. He's smiling. Get back in the water so I can wash your hair."

Carol hesitated, so Rita bribed her. "Then I'll curl it."

Kitty giggled while brushing her teeth. "Daddy's in the bushes? That's silly." She tried to join Kevin at the window, but Rita moved them around the cramped space like pawns on a chessboard, her hands on their heads.

In the back bedroom, the kids put on pajamas and crawled between threadbare sheets. Carol, Kevin, and Kitty got a quick song and a prayer, but the whole time, Rita was distracted by the giant turtle in the shrubbery.

She closed their door, then peeked in on two-year-old Teri in the crib, and eight-week-old Noreen in the bassinet. Angels. She tossed dirty laundry into a wicker basket. On top of the pile, Rita placed Carol's dress for kindergarten, Kitty's nightgown, and Kevin's dungarees with holey knees that needed mending. Rita crept down the stairs, balancing the laundry and her nagging despair.

Out of dog food, she filled a bowl with table scraps for Bruno, setting it on the back step.

Kids. Dog. Now she was ready to help Bob.

"I can't lift you, Bob. You have to turn over to stand."

Rita pressed one hand to her poufy abdomen, the other to her aching back, annoyed at being frail after giving birth. She missed the strength and speed that usually powered her day. To get Bob's attention, she called his name and kicked his boot. He smiled in a dreamy haze, impervious to the dirt he lay in, the light mist, and his recent fall.

"Hi, sweetie." Bob crinkled his eyes.

Rita bent over. "Get up you drunken fool. And be quiet. I don't want the children to wake up." It was too early for the neighbors to be sleeping on this autumn night, but a light went on next door at the Leahys', as if to mock her.

Rita bristled, "Turn over."

Bob put one foot between his planted hands, like a racer waiting for the gun. When his other foot met it, Rita lifted him by his arm. She turned away from his boozy breath to tug at his limp body. God forbid her father drive by. He hated Bob. At this moment, Rita did, too.

She took a sleeve to forcefully steer him up the steps, something she could never do if he were sober. Rita pushed him over the threshold to their home.

"Ah Rita, it's Friday night. Just a few with Joe, my only bother. *Brother.*"

He grinned sheepishly before sitting down hard on the couch opposite her. Bob was charming. My God. He was good-looking, twenty-five years old, brown eyes, tanned skin. He was fit and strong. She smiled wistfully.

"There she is, the queen of my, beauty, beautiful wife and Mother Supreme." He reached out, trying to pull her onto the couch.

Her smile faded.

"Stop acting like we're okay," Rita whispered as tears rolled down her cheeks. She wasn't raised like this, in debt, scrounging for money all the time. Rita looked beyond Bob, lolling on their scratchy brown couch, to their faded rug, the scarred maple coffee table. Everything in their home was tired. She closed her eyes, and envisioned a blue Castro Convertible sofa, and huge potted plants, then shook the magazine dream from her head.

"What's with the tears, love?"

"I want to pay the gas bill on time."

Bob jerked his head up. "Who? Who says I can't pay? They'll get a damn check when I say so."

She moved back a step, having gone too far. She'd have to stay out of his reach.

"No, no one is saying that. But Bob, I just need a little household money. Mother can lend—"

"Your *mother*? Was she here again? That old bag . . . can mind her own business, thinking her precious daughter married a bum."

He felt his pockets for cigarettes and struck a match with a calloused thumb. He inhaled deeply, using the cigarette as an underliner to his words. "I'll tell you what, baby. Just write the check. I'll put a God-damned h-hundred dollars in our account. S-soon."

Rita crossed her arms, thinking of the degrading ways she kept them afloat, buying cheap meat and patching tattered clothes. But now she had to placate him, so his anger would lessen.

"Oh, that's a clever idea. Just write a check and cover it later."

Bob's head rolled back, and he started to snore. Rita, a lefty, took the cigarette to squash out, then snaked her hand into his right trouser pocket, sliding out a mishmash of fives and tens, coins falling between the cushions. Pushing straight-armed off the couch to protect her healing body, Rita tiptoed upstairs, leaning heavily on the railing.

Early the next morning Rita, dressed in a cotton housedress, went to wake the baby. Noreen, the brown-eyed doe, their Chocolate Girl, sparkled at her. Rita's heart sang with each of her babies. Her chest rose with wonder, making her smile, tiptoe, and whisper like she was unwrapping a present each day. Rita sang "You Are My Sunshine," lifting the baby to the bureau used as a changing table. She folded the cloth diaper around Noreen's chubby legs, secured it with duckie diaper pins, pulled on tiny rubber pants. Rita dropped her head into the baby's stomach to elicit a happy gurgle.

Noreen kicked her feet as she grasped her mother's cascade of brown hair.

"Come on, let's get you a bottle, angel."

On the landing outside Noreen's room, Kitty and Teri were hopping around in pillows Rita stripped from the beds for Saturday's laundry.

"Can we slide down the stairs in the *pidlow* cases?" Kitty asked, her eyes bright with hope.

"No. How could you? Why would you?" Rita laughed. She draped the baby over her arm and moved them along. "Come, girls. Breakfast."

Slipper-footed pajamas slapped down the stairs ahead of her, as Kevin ran up, wearing a cowboy hat and a holster slung over his skinny hips.

"Stick 'em up." A silver cap gun was drawn, pointed at Rita.

"Oh, but I can't, sir. I've got a little baby here," Rita pleaded. "Where're you going?"

"To see Daddy in your room. He called you, but you *diddin'* go, so I did. He wants these." He whipped out a pack of smokes from his holster. "I got matches, too."

"Oh, no, you don't." Rita took the cigarettes and matches from Kevin. "I'll bring these to Daddy. You get Carol, then go down. Grandma will be here any minute."

Rita turned around mid-staircase as kids streamed by her in both directions. She switched Noreen to her left arm, slid the contraband matches into her pocket, and went to see how hung over her husband was. Bob sat on the edge of their brass bed in boxer shorts, his skinny bowed legs stuck into old slippers. His T-shirt was white—he was a clean man—but his eyes were bloodshot, and his hands trembled.

"Where's my little buddy?" Bob rasped.

"Forbidden from delivering matches. He's four years old, for God's sake."

She slapped the goods on the dresser, glancing at him in the mirror, ready for Bob's humble, useless apologies. Rita grimaced, thinking back to Bob's suggestion to just write bad checks. Bob would be ashamed of himself once he remembered, or didn't remember, the night before.

He gave a knowing nod and asked to hold Noreen.

"She might spit up on you." Rita hoped she would.

Bob responded, "Ha, I might spit up on myself."

"I'm not ready for your jokes yet. Maybe later when you've flogged yourself enough."

Rita left to heat the baby's bottle, organize breakfast for the rest of the kids, and to check if Mother had arrived. When she came back, Bob was walking around the room, holding tiny Noreen in his arms, explaining the big brass bed he got while on a job.

"This was from a mansion on South Whitney Street. They wanted something new. Ha, I knew Mommy would like this. I brought it home in boxes. Mommy and I put this together and polished it until it gleamed. Took two months."

Rita returned with a coffee for him and a bottle for Noreen, meeting Bob's gaze. She did love that bed.

Bob held a corner of their quilt. "We got this Double Ring quilt for a wedding present. It means your marriage goes on forever and ever." He rubbed a gentle finger down her button nose. "You'll inherit this, being my only daughter with brown eyes. Smart move, Noreen, looking like your dad."

He was a tile setter by trade, and renovated kitchens and bathrooms in big houses, nights and weekends. Rita didn't like knick-knacks, but sometimes, he'd be offered something she'd enjoy, like the pair of cobra-shaped candlesticks on their mantle.

Rita fed Noreen in the Boston rocker, watching Bob lift his pants from the footboard, cringing at the ground-in dirt at the knees. He swallowed hard, then lumbered to the hamper to drop them in.

"How bad was it . . . was I . . . last night?"

"I don't know how much you drank, or how much you gambled, or how much money you wasted. You were swearing and yelling, slurring your words. You fell off the porch."

Bob fingered his scratched elbow, shaking his head, not surprised by any of this. He ran his fingers through his thinning hair.

"That's the evidence of your decisions, Bob. But more importantly, the children wait for you. I told them you were still working, so we ate supper without you. And I wait for you. I wait for . . . your company and your paycheck. You insulted Mother as well in your ramblings. I couldn't get through a day without my mother . . . not one day. And I think she doesn't feel well."

"Oh, God, I'm sorry, I'm sorry." He reached out to rub her arm. "I was at the Beacon. I didn't get that raise . . . so, it was a pity party. Party of one. Then my brother Joe and the firehouse guys came in . . . buying drinks for the Leonard brothers."

She clucked her tongue. "And then you had to buy a round for the guys?"

Bob shrugged his shoulders.

Rita pulled a ten-dollar bill out of her pocket and held it out to him, keeping $75. He knew better than to ask. He brought her free hand to his lips, kissing it.

"This little baby needs you." Rita pulled her hand away. "They all do. I need you, Bob. I pray to God you stop drinking."

"I pray too. I'll stop. This time, I will stop. You deserve so, so much."

When they both stood, Rita folded into Bob's embrace, with the baby between them, and he gently rocked them all. But his red eyes, parched lips, and shaking hands reminded Rita that she had work to do. Next Friday, she'd meet him at work, to stop him from heading to a bar.

2

STORM

Bob came straight home after work all of that chilly New England autumn. Under Rita's watchful eye, he controlled his drinking. The holidays would be hard. He wanted to stay home, skip church, and forgo the party, but every year they went to Rita's parents' house for Christmas Day. He'd have to bestow fake warmth on his father-in-law, and go easy on the cocktails, with Kieran judging Bob's every move.

Christmas morning, Carol, Kitty, and Kevin tore down the stairs at six, pulling each other back, trying to be first to the living room, knowing Santa visited in the night. Rita was behind them, carrying Noreen and leading a sleepy Teri by the hand.

Bob knelt near the tree to plug in the lights. He paused a minute, hidden by the pine boughs, as his children widened their eyes and dropped their chins at the pile of presents. Their excitement was infectious, raising Bob's spirits.

He bought their scrawny tree from a gas station lot. Rita's dad was a landscaper with access to trees, but Bob didn't want a handout. Rita and the kids decorated it with silver tinsel, random bulbs, and the pinecone ornament Carol made with Miss Rosetta.

The children squinted at names scrawled on little white tags, though none of them could read. Once Rita handed out presents, they ripped papers and threw ribbons to the floor. Bob and Rita sat on the couch directing the big kids, holding the little ones on their laps. Each child opened pajamas, two toys, and a coat or a pair of boots.

This was the happy, controlled chaos Bob liked. He helped Teri unwrap a stuffed panda bear.

Bob wanted to be with his family, light a fire, and listen to Nat King Cole sing "O! Holy Night" on the record player. Maybe they could at least go late to dinner.

Rita handed Bob a gift, a brown terry-cloth bathrobe. "This is very Marlon Brando," she smiled, "I hope you like it."

"I hope I wear it as well as Brando." Bob gave Rita a long Christmas kiss. He traced a finger from her ear to her chin, then handed Rita the package wrapped in G. Fox & Co.'s signature paper and an oversized bow. It was a subtly shimmering green plaid dress, nipped at the waist, with a black velvet belt and collar.

"A dress to show off your post-baby figure. You'll look gorgeous in that. Sure we can't stay home today?"

She nestled into Bob. "I'm sure. But there's always tonight." She tilted her head, stirring him to the core.

Bob shaved, dreading having to go to Mass *and* the party. "Yeesh, what a way to wreck a holiday," he grumbled, flicking foam off the razor.

In the front hall, he pulled on a weary wool coat. Christmas 1958 dawned cold, and Bob had doubted the Fairlane would start, so he parked face-out in the driveway for a running jump. He blew on his fingers and turned the key. It started. He patted the dashboard in thanks when the engine warmed up, because Rita looked so forward to her version of the perfect Christmas Day.

Bob loaded the car with food, presents, a diaper bag, and a coffee urn. It was a disaster getting out in the snow and slush, and Bob's black rubber boots leaked. The children were useless. They were alternately playing and fighting over the new doctor kit, eating ribbon candy, and teasing the dog.

"Who let that mangy mutt in?" Bob raised his voice, knocking snow off his shoulders, shuffling into the living room.

"I did," said Kevin, dangling Kitty's new Raggedy Ann just out of Bruno's snapping reach.

"Why? He's an outside dog. He has a doghouse. Take him out." Bob was getting irritated at the mess and noise and doing everything himself. He exhaled through his nose.

"He likes me. He wants to stay." Kevin patted Bruno's head, calming him.

"You little sh—" He stopped himself in case Rita was listening. "Yeah, well, pal, he can't stay inside. He chews table legs and shoes." Bob cracked his knuckles, getting his anger in check. "He might eat your new boots. Do you want that? Or your new bow-and-arrow set? Huh? Bruno will chew all the stuff in this room." Bob ended his tirade like a joke, but also a possibility.

Kevin's little lip pulled down. Bob touched his son's shoulder, remembering it was Christmas. "How about I put him in the cellar, this one time, while we're at the party?"

Kevin smeared the lone tear that snuck out of his eye. He nodded.

Bob yelled at the rest of the house, "Let's go, for the love of Pete."

He helped Kitty and Teri into coats and carried them to the car, where he drummed the steering wheel as the others drifted out.

Kevin bounced down the steps wearing his new winter boots, but he wore a summer jacket. Carol's tights were falling down at the crotch, but she was making good time. Rita looked resplendent in an old coat over her new dress. Baby Noreen, the little bunny, was dressed in a blue quilted car suit.

The family looked well put together, making him proud. He smiled. The car was warm, and the windshield wipers were doing a valiant job. The family sat in their usual spots, with Bob at the wheel, and Rita holding Noreen on her lap. In the backseat, Carol kept peace between the twins, Kitty and Kevin. Teri stood up. They had to allow room to pick up plump Aunt Rose.

The family filled the church pew. They kneeled, sat, and stood, repeatedly, which Aunt Rose did piously. Bob went through the motions, setting an example to wriggling children. To get through this charade with the promise of tonight, Bob tried to catch Rita's eye in camaraderie, but she was clawing the squirming kids apart. Rita fake-smiled to the nuns and neighbors, her nostrils flared in annoyance as she herded the children through the throng after the final hymn. To change her mood, he offered to bring the car around, kissing Rita's cheek.

Bob palmed his hat onto his head and moved toward the parking lot, thankful to be outside, one of his Christmas chores done, one to go, all to be home with Rita that night. He creaked the frozen door open to slide onto the driver's seat, and now the rusting hulk of a car wouldn't start. Inside and out, the frosted windshield was opaque. Bob rolled his window down to whistle to neighbors as they clomped toward their cars.

"Hey, Tony, Marty. Could you give me a push?"

The two guys stepped into slushy ruts to push the back end of the Ford. Bob's breath was pluming, and his fingers were frigid on the wheel and gear shifter.

"Go," he yelled. They pushed as Bob popped the clutch to get a bang and a start. He revved it in neutral, charging the battery, then let it idle. Taking a flask out of his coat pocket, Bob stepped into the rutty parking lot and held it out to Tony and Marty.

"Merry Christmas, fellas." While their cars warmed up, so did the three dads. What was the harm of a little nip, when Bob had the entire day to pace himself?

Rita's whole family gathered at Kathleen and Kieran's home. Her sisters, Mary Alice, with Mac and their four kids; Nancy and Jack, with their three kids, and the youngest Horan daughter, Carolyn, too old to be a kid, too young to be an adult.

Aunt Rose helped to stock the buffet table with a huge roast turkey.

The sideboard bar was loaded with a paltry amount of ice in a bucket, but whiskey, rye, and port were in abundance. There was a plaid cooler filled with beer. Bob planned on sticking to beer, so he'd be relatively sober at this family event. He shook hands all around, but his eyes were on Rita.

"Look at that dress. Wow, wow, wow." Mac greeted Rita with his perceived Southern charm and actual Southern accent.

All of the Horan daughters married Irish Americans. Nancy, fashionable and witty, was usually the center of attention, but Rita was glowing. Bob winked at his wife, and she gave a little wave and mouthed "*Behave*," their new codeword for being careful what he drank. He planned on being the perfect husband and father to get Rita to leave here sooner, so he could stop acting like he gave a shit about all her relatives.

Irish music by Bing Cosby wafted from the Hi-Fi. The parlor smelled of wet wool, overcooked turkey, and a bit of the older folks' body odor. Jack handed Bob a highball of rye and ginger. The adults got louder singing Christmas carols as the eating and drinking went on. Rita got silly. She and her sisters joked about Christmases past. They sipped whiskey sours and giggled. Bob settled back in his chair, knowing a tipsy Rita would forget to monitor him.

Rita envied Nancy and Mary Alice's elegance with their cigarettes, although she didn't smoke. Whenever her sisters tied a shoe or cut meat for one of their kids, they would stick the cigarette between red lips and squint their eyes to complete the task. They puffed, laughed hysterically, then blew the smoke out.

Rita watched Bob. The men sat in clumps and told well-crafted, lengthy stories or limericks that had dirty endings. They slapped each other's backs, coughing, interrupting. Was Bob over-laughing? Was he drinking too much? Rita put down her drink, twisting her hands.

The snow was falling and so was the night. One cousin slept on the pile of coats; another threw up into the tub. Siblings started to fight and cry. A new toy got broken. It was time to go home. Rita stuffed her kids into coats and mittens and gathered presents from godparents. She had to get Bob out of there.

Bob put his coat on, took Rita's hat from the stand, and clapped it on his head. Nancy and Jack roared from his antics. He switched it out for the right one, but he couldn't get one hand out of his pants pocket. It was clenched around his keys. He looked confused; he swayed.

"I'll drive," Rita said, suddenly quite sober.

"No, no, no . . . I'm fine." He managed to get his keys out, saying, "Thank you, all, for a l-lovely party."

He walked onto the porch, then slid down the ice-covered steps, mostly on his heels. He fell at the bottom, which Rita saw, but hoped her parents had not. She prayed he would get to the car, and it would start. He did, and it did.

By the time Rita gathered the children, sixty-year-old Kieran was outside chipping ice with a pick. He reached out a hand as she side-stepped with the baby wrapped in her arms.

"Watch it here, *Reeta*." Kieran took her elbow.

Aunt Rose stomped down the steps, determined to hold onto two-year-old Teri. Kevin skirted the helping uncles by scrambling over a snow mound, then hopped into the waiting car. Rita faced the backseat to organize the ride home. "Climb over, Carol, to come sit with Daddy and me. Rose, hold Noreen."

Kitty, Kevin, and Teri snuggled into Rose's bulk, sleepy after the long day. The heater whimpered to life. Bob rocked the car to dislodge it from the icy roadside. He shifted forward, reverse, forward, as tires whirred in a high pitch, and then shot ahead. He stomped the brake pedal. Rita threw her arm out to keep Carol from smacking her head on the metal dashboard.

"Bob. *Bob*," Rita warned, putting a hand on the wheel, "not so fast. Want me to drive?"

He swatted it off and shifted into gear. The car wobbled, then hit the curb. "Damn snow," he muttered.

The car moved to the center of the road. Rita drew in a sharp breath, focusing on the bright lights in their path, also in the center of the road. Bob cut to the right, the other driver's horn bulling through the dark. Rita heard Rose being tossed around, a yelp escaping her lips, and the baby was crying.

Carol, sitting at his elbow said, "Daddy, I can't see the road. I need to be higher up."

"You don't have to, Carol. I'm drivin', not you." He wasn't smiling at her.

"Daddy, look out there."

Rita saw what Carol saw. "Bob, there's a stop sign. Brake, brake!"

"Shut up. Shut up. . . . uhn . . . ah, shit." Bob sailed through the intersection, which was empty, thank God.

Carol buried her face into Rita's wool-coated armpit. They hit a pothole with a thunk, and three shrieks erupted from the backseat.

"What was that?" Kitty pulled forward to grab Carol's collar.

"We can't see, Daddy and me. We can't see the road, with the snow." She pushed Kitty's hand away, concentrating.

Rose sat forward, squishing Noreen with her giant bosom. She pulled Kitty back and shoved her next to Kevin, who placed an arm around Teri.

"Bobby. Bobby, let Rita drive."

Rita twisted in her seat. "Let me drive the children home, honey."

Bob snorted and hiccupped. "You can't drive at now . . . night . . . night. Drive like shit at night." He stepped on the accelerator, going too fast but not seeming to care about kids falling off the seat and getting knocked around.

"Oomph," Teri, two, yipped in surprise as she hit the floor.

"Stay on the floor, then, Teri. Kitty, stop whining." Bob glanced around the car. All the girls were crying.

"I can drive, Bob. Yes, honey, please . . . pull over. I can see well enough." Rita reached across Carol to get his attention, patting his coat sleeve.

Kevin dared to speak. "Daddy, you're too drunk to—" He dodged Bob's fisted blow, which landed on the seat right above Carol's head, as they skidded crazily in the road. Rita held Carol close.

"Rose, stop crying, you're scaring the *shildren*." Bob bellowed, then whispered, "You old bat." He snickered.

"Please, Daddy," Carol said, oh-so-small, her face pensive, hopeful, because she loved her father. "Please, Daddy. Let Mommy drive."

Bob glanced at his Carol, twisting a button on her coat.

Please, do it for her, Rita prayed.

He slowed the car, moving it toward the edge of the snowy street. Bob rolled to a stop and pulled the handbrake. The car stalled out.

"Rita, it's clearly . . . it's nearly . . . " He couldn't get out what he meant to say. "You never drove in a *blizzar*. You gotta be sure . . . careful to drive."

Rita faced Bob, swallowing hard. "We'll be safer if you walk, and the cold air will do you good."

Even Carol nodded yes. Bob got out. He buttoned his coat, fixed his hat, then climbed over the snowbank to the sidewalk. He had no gloves, so shoved his hands into his pockets. Bob started tilting and slipping home on that snowy Christmas night. He was too drunk to drive, but at least now with Bob walking, nobody would get hurt.

Rita had lip-trembling Carol sit by the window, off-duty, and told Kevin to climb over to help, because his anger needed a job. Straightening her spine, she depressed the clutch. She could do this. And she knew the damn car would start this time. God owed her this one.

Despite Rose's protests, Rita dropped her off at home.

Rita was driving fine, going slowly, and signaling early for the turns. In her own driveway, she unclenched her hands. She woke the sleeping children and told them to walk inside themselves. She could carry only the baby. Rita helped them into new Christmas pajamas, and into beds and cribs, then remembered to let Bruno out of the basement, and into the backyard for a cold minute.

While gathering wrapping papers from the floor, Rita heard the door open and exhaled in relief. Bob had made it home.

He stood wavering in the hall, a bloody, weeping mess.

Rita put one hand to her mouth before leading him to a wooden kitchen chair. He managed to tell her he'd been walking home with his hands in his pockets, then tripped and fell face-first on the iced sidewalk, smashing his nose.

Rita took shallow breaths to calm down and gather strength to doctor this moron. Ice wasn't the culprit here. It was his own fault. Rita wet a dishcloth with warm water and tried to clean his mangled face. Her hands shook and saliva collected in her mouth, as she blotted gently.

"Your nose is broken. I'll call your brother Joe. He can take you to the hospital."

Rita was glad someone else could see how bad Bob got. Let his brother manage him for a change. The hospital would keep Bob overnight, or perhaps longer.

A glimmer of hope tugged at her lips. A few days without him would be a relief.

3

RAT

I n the early hours of December 26, 1958, Bob was admitted, against his will, to Hartford Hospital after having his broken nose set. It was no big deal, as he wasn't staying. He was wheeled to an overheated room, where falling snow was illuminated under a streetlight outside. Seeing that, Bob remembered he had to be home because it was some special day.

He pushed the nurse's hand away as she tried to take his temperature. Two orderlies were called to assist, but Bob lurched out of the wheelchair, and turned to confront them. "Unhand me, you lunatics. It's Chris . . . Christmas time . . . I gotta go home." He wanted to see his son and daughters playing with their new toys under their tree. And he had a new bathrobe.

A doctor walked into the small space, glancing at Bob's intake form and waved the orderlies and nurse out. "Yes, you do. You have to get home. Why don't I call you a cab? I'm Dr. Paul. I'll give you some medicine, then make that call."

Bob sat down on the proffered bed, calmer, and swallowed two pills. He liked watching the snow fall, but his eyes kept closing. The bed was soft and warm. "Hey, Doc, I'll just . . . lie back here until the c-cab comes."

"All right, Mr. Leonard. You'll feel better when you've rested." Dr. Paul uncapped his pen to scratch notes in his chart. Bob slept the sleep of the very medicated.

He woke to an IV line in his left arm, and a well-bandaged broken nose that hurt. It was morning. He'd been duped into staying. He sweated through his johnny and ripped the ties trying to get it off. He had the chills. His head ached, his mouth was dry, his eyes watered. He vomited, had dry heaves, fell asleep, then bolted upright in bed. He had to get home. Or maybe Rita could come here? Whenever Bob's door swung open, he turned to face her, to greet Rita. He'd go home to her right now, but he was too sick. Had she given up on him? Bob slipped between being asleep and awake, tormented.

On the third day, Dr. Paul pulled a chair close to Bob's metal bed. "How are you feeling?"

"I feel great. I just need a ride home . . . kinda cold out. Plus, I could use a smoke." Bob was trying to be charming to get out of this place. He had to check on his marriage. His family. His life.

Dr. Paul began, "We can't let you go yet—" He held out an arm to keep Bob in bed. "What I'd like to do is go over some of your options, so you can . . . you know, go home. Start over."

"Yeah, Doc, that's what I'm gonna do." Bob missed sleeping near Rita, wearing his own clothes, shaving in his own bathroom, with Kevin propped on the radiator, watching him. He wanted to get back to giving the girls piggyback rides and eating Rita's pot roast. Bob scratched his stubble and tapped the tape holding his nose together. He cringed standing up, then slowly walked around the room, holding onto furniture, looking for his pants. "I want to see my wife."

The doctor said it would be best to stay a few more days, as Bob needed to detoxify the alcohol from his body. With sagging shoulders, Bob agreed. "I'll stay. I'll stay a couple more days. I'm no good to her right now . . . you got a plan, Doctor?" He lay back on the bed and shut his eyes.

"Number one: continue keeping you in the hospital for rest, fluids, and a balanced diet, and be given anti-anxiety pills. Number two: Give you paraldehyde. Enough to knock you out for a few days, enough time to diminish your desire for alcohol consumption."

Bob opened his eyes. "That might work. Sleep through it . . . sounds like a dream . . . get it?"

Paul twisted his mouth. "It's not that easy. There are drawbacks." He put a hand on Bob's shoulder. "The drug has a pungent odor that'll make you nauseated. It's also administered rectally. Plus, it's bad for your lungs, and you're a smoker."

"A . . . a . . . up my bum? Hell, no, no . . . I'd rather be a rum hound." Bob bristled with insult. He would not do any of that. Blood coursed through his brain, pounding his recently re-set nose. "You're outta your ever-loving mind."

"I can refer you to some people in AA. Alcoholics Anonymous. They rely on a higher power, take the pain away from you and give it to God." The doctor held out a hand.

Bob pushed it away, turning his face to the glittering scene outside. The radiator hissed. "I had a God, Dr. Paul. I had a God. He has forsaken *me*. He's *left* me. I said my prayers, went to church . . . I have been . . . I've been on my knees asking him for help. In a back alley, in my truck, in my basement . . . alone, on my knees." His chin quivered. "I'll stay a while. But I'm doing this my way when I get out. *With my wife*. Not your drugs, not your programs, and not your God. Rita depended on me, believed in me. I've got to get that back. I gotta be a better man."

"Mr. Leonard, sounds like you have a champion in your corner, in your wife."

Bob glanced at the doctor. "She's strong. I don't know what I'll do if she's had enough. I can't do this without her. Any of it."

Rita's stomach flip-flopped as she spoke with Bob on the phone. Their polite conversation was about his care, then the logistics of his cousin Fran picking him up. Rita didn't know how to feel and didn't want to talk about his hospital stay until she did understand. Was he a heavy drinker, or, a word she was afraid to say, an alcoholic?

She plugged the vacuum in, moaning as she bent over. With a newborn, she shouldn't be working this hard, but the whirring of the machine blocked the kids' noise. They were playing with plastic soldiers in a fort under the dining room table and Noreen was cuddled in her Swing-o-Matic.

Rita could think, driving straight rows over the old carpet.

She dreaded Bob's return. This past week, there'd been order. The family ate simple meals the children loved. Bedtimes were peaceful. Rita didn't worry about a nosy neighbor or a dented fender. Money stayed in her pocket. Rita didn't miss his mood swings, or the sound of his retching before vomiting in the toilet. Could Bob stop drinking? Would he change?

Rita moved into the kitchen. It was neat, as Mother had been there this morning. Rita dried the dishes in the rack, forcing herself to think of what she missed about Bob, wanting to be fair. She loved his laugh and sense of humor, like when he wore her apron and danced with a mop. He worked hard and was a good dad when he was sober. His strong arms were tight when kissing her and tousling her hair. His masculine scent was a mix of sawdust, fresh cigarettes, and Old Spice aftershave. A blush warmed her cheeks.

Rita's pleasant reverie was interrupted by a faint scratching. She stopped drying a plate and tipped her head to listen. Nothing. Maybe it was just Bruno clawing to get in.

Rita began to clean the pantry by putting a sudsy dishpan on the counter and climbing a step stool with a clean cloth diaper over her shoulder. Moving cereal boxes around, she wiped down every sticky shelf. Her ears perked up when she heard that sound again, like fingernails on a chalkboard. She stopped short. There was a ragged hole in the front of the Ritz cracker box, as if a child sawed through it with a plastic knife. The scratching was joined by a slight wobble of the box.

"What in the world is this?"

She pushed soup cans aside and cocked her ear to the shelf. Whiskers, white and probing, emerged from the hole, attached to a wet and pointed brown nose, followed by two big, yellow teeth. It was the face of a . . . a rat! Rita shrieked, falling off the stool, which clattered on the linoleum and knocked over the basin of soapy water. She landed on her butt, then crab-walked to the doorway in her struggle out of the confined space.

"A rat!" she screamed. A disgusting, flea-bitten, chewing, dirty rat had gotten into her home, her kitchen, her food.

Kids came streaming onto the scene.

"There's a rat, children, move, go," she directed. Scrambling to her feet, Rita pushed the kids into the front room, then guided them a few steps up the staircase. "Stay there."

She ran to check on Teri in the playpen, and Noreen in her swing, both of them off the living room floor. She leapt back to the stairs and stretched over the railing to reach the rotary phone.

"What is it? What happened?" Kitty blanched, then shrieked. She grabbed Rita's skirt and twisted the fabric into a swirl. "Call Daddy."

"Kitty. Shh. Quiet. Grandma is closer." Rita spoke into the receiver, asking the operator for Adam 296. Kevin snuck around Rita and was climbing outside the banister for a better look. Kitty escalated to loud blubbering.

Rita was squeaking into the mouthpiece, "Mother. Mother. Come quick. There's a rat in my house."

"Stay where you are," Mother's calm voice washed over Rita like a wave, "and stop that child's blathering. I'll be right there."

Rita smooshed Kitty's cheeks together and told her loudest child to be quiet. Grandma was coming to take care of the rat. They didn't need Daddy right now.

Kevin's eyes lit up. "Listen."

Rita heard the furtive chewing of cardboard by their unwanted guest, so steadied her own hands by clasping Kitty's.

Carol wanted to know what the rat looked like.

Kevin volunteered to find out. He could see into the pantry by straddling the staircase and the kitchen doorknob. It was a straight view from there.

"It's kinda waving his paws around when he sits up."

Rita cringed thinking what she might have served with rodent germs on it. Biscuits, pancakes, pie crusts. She held her breath. The gnawing continued, so Rita braved a peek. The rat's whiskers waved about, its teeth chomping, and its beady eyes moved back and forth in the box's opening.

"Hey. I liked those Ritz." Kevin bucked his teeth and wrinkled his nose, hanging off the railing by one arm. Carol laughed at his rodent imitations.

Mother burst in the front door with a spade in one hand, and a dust bin in the other. Her purse, as always, hung from her elbow. "Where is it?"

"The pan . . . the pan . . . the pantry."

Rita was glad to have Mother lead the fight.

She marched in, put her purse on the table, the dust bin on the floor, and entered the pantry.

Kevin leapt from his perch to follow her. Rita trailed behind him, then came Carol. Kitty stayed on the stairs, watching from a safe distance.

Mother knocked the wrecked box from the shelf with the spade. The box, loose crackers, cans of soup, and rat tumbled to the floor. Carol and Kevin came forward to witness the assault. It scrambled to run away, but Mother clubbed the spade onto the rat, flattening it, the crackers, and smashing the potty chair, an innocent bystander. Its body was a flat mass of oily black fur, bloody guts, a skinny bald tail, and claws.

"He'll not be bothering you now, Rita. You have to show 'em who's the boss."

"Wowie," Kevin admired, "can I touch it?"

"No, you ninny, it's full of fleas and disease," Grandma *pffted* at Kevin while she scooped the rat mess into the dustbin, which clanged shut.

Mother started to giggle. When Rita finally closed her mouth, she burst out laughing. The kids laughed, too. They tittered at Kitty's crying, at Kevin wanting to touch the dead rat, at Mommy's fear of something tiny, and at Grandma's bravery.

After dumping the dustbin into the garbage can outside, Mother stayed with Rita for a cup of coffee, time they rarely shared. The children went back to their fort.

"Two things, Rita. One, when are you going to stop calling me to solve your problems?"

"I always call you, Mother, because you always come," Rita dropped her eyes. "You always know what to do. I don't know how to handle a rat. What if it got into the baby's cereal," Rita suppressed a gag, "or the flour? That's disgusting. I feel like a dirty housekeeper."

"Ah, they're all over the place, even at my rental apartments. But you'll still have to clean that pantry. Take everything out, check the shelves."

Of course, Rita would finish the pantry, the things smashed by Mother's shovel, the boxes, cans, and the potty chair, but it was annoying to be told what to do. Rita put out a glass sugar bowl and creamer, poured coffee, and sat across from Mother, who then laced into her.

"Two, what did you tell the children about Bob?"

Rita fiddled with her sugar spoon, then took it to the sink, to turn her face, her whole body, away.

"I told them he tripped . . . and got hurt. That he was in the hospital and would be home soon. Carol made him a 'Get Well' card."

"And what about you?" Mother scraped her chair out to face Rita.

"What can I do, Mother?" Sitting back down, Rita ran her thumbnail down the seam in the yellow Formica tabletop, clearing out bits of gunk. What about me? Rita thought. I want a whole man who can quit his bad habits and love his wife and children.

Mother returned to her original position and stirred her coffee. "You remember that Daddy warned you? About marrying Bob."

"That's not helpful now. I phoned Father Fitzgerald." The Catholic church didn't allow divorce. But she'd hoped for some decent advice, at least. "He reminded me of our wedding vows. For better or worse. But priests don't know what it's like to be married."

Mother's head popped up. "They know about church law, Catholic law. What did the priest say? You didn't say anything to him about splitting apart, did you? That can't be done, you know that." Her mother squared her back now, aiming to drive home her point.

Rita was flustered and embarrassed, the blush rising on her cheeks, but not in a pleasant way this time. She hadn't said that to anyone, but she'd thought about it. Often.

"What more can I do?"

"He's got to stop drinking liquor. You have to find a way to make him stop, or he'll be your financial ruin. He will ruin your family."

The baby started fussing, waking from her nap in the swing. Rita was grateful for the interruption, ending this painful lecture. Mother, pale, stood and collected her purse, then walked to the back door, where she'd left the dirty shovel and bin. Rita dutifully thanked her for coming.

She changed Noreen's diaper and wondered what else she could do. Why *did* she rely on her mother? Was Rita to blame for Bob's drinking? Was she too weak?

Rita put Noreen in the baby carriage and rolled it into the kitchen. Noreen giggled and kicked happily while Rita finished washing shelves, pots, boxes, and tins. Rita threw out the flour and sugar, not knowing if the rat prowled those shifting depths in paper bags. She knocked a broom handle into crevices in the pantry, warily looking for any hole a rat could crawl through. As Mother had rid the house of the rat, Rita vowed to rid her home of alcohol and to watch Bob like a hawk as soon as he got home from the hospital.

She packed peanut butter and jelly sandwiches into a basket. Rita swaddled Noreen and then handed her to Carol. She crawled into the fort to have a winter picnic with the children before afternoon nap time.

Ruin? Rita was not about to let Bob ruin this family.

4

BED

That evening, Kevin excitedly retold the rat story, pretending he killed the varmint, but promised Carol and Kitty the ghost rat would be back, then crawled under their beds, scratching and sniffing. Kitty and Carol laughed, screeched, and threw their pillows at him.

Rita, setting her hair in rollers, called for them to quiet down. She then sat on their old couch with a *Reader's Digest Condensed Book*, but the book fell open on her lap. Had *she* failed? Her anger at Bob was lessening, but she still wanted to shake sense into him. What was his need to get drunk, to turn evil, mean, ugly? Sipping her tea, she stretched her feet out to the coffee table. How could she help Bob, other than hiding his alcohol? What was she missing?

They used to laugh a lot. That's what she liked about him at first. She was shy. He coaxed her to tell a joke or make a flip remark, and Bob laughed with her. They were madly in love when they married at 18, had Carol eight months later, then twins and two more babies within six years. As he failed to become more responsible with each additional child, she got more . . . what? Determined? Aloof? Headstrong? Did she devote so much time to the children that she ignored him? Who could she talk to about the intimacies of marriage, except her sister Nancy? She'd brave the call. Rita had no saliva, so took a sip of tea and turned down the lamp.

"You're a slave driver, Rita. You tell him what to do, even in front of other people."

"I do not. What are you talking about?"

"Do you, or do you not, tell the man how to deal with Daddy? Or tell him how to dress? Which, by the way, he always looks nice at parties."

Rita dropped her chin, pausing a moment to think. "Bob needs telling. To talk to Daddy, who always makes Bob feel like dirt. I try to talk him through—"

Nancy stopped listening, "Oh, by the way, are you going out on New Year's Eve? Bob will be home by then, right?"

"That's beside the point, whether we're going. I don't know if he'll be out of the hospital—" Rita was cut off again.

Nancy snorted. "You work at the hospital two nights a week, right? Find out some things, such as: when he is being discharged, and what the doctors wrote in his chart about you."

"Me? What does that matter?" Rita's voice rose. "Bob's the one with the drinking problem."

"Listen, little sister, they *all* have drinking problems. Maybe you're a nag, with too much church crap."

"How can you say 'church crap' after how we were raised? Nancy, there are rituals and prayers that we learned to keep us, I don't know, good." She needed advice on love and sex and marriage, and Nancy was talking about church.

"So what? You want to be good? Boring. Were you thinking about the church when you seduced Bob?"

"I did not seduce him." Rita pressed her hand on her chest thinking of that possibility.

Nancy crinkled her cigarette box wrapper and snapped open a lighter. "You wanted 'it', and you wanted him, way before you should have. Do you remember coming into my bedroom? You were, what, 17? You knelt by my bed to wake me."

Rita patted her curlers. "No, no . . . I don't remember that." She blushed in the darkened living room.

Nancy was enjoying this. "You said, 'I've just gone to heaven with the most amazing man.' You were all, how shall we say this, 'aglow'?"

She did remember that night, and a warmth washed over her. "Yes. Yes, I remember. I was in love."

"Are you still?" Nancy waited.

Rita exhaled audibly, "Yes."

"So that brings me back to my point. See what's in his hospital chart. Does he resent you—do you 'drive him to drink'? Or does he think you can help him stop? I'll say now what I said then. Don't get caught. And Rita, when your husband gets home, seduce him. Again."

"Um, oh. I can do that. Yes, that's a good idea." Rita's face flamed, but she liked the challenge. "I know what *not* to wear. I'll call you after to tell you how it went."

Nancy hooted. "Yes, do that, I'll be waiting by my phone."

Aunt Rose came over to babysit the next time Rita had a night shift as a switchboard operator at Hartford Hospital.

Her sister-in-law Pat was a floor nurse. While Bob slept, Pat jotted pertinent notes. Waiting in the hall, Rita peered into his room, gasping at how fragile he looked in blue hospital pajamas. Except for purple raccoon eyes, he was peaceful. His arms rested by his sides, not flung out like at home, and he wasn't snoring. Pat passed the folded note to Rita, pulled his door shut, then kept walking.

The doctor's three choices for recovery help (refused), PT states wife will help him get sober: 'If she can't, no one can.' Confinement to end 12/30/1959. Rita pondered this her whole shift. He needs me. He believes in me, in my help. Pat had told Rita the options that Bob was facing, and Rita agreed she was the best chance to help Bob stay sober.

Cousin Fran drove Bob home the day before New Year's Eve. The children were dressing for outside play. Rita received both men politely, and kept the kids from swarming their father. She poured coffee and sliced a warm Bundt cake, made from a box because she had no flour. Kevin took the largest piece, staring at his father's bandages across his nose and the half-moons below his eyes.

Rita sat awkwardly, glad the kids jostled for cake and attention.

Fran reminded Rita and Bob of the New Year's Eve dinner dance at the Hilton Hotel. They had a reservation with ten friends, who were mostly relatives.

Fran shook Bob's hand goodbye, and warned, "Be good."

Bob lifted Kitty, in her snow pants and boots, onto his knee. She had her worried look on. "Your eyes are purple. Do they hurt?"

"Were you in a fight?" Kevin zipped his jacket.

"Yeah, you should've seen the other guy." Bob smiled, lightly punching Kevin's shoulder.

"Bob." Rita's concern for the children clipped his joke. "Daddy fell, that's all."

"No, no fight, Kevin, I was kidding. I fell and hit my head. Good thing it's hard." He rapped his skull.

Carol padded to her room in a snowsuit, coming back with a crayoned card, "For you, Daddy."

When the kids went outside, Bob and Rita sat staring at the floor. "You start," she said. "Tell me why you were drunk at a family Christmas party."

"Jack kept pouring drinks. I let my guard down, your father watching me, the kids running around, and Mac was bragging about his job again. It just got to be too much." Bob drummed his fingers.

"So, you drink more and more? Does that make you feel better?"

"Yes. Less nervous. But I got good advice in the hospital. Me and you, we can do this, stop drinking."

"I'm not the one with the problem, Bob. But you make it my problem. I was so angry at you, I wanted you to rot in that hospital, to choke on whatever medications they gave you. I hoped you fell down the stairs and stayed down."

"I know." He whispered, "I did too. I slept a lot, then thought a lot. I was medicated and my thoughts were . . . jumbled. But, yeah, I thought about dying."

"Did you? *Want* to die?" She was shocked, especially how complacent Bob had looked in the hospital. Rita wiped her eyes and twisted her tissue into a rag. "But . . . then I remembered how much I love you."

Bob's face folded in pain, "Me, too."

Rita brought him his ashtray and cigarettes. She cleared the dishes, giving him a few moments of privacy, hoping he wouldn't cry.

"Here is the plan, for now. I'll pack the kids into the car on Friday afternoons. We'll pick you up from work, then go to the bank to deposit your paycheck.

When we get home, I don't know, shovel the walk, or play with the kids. I'll write checks right away to pay bills, then give you an allowance. And I'll start supper—"

Bob's humiliation darkened his brown eyes, then a pang of anger flashed through. "What am I, a baby? A moron?"

Rita toned it down. "I know you rely on me, and I'm going to be stronger for you, Bob. I'll do whatever it takes to make you better, for you and the kids. When you're not at work, you'll be with me. Can you do this?"

"Yes. Yes, I can."

Sounds of the children laughing and playing drifted in from outside. Rita brought her coffee cup to the window to watch them build a snow fort. The clock ticked and the radiator knocked.

Eventually, Bob came behind her, and circled his arms around her waist.

She turned around to kiss him.

They hugged, cautious of each other, wanting to get this right. Rita felt this embrace to be good and hopeful, maybe a new beginning.

On New Year's Eve morning, Bob braced himself for their plan of no drinking. Rita was nervous about Bob, but also hopeful, excited to keep her appointment at Wee-Two Beauty Salon for a wash and set and a helmet of hairspray. They hadn't been out to dinner since before Noreen's birth in September.

That evening, Rita put away towels as Bob stood at the bathroom mirror and gingerly pulled the white bandage strips off his face. She hoped all his pain would be a reminder to keep sober. He lathered carefully, and she left him to shave and shower.

Back in their room, she laid out his pressed shirt, a narrow tie, and suit pants, hung from the closet door. Standing in her satin slip, Rita pulled a shimmery blue dress, which she made using a Butterick pattern, over her head. He came into their room, whistled, and slid his hands along her waist.

"Bob," she giggled. "Just zip me up."

"If I must," he acquiesced.

She needed Bob to clasp her pearl necklace, a gift from Mother. Rita clipped on sparkly blue earrings, dashed on red lipstick, and spritzed herself with L'Air du Temps. In the mirror, she saw Bob scowl behind her.

"Come here a minute." Rita blotted a cotton ball with foundation and rubbed two small dots below his eyes. She blended it, ever so gently. "That will get you in the door without too many questions." Rita capped the foundation bottle. "I saw Kevin clunking around in your shoes, downstairs. Go."

On the frosty New Year's Eve ride, Rita, wrapped in wool, asked, "Bob? Did you notice how much we helped each other? Just to get dressed?"

"Yes, and I'd wink at you, but I'd mess up my makeup." Bob kissed her hand.

Their plan was to have as much fun as possible, eating and dancing, and being very casual about not drinking alcohol. Rita and Bob's party included Pat and Joe, Fran and Marilyn, Nancy and Jack, and Rob and Ceil, all of whom knew about Bob's drinking. Rita was strung tight, hoping Bob would be okay.

The table was crowded with glassware, ashtrays, and ladies' evening bags. Uniformed waiters presented prime rib, mashed potatoes, and green beans festooned with slivers of almonds. At the party, friends chatted warmly, laughed at Bob's jokes, and joined them on the dance floor. At 12:05 Rita and Bob kissed each other and everyone else. At 12:10, their perplexed, drunk buddies clapped and hooted when Bob picked Rita up and said, "Your chariot awaits, my lady."

Rita was carried from the ballroom, a little embarrassed, but she liked that Nancy got to see this.

To seduce, which was Rita's plan, in one sense, failed. To seduce means to persuade someone into sexual activity, but no persuasion was necessary. Being all "aglow" was back.

5

STORE

B ob was sober, pleasant, and attentive on New Year's Day. He agreed to
Rita's plan of no alcohol and close monitoring.

The remnants of the holidays, the Christmas cards, wrapping paper, and a
tin of cookies, still littered the dining room sideboard two weeks into the new
year. Rita was happy she'd tossed the booze as she organized the crowded room.
She put Noreen and Teri into the playpen in the living room so she could keep
working and thinking.

Only she could help Bob. AA helped a lot of drinkers, but Bob would not
join because it was too religious, and he was a skeptic. Her own faith in God
was weakening. Her prayers hadn't helped Bob.

Rita stubbed her toe on the playpen while winding up a sheep mobile. Rita
flipped Noreen onto her back and opened a play toolbox for Teri. "There you
go, ladies." The twins, playing with Lincoln Logs and plastic animals, made a
zoo in their room. Carol came home from a neighbor's house.

After lunch, Rita pushed the flock upstairs to rest. During naptime, Carol
tiptoed over to sleep against the closed bedroom door. Rita opened it with her
sore big toe, one inch at a time, to catch whatever little bird, Carol, Kitty, or
Kevin, peeped first. This house was getting too small.

She was hoping to trust Bob more, but for now, Rita needed to retrieve him
and his check every Friday. She managed money and time to keep him sober,
and it was working. Rita roused the children for the drive. It was raining crazily,
coming down in slants. The car windows were steamy. She splashed into the

parking lot at the tile store, and Bob ran out with a newspaper over his head. Kids dripped over the front seat to say "Hi" to Daddy.

"Hello, family. You look like drowned kittens, especially Kitty." Bob shrugged as rain dripped off his head and down his neck. He had been sober for nine weeks. Rita wanted to stop driving to the bank on Fridays. This was too much.

"Tough driving, huh?" Bob threw his wet jacket near the heater, inspecting his bedraggled family, then turned to Rita. "I want to drive my own self. If I don't drive my truck to work on Fridays, I can't get supplies for weekend work. I swear, I'll bring every check to you. Deal?"

"*Own self*? That's not a word. But, yes, I was thinking that too. Thank God, I'm sick of dressing five kids for a ten-minute ride, then listening to their complaints at the bank. Well, except for the lollipops. They like that."

They slogged into the bank for the last deposit by Bob, Rita, Carol, Kevin, Kitty, Teri, and Noreen.

When two more months of Bob's sobriety passed, Rita begged her parents to put a deposit on a building for his dream business, his own flooring and wallpaper store. The three-level building was a wreck, but he could fix it all. The first Saturday after they bought it, Bob came home abruptly, and said, "I need your help."

"What happened?" She came around the coffee table to confront him.

He laughed. "I need your help cleaning out that place. It's a dump. I asked your mother to watch the kids. Go get ready."

She happily changed out of her housedress. In dungarees, with her hair in a red kerchief, Rita helped take debris out of the store. She enjoyed the transformation, happy that Bob was relying on her. She swept broken glass and knocked down dangling cobwebs, going at it like a tornado, not afraid to get dirty.

"I'll get Chinese for lunch. Can I have a few bucks?"

She pushed his shoulder. "You really don't have lunch money?"

"No, boss. I give it all to you, except change for a coffee now and then."

They sat on his unfinished check-out counter, eating egg foo young, laughing when bits fell off their chopsticks. Muted light streamed in from the stained-glass window in what was once a dining room. Rita swung one leg. "Here's what I want to do with this place. Order from Waltex or Atomic Design, the modern wallpapers. So, you'll need to build racks and tables for those."

"Uh huh, go on."

"I'll paint all the walls and do the books. You decide on the flooring and the wood and carpeting."

"I know exactly what to choose, my dear. After all, I chose you." He tilted in to kiss her.

Bob ordered cylinders of linoleum, which he stood up, creating great canyons of merchandise. He bought oak and fir planks, wall-to-wall carpeting, and bathroom tiles in turquoise and pale pink. Pyramids of paints and smelly solvents crowded the register. Rita polished an antique spittoon to hold 24 yardsticks. When Rita and the kids visited, Bob jumped out and yelled, "En garde!" They grabbed yardstick-swords, and father and children swashbuckled through the rows of merchandise until Rita insisted it was time to leave.

At home, Rita did his accounts in a dark green pegged notebook. She squeezed every penny from incoming payments and called customers to pick up materials in order to get paid. Rita wrote outgoing checks slowly, hanging onto the money as long as was honest. She squirreled away bits of cash.

Bob was proud when he'd painted #1 on the driver's side door and #2 on the passenger side of his 1954 Dodge panel truck. Rita, in the store to gather receipts, heard their friend and employee, Big George, ask him why. Bob said, "If someone sees me in vehicle #2, they'll think I have a fleet. They gotta know I'm doing well."

6

MOTHER

Once spring arrived in early April, Rita welcomed opening the windows, but needed to wash them all: inside, outside, storm windows, and sills. Hot water and vinegar in a bucket perfumed the whole first floor. Looking into the yard, she saw Mother and her sister Rose watching the children. They sat on metal lawn chairs, warning Kevin and Carol about stick fighting, and Kitty to stop teasing Teri. They laughed at Noreen's attempts to crawl on the grass. Rita sang as she balled pieces of newspapers to dry the glass.

Mother was slowing down, Rita noticed, and the kids kept getting more daring even as she or Rose snapped, "Mind me, or you'll get a crack." It didn't work back when Rita and her sisters, as teenagers, ran out to whichever beau was waiting, sitting low-slung in a clunky car, and it doesn't work now. Rita heard Mother come inside early and glanced at her watch. It wasn't even ten o'clock yet, and the women promised to stay until noon. She threw all the debris into a paper bag and carried the dirty bucket to the kitchen, to look for her.

"Mother? Mother?"

Mother was sitting on the sofa, wheezing, shivering, and sweating. Copious amounts of sweat bathed the bodice of her dress. She didn't open her eyes, as Rita squatted in front of her. "Mother, what is it? Are you ill?"

"Yes." She rolled her gray head back and forth slowly.

"I'll get Rose."

"No. She's minding the children." Mother dabbed a handkerchief around her neck and chest. "She knows. Let me rest here a moment, Rita."

"I'll get you a . . . a cool cloth." Rita's mind slowed. "Lie down, Mother."

She helped take off the sturdy old lady shoes, thinking of the times Mother paused just climbing steps. When Rita was sure she was sleeping, she ran out to her aunt, crying.

"You know? You know what's wrong with Mother?" Rita took Noreen out of Rose's arms, as if she wasn't honest enough to hold the baby. Rose gasped, then teared up. She looked across the yard filled with children, colorful chickens pecking about.

"She told me not to. Oh, Rita, Kathleen has *the cancer*. Sit, sit. Is she resting? These . . . these episodes come and go. A few days earlier, I walked over for a visit. I would take tea, with a tiny splash of gin, if offered. It was."

Rita sat down, shocked. "You two drink gin? During the day?"

"A tiny bit. Settles the nerves."

"I never knew that."

"She was looking poorly and acting tired. So, I says, 'Now Kathleen, if you're ill, go to the doctor.' She says, 'Bah. Rose. What a waste of money.'"

"I told her Dr. Casey's wife died of a stroke," Rose went on, tacking on some gossip.

Rita stopped bouncing Noreen on her knee. "You don't think she's having a stroke now, do you?"

"Hold on, I'm getting to that, but no. Kathleen goes, 'I'm not having a stroke, saints preserve us. I'm bloated . . . but not eating.' I tell her, 'That's because you are a terrible cook. You could eat those . . . those . . .'" Rose started laughing, shoulders shaking and covering her big teeth with her hand, "'those cream cheese and dill . . . disasters. Club food. Bits of junk on toast. Canapés.'"

Rose worked at the Town and County Club serving luncheons for the wealthy ladies of Hartford. She also volunteered at Irish wakes, pushing small sandwiches around trays and stacking squares of sugar in silver bowls, skills she learned at the Club.

Rita and Rose encircled Noreen, crying, their arms hugging each other's necks. They only stopped when Kitty approached, "Mommy. Why are you sad?"

Rita reached into her pocket for a tissue to wipe her eyes, "Don't worry, Kitty. It's Grandma. She's a little sick right now. Go play, honey."

Kitty stood by her mother, stalwart, then scrambled onto her lap, sharing the space with Noreen.

Kathleen told her daughters she had ovarian cancer. Rita lessened expectations of her and became a caregiver instead.

Two weeks later, Nancy called Rita to come to the hospital to see Mother, as she wasn't doing well.

Rita needed money for a sitter and coins for the parking meter. She held $2.28 in her hand. Money was tight, what with the new business. Bob was on a job and would have cash that evening. If she paid the sitter, she would have twenty-four cents, enough for two hours of parking. With four cents left she could buy . . . nothing. She was a grown lady trying to visit her sick mother.

As she paced the kitchen, she noticed the Bisquick box, and started mixing ingredients. The kids had to eat. It was a Tuesday morning, so she called friends to watch the children. She tried Marie Zambrello and Eleanor Malm, but neither answered. The biscuits were smelling good, so the children drifted in. They climbed onto their seats, and Rita swung Noreen into her highchair.

Rita mumbled, "Twenty-four cents."

Kitty noticed, "Can you buy something with *twemty*-four *cemts*?"

"No, sweetie, I can't."

"How about some peanut butter?" Kevin asked, splitting his two biscuits.

"We don't have any. We have jelly," Rita offered as she poured half cups of milk. That satisfied them.

When Rita sat down, Kitty knelt and whispered, "I have four big coins and ten little ones in my piggy bank. Can you buy something with them coins?"

"Yes, Kitty, I can." Rita blinked to keep from crying, and smoothed Kitty's fine hair. "I'll call Tina to come babysit."

Mother's ovarian cancer had spread to her colon, which necessitated an ileo-transverse colostomy.

The family learned that cirrhosis of the liver contributed to her illnesses, but it didn't matter to Rita how or why Mother was sick. Weary, Nancy and Mary Alice hugged Rita, then slipped down the hall to the smoking lounge.

"Mother, hello." She lay in bed, rosary beads intertwined in claw-like hands, her skin white as parchment. Her sharp nose no longer supported wire-rim glasses. Her eyes were closed. Rita put her sweater and purse at the end of the bed. Mother turned her face to the wall, exhaling, already separating out. Rita wanted to shake her bony shoulders. But they never had outbursts, she and Mother.

A nurse swung into the room, gave a thermometer a professional shake, and inserted it between Mother's thin lips. "Not long." The nurse checked the patient's pulse.

"Not long?" Rita grabbed the nurse's arm, digging her nails in. "What do you mean? Not long for what? She's only sick. Not dying."

"I'm sorry . . . I meant, don't stay too long. I'll be outside."

Rita knelt by the bed, resting her head on the cotton spread near the pillow. Closing her eyes, she felt a hand on her hair, a flutter. Mother was touching Rita's hair, so she kept her eyes shut, as this tender moment was too rare to ruin. Tears slid across Rita's face and onto the bedspread.

She spoke softly and slowly, "I can't help you anymore, Rita. I want you to take care of your sister. Your father won't know what to do with a teenager. I have some money–"

"I don't want your money," Rita's eyes were still closed, but the tears could not be held back.

"Don't be foolish, of course you do. You may not want it, but you . . . can help your family. Find your strength, Rita."

"Mother." Rita sat upright.

Mother opened her pale blue eyes. Rita took a fragile hand and kissed it. This once-stout lady, who was now a tiny replica of a dashboard saint, withdrew her hand and shut her eyes.

Rita took uneven inhales. "Mother, I don't know what to do without you. How do I start my day, what do I tell the children?"

"Go home now, Rita."

Ever obedient, Rita gathered her things. Squaring her shoulders, she walked away from the one constant in her life.

Mother passed away during the night.

The wake was at Ahern's, and the Irish community rallied.

Kathleen's lips were sewn shut and her waxy skin was powdered an unnatural pink. Kieran stood sadly, dutifully, by the open casket, with his four daughters and Aunt Rose. After being on their feet for two hours in the receiving line, Rita, Mary Alice, Nancy, and Carolyn were cried out, dried out, and sighed out. Bob brought pointed paper cups of water to the ladies.

The funeral was almost regal because of Kieran's donations to Our Lady of Sorrows Church. Candles were flickering as incense did its job of wafting to the arching ceiling, guiding Kathleen's soul to heaven. Rita, in a black suit and small feathered hat, sat in the second pew, with Bob and Carol beside her. The rest of the children were home, too young to understand.

The hearse, limousine, mourners, and adjunct parishioners traveled through Hartford to Mount Saint Benedict Cemetery. More prayers were whispered, more tears were shed.

The route was retraced to Rose's house to finish Kathleen's send-off in style, with an Irish ending. It was a mix of music, Latin, Gaelic, tears, shots, snots, and food, and being a good Irish funeral, it would end with dancing until quiet exhaustion forced its conclusion. Bob did not drink any alcohol; he just sat with Rita as she clung to his hand.

Mother's passing hit Rita hard. Her mother had been the voice of reason and tradition, whisking into the Leonard home five days a week. Rita acclimated to running her own life when her mother entered the hospital, but now she was without hope of Mother ever coming back. Kathleen died young, at age 53. Rita had to create her own show, and the only way she could get through a day without sitting down with head in hands was to push any sad thoughts away, to a deep cellar, to be visited another time.

Rita worried about Carolyn and Daddy. The sisters got together to clean his house. Nancy offered critiques and solutions, always looking to improve everything: "Take down those velvet curtains—it looks like the Globe Theater in here."

She threw out old shoes and mothball-scented coats, and tossed food from the back of his monitor-top icebox. Daddy sent Carolyn to boarding school. Mother was gone, and now Carolyn was too.

Rita was lonely, despite her children fluttering around. At least now she could rely on Bob again. He was sober and kind when home, but he seemed to be doing a lot of extra work at night.

7

BUILDING

Without Mother, Rita was forced to take all five children to the pediatrician for a May visit. Kitty and Kevin, starting school in the fall, needed physicals, and the rest needed booster shots. She drove toward Elmwood Center, noticing a new sign at the corner of—what was it? Exeter Avenue? *Ready to Build Your New Two-, Three-, or Four-Bedroom Home?*

Rita nearly rear-ended a Studebaker turning around. The kids flew off their seats, falling to the floor. Carol did a fine job holding onto Noreen. Rita glanced in the mirror, "Whoa. Sorry about that, kids. Hold on." She pulled down a short street with no sidewalks. Three lots were marked by wooden stakes, with little flags tied to strings. Children's clothes hung from the lines. The names on the mailboxes, Pistritto, Maschi, LaPenta, were Italian. Beautiful flowers were in front, with vegetable plots in back. This was five blocks from home, yet a world away. Who was building these homes? How much did they cost? And, who, in their right mind, would buy a two-bedroom home?

Kevin pulled on the back of the seat, standing close to her shoulder. "Who lives here, Mommy?"

"No one. Just looking." Her pulse quickened. This might be perfect for their new home. Under her breath, she answered him, "Maybe we will."

At the doctor's building, Kevin opened his door before the car stopped, "Come on, girls. I'll race you." He led them to the frosted "Doctor's Office" door, waving Kitty and Carol through. They sped to see two turtles lying around a fake pond container with an island, complete with plastic palm trees. The water was murky. Kevin picked up one who pedaled its legs in the air. His sisters were laughing until giant Nurse Sherry walked over and snapped, "Put that down."

"Oh, okay." Kevin scrunched his shoulders and put the turtle on the wooden floor.

"Not there." She loomed large.

"Oh, sorry." He put the turtle in its dish, patting its back with one finger. He smiled at Nurse Sherry, who stomped off to her desk. Kevin slit his eyes to watch her walk away, wondering why she was crabby.

Nurse Sherry was squeezed into a white cotton uniform. He noticed her speckled legs through her white tights. Falling-over white shoes. But she wore a nice paper hat with some gold pins on it.

Mommy came in carrying Noreen and prodding Teri along, "Hi there, Sherry." Mommy smiled. "Everyone has an appointment, so you can start at the top or the bottom."

Nurse Sherry made a show of looking at her watch.

Mommy said, "Take your time. I know we're early." She settled Noreen in her lap.

"Ah. . . Mrs. Leonard, I'll start with the baby. Why don't you take the boy, Kevin, into the examining room and help him get undressed?"

"Oh, he can undress himself. Kevin, go in and put on the blue robe, then wait for the doctor." Mommy pointed to a room.

Kevin, in his skinny underwear and robe, soon forgot to sit still. He stood on the scale. The base wobbled, but the top part didn't move. He got off, pushed a chair over, and climbed on to move the clunky part to 100, a big number. It didn't move. It's broken, Kevin thought. He assembled some junk to make the scale respond: a stool, and a plastic life-size torso cut open to show some pink and red parts.

Dr. Saunders breezed in. Kevin remembered him from his house visits. The doctor smiled, but Nurse Crabby, behind him, scowled at Kevin's project.

While Dr. Saunders pushed down Kevin's tongue with a popsicle stick, the nurse put the room in order. He took Kevin's height and weight and showed him how the scale worked. The doctor sat him on the table to knock his knees with a small hammer.

"Can I do that?" Kevin asked. It was a cartoon hammer with its red rubber end.

"Sure." The doctor watched and laughed with him. The nurse clicked her pen and wrote notes on a clipboard. Dr. Saunders stated, "Well, you are a normal, inquisitive, active, clean, and skinny five-year-old kid. How does that sound?"

It all sounded fine, except for the big word. The doctor held the vaccination in a tiny glass bottle, stuck a needle in it, tapped the syringe in the air, and pumped drops out.

"Kevin, this may hurt. Do you want your mommy?"

"No." He smiled. He wasn't some big baby.

"Do you want to look the other way?"

"No." His smile lessened. His mom was probably with Noreen or Teri.

Kevin cringed when Dr. Saunders plunged the needle into his arm.

"Did that hurt?"

"Just a little." That hurt *a lot*. But he didn't cry because he was big.

"Good man. You can hop down. And you know what else, Kevin? You're brave. Put that in your notes, Nurse Sherry."

Nurse Crabby sneered, pressing on a Band-Aid. "Get dressed, then go to the waiting room and send in the girls. And don't touch anything."

When the girls got poked, emitting cries and yelps, their mother was with them, so Kevin was alone. He told himself how brave he was, like the doctor said. Smiling, Kevin put both turtles on toy trucks and drove them around the floor, giving them a taste of freedom.

On the way home, Mommy turned down Exeter Avenue. "Kids, what do you think of this neighborhood? Would you want to live there?"

Kevin hunched over from the back seat, "Yeah, it's got lots of trees and dirt, but will there be a house?"

There was a small bottle of vodka in the garage. It was always there, it, or its predecessor. Bob ignored it for January, February, March, and April, but one day in May, tired of being perfect, he took a quick slug, and this old friend lightened his mood, slowing his mind's racing. He lit a cigarette before going into the house.

The garage was filled with junk because it was too wobbly to actually protect a car. Bob thought of a reason to get out there, often, a reliable get-out-of-jail-free card. With pieces of leftover tile, he created mosaic inlays for wooden tables, which Bob sold in his store. After supper, he'd call out, "Rita, I'll be in the garage making furniture."

On the Saturday following Kathleen's funeral, Bob was out there, listening to the Yankees on the radio, while his kids played in the yard. Occasionally, he would give someone a push on a swing. He didn't want to play with the children until the game, his table, or his little bottle was done, whichever came first. By three o'clock, his mood had changed, and Bob roared into the yard and scooped the kids up, tickled them, and pushed their swings too high.

"Ssh," he winked to his conspirators, "do you want your mother to come out?" They were his gang, his posse. He filled the rubber and metal baby pool, even though it was only May. He sat right down, in his khakis and white tee shirt, laughing and daring his kids to jump in. Then he knelt up, swaying, growling.

"Nuh-ah," Carol smiled at him but crossed her arms over her red playsuit. She was the smart one but wanted to play, so she danced away a little. Bob tried to grab each kid as he or she ran by. A pool and kids in a yard always equal laughter, Bob thought. "You're getting too close to the Creature of the Black Lagoon."

He lurched out and tossed Kitty into the water.

"Yikes. Yikes. It's *fweezing*," Kitty hopped back out, soggy socks, sneakers, and bottom, and squawked for someone else to get captured. "Get Teri. Get Kevin."

The dog was yapping while Kevin buzzed in and out of reach, escaping like a football player, slipping in the mud forming around the pool. Bob snatched Carol and plunged her into the black lagoon. She popped right out, arms akimbo, wide-eyed, and then pointed at the back porch.

Rita was out to gather the sheets off the line. "What in God's green earth is going on?" She jutted her chin in the direction of the out-of-season pool, the wet grownup, the kids, ranging from damp to dripping, with globs of clinging mud. The dog was trotting at the end of his chain, barking, barking, barking.

"Stop it, Bruno. Bob?" Rita turned around, but Bob saw her laughing.

"Uh, yes, dear?" Bob rubbed his muddy hands over his face and hair. He slipped in the pool, then regained his footing.

"I heard on the television news. Walter Cronkite says that the real Creature of the Black Lagoon has escaped. Can you please get the kids into the house right away, and into hot showers?"

"Look, kids, Mommy smiled. Did you see that?" He was glad she was getting less sad since her mother's passing. "Get on in there."

Bob went back to the garage for a while until Kevin called Daddy in for supper. He hid his vodka bottle behind a can of paint.

Later, Rita went on and on about the building lot she saw, what a great neighborhood it was, and how they could use Mother's money. Bob nodded and prodded. He congratulated himself on how relaxed he was, and how well he hid his boozy euphoria from Rita. This was the happiest she'd been in a while, excited with the possibility of a new house. He didn't want to mar any part of her day.

8

CAR

Rita was buoyed by the fun Bob and the kids had the previous Saturday, so she asked to run an errand with Nancy. She wanted to get a surprise for the new house. Being alone with another adult was appealing, too. He was drinking coffee in the kitchen, reading the *Hartford Courant*, still in his robe.

"Sure, why not? When?"

"Well . . . now. I'll telephone Nancy to come soon."

He wouldn't have to do much. The children were watching cartoons. Rita wiped the countertop and coffee pot, then checked her lipstick. She told Teri to get off the coffee table, took a ball of yarn from Noreen, and turned the TV down a notch. To Carol, Kitty, and Kevin she said, "Listen to Daddy. I'll see you later."

With a sweater over her dress, and a large box in her hands, Rita kissed Bob goodbye. Nancy was honking out front.

"Look, look." Rita grasped Nancy's arm as she drove to the S&H Green Stamps store. Nancy was overdressed for shopping, with her blonde hair held back by a silk scarf and her yellow dress a smidge too tight.

"For God's sake, I can't look. I'm driving Jack's new car."

"Well, at the stop light, then," Rita waved a brochure from the builder. She parked the box of stamp booklets by her feet.

"What?" Nancy looked left and right, but not at Rita. The light changed. "This will be the den instead of a dining room in the new house, for the kids—"

Now Nancy glanced at Rita. "That's tacky." She pulled into a far parking space.

"What? That's so RUDE." Rita should be used to Nancy's tongue.

"Oh, sorry, I meant . . ." Nancy opened her door, reached for her envelope of stamps, looked over the top of the car to Rita, "You're buying a new house, and you're not having a dining room?"

Rita bumped her door shut with her hip.

"What if the principal or your boss comes for dinner?"

"For dinner? Why would they? My dinner guests are all under four feet tall or are family."

Nancy whisked ahead to the store, in cute yellow heels, looking like a daisy. Rita imagined Nancy's little heels making small depressions in the warm asphalt. She smiled to herself. The *Come In! It's Air-Conditioned* sign beckoned to them. The sisters walked to the counter to fill out their orders.

"So, look. I'm buying a vinyl footstool with secret built-in storage. It will be modern."

"Your den?" Nancy was flipping through the Corning Ware catalog.

"No, the stool. But, yes, we are getting a vinyl sofa from Puritan. I'm putting nautical décor in there . . . "

Nancy huffed, "How are you affording this? A new house. A sofa."

Rita stopped her pen mid-air and lowered her voice, "You know, with Mother's money."

"Be careful. You don't want to go into debt."

A clerk directed Rita to the pick-up counter, warning, "That footstool box is heavy."

Nancy met Rita there, and promptly said, "Oh, no, we're not carrying anything. There's people for that."

A young man in a green pinny loaded the hassock and the diminutive casserole box onto a cart and followed them to the car, where he whistled at it, in all its gleaming glory: a 1960 Carnival Red Plymouth Fury. Nancy smirked at the kid's response. She held out a dollar. Rita thought, who tips at the S&H store? Once the peon was tipped, Nancy pushed buttons to drop their windows. They continued the conversation, while Nancy fiddled with the radio.

"Why are you worried about me? We all got the same money. You moved, bought a patio set—"

"That's because of Jack's promotion." Nancy got testy.

"Oh, I get it. You got *this car*. What *is* this anyway?" Rita was now running the conversation, and her hand along the futuristic dashboard.

"Plymouth Fury, with a slant-six, excellent 225 cubic inches—'"

"Push-button everything. *Fury* is anger from Greek mythology. I bet it can go really fast." Rita got excited, "Let's see, sister dearest, we are on Trout Brook Drive, a nice straightaway. Push that pedal."

A racehorse, the Fury leapt from zero to 60 mph in two blocks. That was as fast as Nancy dared, driving across town, through two (thankfully green) lights. The wind blew up their skirts, tossed around their hair, and threw joy into their small-town, house-wifey lives. The speed was exhilarating. Rita forgot she was the 26-year-old mother of five children.

Nancy parked at the curb, and asked, "Where are the kids? Your kids are always outside."

Rita hoisted her gift from the trunk and said, "I'm about to find out. Thank you." She juggled the box up the back steps. A nudge in her brain hurried her on.

Bob was sitting at the kitchen table, all sweaty, legs straight out, scraping an ashtray from one hand to another across the table. Rita looked at him, and looked beyond to the torn-up house with toys and shoes strewn everywhere.

"Where're the kids?" A slight panic rose in her chest.

"Napping and crapping," Bob scoffed.

"What?" she asked. They didn't usually talk that way.

"I mowed the lawn." He narrowed his eyes.

"Good. Good, it looks nice. Where are the babies?"

She heaved the box onto the counter and made a wide berth around Bob's outstretched legs.

"They are the ones napping, Kevin's been in the can awhile, I assume, crapping. Carol and Kitty are playing with some . . . some dolls. I told them to all play inside—"

"Why? It's a beautiful day."

"*Why? Why?* Have you ever tried to mow a lawn with brats all around you?"

Rita paused, thinking of all the times she took them grocery shopping or to the post office. Big deal. Then she glanced at the two triangles punctured in the top of a beer can. He noticed her noticing.

"Ah, lighten up. It's one beer. Everyone's fine. Except Kevin fell out of the tree again. Teri got stung by a bee or something, cried blue blazes . . . Noreen blowing dandelions . . . Lucky I didn't run her over."

Rita widened her eyes and opened her mouth to say something . . . to . . . to protect these little people. She rubbed her arms, then took her time walking toward the stairs. "I'll go check on them." She was afraid that Bob would launch at her. He was drinking beer. How many? Where'd he get it?

"You do that, Miss High and Mighty. I'll put the lawn mower away." He stood and slowly pushed his chair in. He opened the back door and Bruno barked. Bob said, "Asshole," but Rita didn't know if it was to her or the dog.

Rita hit the steps quietly. Noreen was asleep, sucking her thumb and Teri was snoring in puffs. Carol and Kitty were playing with paper dolls, unharmed. She knocked lightly on the bathroom door.

"Kevin?" Rita pushed the door open.

Kevin was playing at the bathroom sink, marching toy soldiers around in an inch of water.

"Ah . . . it's too deep." He used a high-pitched whine for the blue soldier. "You're going, in, ya big baby." He gruffed his voice for the red one, the mean guy.

"Kevin. Hi." Rita knelt beside her five-year-old son. She noticed scratches and yellow and mauve bruises on his arms. "Are you alright? You look a little banged up."

She put her arms around his skinny shoulders. He smelled like a summer kid: dirt, sweat, grass, sun, and water. He blushed, seeming relieved she was home, but embarrassed to be talking to himself.

"I'm okay. A little better. I fell out of the tree." Kevin lifted his shirt, checking the damage. His entire left side, from armpit to waist, was scraped raw.

"You know what, Kev? How about a whole bath, what do you say? You could bring more toys."

He had to like the idea of a full tub, a bathroom without sisters, and his mom all to himself.

"Yep." He came back from his room with a Barrel of Monkeys and a fishing net.

He was smiling the whole time as she gently attended to his wounds. Her fingernails combed his soapy scalp, loosening all kinds of bits from the lawn and tree. Rita used a cup to rinse the debris away. She sang softly, wrapping him in a clean towel.

"Mommy?" Kevin twinkled at her. "You know how when you tie my shoes, they keep tied? I think my hair will keep nice now 'cause you really did a good job scrubbing me up."

She laughed. "You think you're going to stay clean now?"

"Yup. For a long, long time."

"Let's check tomorrow, shall we? Take a rest in my room, and I'll call you for supper."

As she walked toward the door, Kevin paused, "Mommy?"

"Yes, Kevin?" She turned around.

He got shy. "You're pretty."

"Thank you, Kevin. I love you."

He fell asleep in her shade-darkened room.

Rita ushered the girls outside, then started making a supper of meatloaf, green beans, and rice. Bob was in the living room, probably performing an act of contrition by picking up games and sneakers, knowing he'd overreacted to her being late. He next brought dog food out to Bruno.

Coming back in, he wiped his hands on a dishtowel. "Rita. Sorry. I thought you'd be back in an hour. You were gone for what, jeez, three hours? On a Saturday? What'd you do . . . go to confession?"

"No, Bob, no confession for me today. I'm probably boring God to death. But you. You need to think about what makes you mean. Mean is a sin, but I don't know which one. Do you? Thou shalt not what . . . hurt a child?"

"I didn't hurt anybody. I yelled at them, that's all."

She burst out, "Hurt? They're hurt if they're afraid of you. You're supposed to be their protector. They're hurt if they can't run to you with a scrape or a sting or cut finger. You're supposed to fix them. They are hurt if you ignore them, if they are crying, hungry, lonely . . . that's what we do as parents. We help and hold and, I don't know . . . whatever else needs doing."

Rita stirred the rice, banging the spoon twice on the pan. "Bob, can you . . . is it safe for me to leave you alone with our children? Their own father?" Her nostrils flared.

"Yes. Sure. Mostly." He rested against the sink, crossing his arms.

"You can't drink, Bob, *especially* when you're in charge."

"I'm not. I don't. Well, I have a beer on a Saturday, or on a Sunday when I'm watching a game on TV. But, shit, I'm no saint."

"So," Rita held his gaze. "The alcohol is back, is that what you're saying?"

"Sit down." Bob pulled out two chairs.

Her heartbeat clicked as she sat.

"It's under control. I've got a lot to do with . . . with the move to the new house. The business. Fixing this house to sell it . . . We both have a lot to do, Rita. I lost patience today."

He was justifying his behavior, drifting off into the land of denial, moving off the hard path of sobriety into the murky edges of dabbling again in his personal poison. And she was going to let him, at least for a little while, have his beer or two. This was a battle, and she needed to win the war. Rita needed to get the family out of this too-small house, grow the business, and start anew. The wheels were turning fast, now, in her brain.

Rita took his hand across the table. Acting. "Sure, Bob. Have your Saturday or Sunday beer. You've been great getting home from work. If you continue to stay out of bars, we'll get on our feet. I'll be in charge of the kids, unless it's for a teeny tiny time. I'll ask Marie to help out, when we pack to move . . . get out of here, get room for everybody."

Bob squeezed her hand. Rita hoped he was placated by the pardon she offered. He stayed quiet. When he stood and slapped the table, it was in acceptance. "Yes. Will do. Permission to whistle the children in, sir." Bob tried to bring some humor back to diffuse the tension. He pulled the door shut behind him. She pretended to laugh, although her heart was unsteady. She set the table.

"Asshole. You're the asshole."

That was the first time in her life she needed to use that exact term.

9

BLUEPRINTS

Carol pouted, sitting in the front seat of the car to "watch" Kevin, Kitty, Teri, and Noreen, while Rita and Bob met with the builder. The yard was a muddy mess, with a slimy plywood path from their parking spot to the framed house. Rita wanted to be quite sure Mr. Wilbur knew she was making decisions equally with Bob, especially about the den and fourth bedroom, in their forever home. Standing near the hood, Rita heard squabbling, but ignored the children as Mr. Wilbur approached with rolls of blueprints.

"Stop scratching your armpit," Carol snapped.

"I'm not." Kitty was defensive. She probably *was* scratching.

Rita leaned against the Ford. Her attention was torn, and her anger was rising.

"Stop kicking my seat, and scratching."

"I'm not."

"Cut that out. Besides, it's funny. You're a cat, and you always scratch."

"I'll scratch your eyeballs out if you don't quit that." Now Kitty was fighting mad.

Kevin laughed. "You just proved it, 'scratch her eyeballs.' Ha."

"Quit it. I'm telling Mommy." Kitty was out of the car in a flash. Rita glowered at her trudging around in the mud, yipping, "Mom. Mommy."

"We're right here, Kitty, quiet down." Kitty started to tattle-tale, but Rita squeezed her hand, hard. "I heard it all. Bob? Go check on the kids, would you?"

Embarrassed, Rita swiveled her head from the pandemonium in the car to the plans, glad the children were a little afraid of their dad, even now when he was sober.

Kevin shouted at Carol, "Now you're gonna get it, Miss Perfect." Rita saw Kevin roll away from her clawing hand, but not before a button popped off his shirt.

"I HATE you," Carol screamed at Kevin, just when Bob yanked the door open.

"*What* is going on in here? Kitty's crying, you're yelling, a bunch of hooligans. We're trying to show these people we're good neighbors."

Kevin, Carol, Teri, and Noreen clamped their mouths shut and sat still.

"That's better. Now get out and wave to Mr. Gabriele. His kids, Peter and David, are about your ages. And cut the crap if you know what's good for you. This house is a big deal."

The children stood still for three full minutes. Rita and Bob held kids in place by digging fingers into their shoulders, which worked in church. Rita introduced the children, then told them to go play. Kevin and the girls played tag, happy to slip into the muck around the house's shell.

Bob, Rita, and Mr. Wilbur walked around on the boards, pointing out finishing touches to be completed. Although her children were getting filthy, she could blissfully concentrate on the house.

Rita and Bob's good mood lasted all summer, after they sold their old house, and in the early fall, moved into the new one.

For the price of $18,000, in 1960, the Leonards got four bedrooms, a den, and a walk-up attic. They said no to building a garage or paving a driveway, so they splurged on wallpaper, a slate floor in the hall, and wall-to-wall carpet in the living room, which they hoped to keep pristine. The basement was left unfinished, with one wall of knotty pine to separate the work and play areas. The house's best feature was the intercom system. As soon as the family moved in, it became an integral part of life. The NuTone was based in the kitchen, with speakers in the bedrooms and the rec room. Rita turned on the radio, then woke the kids, always in the same order: "Carol, Kevin, Kitty, Teri, and NOReen" in a sing-songy voice, to be funny. Music lilted through the house as the kids hurried to breakfast.

One dark Saturday afternoon, Rita tripped on a pair of kicked-off sneakers. The house was getting messy. She marched to the intercom: "Bob."

He appeared.

"The kids are messing up our home. I don't want it all nicked and dirty, so let's make our rules real. Which do you want to start with?"

Bob chuckled, snorting in agreement. After a few minutes of collaborative scribbling, Rita called the kids to supper, but didn't put out any food.

Carol landed with her elbows on the table. "What's up?"

Bob smirked from his seat. "Mommy and me have some new rules."

"We have plenty of rules . . . more than any of my friends."

Rita and Bob smiled at each other, noticing more bad habits. Kevin came in from outside, carrying a teepee made from pine branches and string. He threw his wet jacket over a doorknob. "Am I late? I'm starving."

It was dark at six-thirty.

"Sit down, children. We're adding new rules. Daddy and I are serious." Rita read the list as Teri and Noreen got into their seats. Kitty brought a yo-yo.

"Only adults use the front door. No playing in the living room. At bedtime, brush your teeth, put on pajamas. Sit in the same seat at meals." Rita pointed to Kitty, "No toys at the table." At Kevin, "Be here for supper at six o'clock OR before it's dark out."

Bob tilted his chair, "No one does this," he hammered it down, and reached for imaginary bread in the center of the table, "Or this." He tried not to laugh.

Rita went on. "We recite grace, then pass serving dishes to the left. Vegetables have to be eaten, and dessert is not a given. No gum-chewing, trading, tattling, and of course, the big ones, no lying, cheating, or stealing."

Carol, at eight years old, simply asked, "Why?"

"It's called manners, and Daddy and I want to keep this house extra nice. And you do, too. It's the best thing we'll ever have."

The rigidity might have been onerous, but the kids were allowed to be as physical and creative as they wanted, as long as it was outside, in any weather, until the streetlights came on. They rode their bikes in the road, roller-skated down the hill, and chased after the Lincoln Dairy man for chips of ice. They had their own trees to climb, either pine or maple. That fall, the children's coats were hung in the hall closet, boots sat at the back door, mittens dried on a basement rack. The parents' rules made sense and kept order. The children fought and played equally hard, pushing, slapping, chasing, capturing, or daring each other to jump off a bridge or cliff. Kevin was the most creative with the dares, starting with one word: Run.

Rita peeled potatoes at the sink on Thanksgiving eve, watching Kevin climb a snowy pine tree until it bowed with his weight. She opened the window, listening as he told Kitty and Teri to build a landing pad of snow, fast. "I'm losing my grip. Help me." They worked hard to give him a soft cushion, and, worried, Kitty called Carol over, "Quick. He's gonna die."

Carol rushed to pack on snow, as Kevin sprang from the tree, yelling, "Geronimo!" The girls ganged up when he landed in the fluff, and stuffed snow down his jacket and tore his hat and mittens off. They pushed him out of the way to climb the tree and took turns dropping out of it, throwing his hat and mittens around the yard. Rita was glad she hadn't intervened.

Their children were friendly to other kids. If Rita got a phone call from school and someone heard the words "Mommy wants to see you," they were fearful, thinking of every bad thing they had said, seen, or done. They confessed to things she didn't know about, but Rita never said, "Wait until your father gets home" as she meted out justice quickly.

"Who wants popcorn?" Rita asked the following Sunday night while the family watched *The Wonderful World of Disney* in the basement. She disappeared to the kitchen to make popcorn and hot chocolate and carried it all down on the metal tray with orange melamine handles. Rita loved this cozy evening with her family. As she snuggled next to Bob on the couch in this unfinished space, with kids crammed in, Rita thought, this was the life she had been waiting for. A beautiful home, a sober husband, and healthy, giggling children. She hoped it would last forever.

10

STITCHES

All the neighborhood kids played in the street, where they graduated from tricycles to two-wheeled freedom. By spring, the Leonards did everything barefoot. Kevin, seven, had to climb higher, run faster, and jump farther than everyone. Even running across his rock driveway, his bike pedals were already moving by the time he jumped on.

Dave Gabriele warned Kevin, "Jeez, skip the rocks, would you? Go on the grass."

Billy Malm snickered from his bike. "Yeah, watch them pricker bushes. Your dog is smarter than you."

If a Pontiac or Chevy came along, games would stop, and some kid would yell "car" and scowl at the driver. But Kevin screeched to a halt when Kitty pedaled her bike down the incline of the Malms' driveway. Kitty rolled into their driveway, fishtailed when her tires hit the rocks, swerved dangerously close to the prickers, and fell on her face.

Kevin threw his bike on the lawn, the back tire spinning.

Kitty's blood gushed out as he helped her up. She mashed her bangs into her forehead and pulled both hands away, shrieking, which was her response to everything, but this time it was warranted.

Kevin was fascinated that blood pulsed out of her forehead, right between her eyes. "Come on, Kitty." Over her howls, he yelled, "Mom. Mommy, Kitty's hurt." He guided his unseeing twin into the kitchen.

Mommy ran up the basement stairs. "Kevin, why are you yelling? "Oh . . . ooh . . . Kitty, let me see."

Mommy dragged Daddy's chair from the table and pushed Kitty into it. "Stop screaming, let me see your cut." She pulled Kitty's hands away.

Kevin's heart skipped when Mommy's eyes went wide, and she turned white. The assembling siblings squirmed in close. Kitty's roaring subsided, but gasping sobs started, and her eyes were screwed shut. Kevin scurried out the door.

Mommy asked, "Where are you going? You're not afraid, are you?"

Kevin brought a bloody rock to the table. He expected a thank you, or a pat on his head, having found the exact one in a driveway of many. He would save Kitty from seeing it ever again. "Here is the rock that hurt Kitty. Here it is." A pyramid, each face about an inch long, dripped deep-red blood on three surfaces.

"Oh, Kevin, this is not a crime scene. Take it outside." Mommy took a wet washcloth from Carol and coaxed Kitty's hands away to gently apply pressure.

"Why? This is the bad guy."

Kitty glanced at the culprit. "I hate that rock." Kitty looked at Kevin through wet eyelashes. At least *she* understood how important this was.

"I'll throw this rock far away." He would protect his sister.

"Kevin, stop it . . . Carol, can you call Daddy at work?" Mommy couldn't reach the phone.

Carol showed off, *telling* Daddy to come home, while looking at Kevin. "Kitty's hurt, but Mommy doesn't know if," Carol cupped the mouthpiece, "if she needs stitches and how many."

Kevin went out to straddle his bike because he had a job to do. Dad could decide what Kitty needed. He always did that deciding.

Rita pulled the cloth away. The kids stood there, riveted, watching her handle this disaster. "Could someone get Kitty's bike out of the driveway before Daddy runs it over? Teri, you go."

"I can't put it away *mysewf.*"

"Get Kevin to help you."

"He rode away."

Just then, Bob's truck rolled in. He punched the horn, and yelled out, "Somebody move that bike."

Rita raised her eyebrows, "Teri, go now. Do the best you can."

She heard Teri say, "Hi Daddy," then drag the bike to the backyard.

Kevin's leaving nagged at Rita.

Bob entered, jingling keys in his pocket, seeking Kitty.

Teri came in and said, "The dog's gone."

Rita wasn't listening, anxious to talk to Bob.

Kitty's shirt was bloody, and she was sniffling-breathing dramatically.

Bob knelt in front of her. "Let me see that, princess." He gently took the cloth away and gave a low whistle, then quickly made his eyes soft. "This is one beautiful cut, Kitten. I think one stitch or two . . . " He mouthed the word "more" to Rita, "and you'll be good as new." He winked at Kitty. "I'll take this girl to the Emergency Room. But she could use some shoes." Bob laughed as he looked down at the kids' dusty feet. "Looks like they all could use shoes."

Rita kissed Kitty's head after lacing up her red Keds. Rita tugged Bob's arm, "Get someone skilled . . . for the stitching . . . not an intern. You know, it's her face, that little face . . . " Rita welled up.

Bob hugged her, taking Kitty's hand. "I know, honey, I know. We'll be back soon."

Their kids, mostly pale with smatterings of summer freckles, were skinny little things, but tough in the long run. Kitty would be fine.

Carol, getting a glass of water, looked outside. "The dog's missing."

"Oh, no, now what?" Rita looked out the window. Bruno's path, a circle of brown in the green yard, was abandoned. Did she have time to fix the washing machine before they got back from the hospital? She couldn't think about that dog right now. Rita never wanted a dog anyway.

"I *knowed* that Bruno was gone," Teri said, "it was right when Kevin left."

"Kevin left?" Rita scrunched her face. "Did he leave on his bike? When? Why?"

Carol explained, "Mom, he was throwing out the rock that hurt Kitty."

"Why would he throw out a rock? Where do you throw out a rock? That makes no . . . but wait, maybe *he* took the dog." Rita's mind was whirling.

"Trout Brook." Carol drank her water, then turned on the radio.

Rita was forming a picture. "So, he went to Trout Brook to throw out a rock, and he took Bruno?"

"I don't know anything about the dog. Kevin wants to be Davy Crockett, so he'd head to the woods. He's *a idiot*." Carol pushed her hairband back.

"Stop calling everybody 'stupid' and 'idiot', which is actually 'an' idiot." Rita was getting off-track. "Where would he go? At Trout Brook?"

"I don't know. He takes off and then comes back." Carol flipped open her illustrated *National Velvet*. "Can I go to my room to read, and listen to the radio? You and Daddy figure it out when he gets home."

Rita was taken aback by Carol's tough words, but was more worried about Kevin's departure and Kitty's wrecked face. She wanted the twins safely home.

Kevin pedaled beyond Exeter Avenue to the woods. Stashing his bike under bushes, he found the path that led to his haven of birds, and a brook with stepping rocks to the far bank.

He felt a kinship with animals who ran fast, either to capture something, or escape from something. Kevin loved watching acrobatic squirrels; he was amazed by slithering snakes and crayfish crawling backward into tiny under-water caves. His dream heaven featured wild weather, heavy rainstorms, or ice crusted over snowdrifts. This evening, tall oak and elm trees swished gently in the breeze and small mammals skittered in the underbrush.

He was going to explore all of Trout Brook someday, but right now he was proud to stand on the rocky cliff, ten feet above the rushing water.

Kevin took the bloody rock out of his pants pocket.

"You're one sorry rock. I'd spit on you, but then the blood would wash off. And I hope I never see you around here ever again to hurt my sister. Now you go to your watery grave."

He hoped he sounded tough enough, and with all his might, hurled that rock. With a satisfying "ker-plunk" Kevin knew it hit deep water.

He looked around, making sure no one saw him talking to a rock. Would Dave Gabriele or Billy Malm work as an explorer, a sidekick? It was getting darker as he pedaled home.

Whew, he was glad he helped Kitty. Hoping she was home by now; he'd tell her about getting rid of that nasty rock.

And he wanted to see her stitches.

11

RUNAWAY

When Bob brought Kitty home that evening, Rita gave the children Neapolitan ice cream in fake-wood bowls, mostly their favorite: chocolate, strawberry, or vanilla.

Kitty dramatically played the hero, as Bob knew she would, with a white bandage covering the gash. The swelling and bruising around her eyes made her look like a boxer.

Rita called Bob into the den, out of earshot of the children, "Bruno got loose. And we haven't seen Kevin yet."

"Did Kevin untie him? Did you look for him?"

"Who?" Rita asked.

"The dog."

"I'm a little more worried about Kevin. It's getting late. You never trained that dog to stick around. He had no license, no collar, no fenced yard. The dog ran away, plain and simple. Right?"

Bob's face contorted at her coldness. He hissed, "It's MY dog, Rita. You never wanted him, so you don't understand." He pulled back the curtains to look at the patch of dirt Bruno usually scratched around in at the end of his frayed rope.

"No, I don't understand," Rita dug in, "why you brought a dog home, when we were barely feeding our children. I'm worried about the twins right now, Bob. Kitty's face will have a scar, and that's tough for a little girl. Kevin is missing. *I'm* worried about my children. I'll let *you* worry about the dog." Rita walked back into the kitchen, throwing out, "Maybe Bruno followed Kevin to the brook. Kevin should be home by now. The streetlights are on."

Bob stayed in the den, heated that Kevin might have taken Bruno off the rope. He paced, thinking. Bob didn't spend any real time with his mutt, but he liked Bruno's wild side.

Ten minutes after his dad pulled into the driveway, Kevin burst into the kitchen, sweaty and breathing hard. Bob watched Kevin notice Kitty, and all the ice cream bowls, as he moved happily toward his seat. He didn't get far.

"Where's your bike, Kevin?"

He slit eyes at Daddy, then went back outside to put his bike away, his ice cream untouched.

"Carol, where's yours?" He asked each kid.

Everyone went to get their bikes off the back lawn, except two-year-old Noreen.

"Kitty, sit down, they can put your bike downstairs for today." Bob was still being kind to the injured one, but he twirled a matchbook around and around in his hand, thinking of her twin.

In the dim yard, Kevin, Carol, and Teri grumbled at this task. Kevin hated it and knew the girls hated it more. He tried to be brave. They scraped and bumped their bikes down the cellar stairs. The hatchway was new, but that didn't prevent spiders from moving into its dark corners, building creepy webs under metal doors that clanked shut. They were scared to be in the spider haunt, so closing the hatchway quickly was important. Kevin banged the doors, then slid the bolt. Scrambling into the safety of the cellar, he pulled at the others to keep Teri or Carol from escaping the cavern first.

As they ran up, Daddy was coming down, and Kevin was caught by the arm. "I want to talk to you."

Kevin's heart stuttered. "Right now? Can I have my ice cream?" Kevin ventured a peek at Daddy, trying to gauge his mood.

"No." Daddy walked him to the bottom of the stairs, through the laundry room now loaded with bikes tilting on kickstands. Kevin followed him into the "office," the boiler room which Daddy fixed with shelving, a big bean pot filled with his penny collection, and a swivel chair. It was a bare room, far from the kitchen above, where Daddy gave out punishments.

Kevin would rather be back in the hatchway. He did a quick inventory of all he'd done that his dad disapproved of. He kicked Kitty in the back when she was running to tell on him, climbed the telephone pole by balancing on the bike seat to reach the lowest medal spike, and ate two bananas when no one was looking.

Daddy indicated a chair for his son to sit in. "Where's my dog, Kevin?"

Kevin's head yanked up. "What?"

"Bruno's missing. Did you let my dog off his rope?"

"No. He's missing? He's gone?" Kevin was surprised, then he frowned.

Daddy held a wooden ruler he used to hit the kids. "Hold out your hands."

Kevin held steady, even though his heart was thumping. Smack. The wooden edge, not the metal one, slammed down, across both palms. He winced and bit his lip, trying not to cry, tasting metal in his mouth. His father hit him again.

"If you're lying to me . . . or if you pull your hands back . . ." Daddy let a finger drift down the metal ridge, "it will be worse for you."

"I . . . I . . . I didn't even know he was gone. I'm gonna go call him and . . . and look for him." Tears rolled down Kevin's dusty cheeks. He was seven years old, his dog was gone, and Daddy blamed him.

"No, you're not going to look for him. It's too dark now. But if you're lying to me . . ." Daddy got quieter, his face in shadows.

Kevin's heart knocked in fear and sorrow. He sniveled, "I'm not, I'm not."

They were interrupted by Rita calling down, "Bob? Kevin? Come on up, boys, the ice cream is melting."

His father handed him a handkerchief, which he always seemed to have. "Blow." He went to the laundry room sink to rinse it out and came back to wash Kevin's face and cool his hands. It wasn't an act of kindness, Kevin knew. It was to get rid of evidence.

"This stays between us, man to man." It was Daddy's warning not to tell.

When Kevin entered the kitchen, the others were gone, getting ready for bed. Unlike in the movies, Kevin ate food even when he was sad. Head in hand, alone at the table, he swirled mostly melted, mostly chocolate ice cream, thinking.

Why was Daddy nice to Kitty, but mean to him? He didn't like Kevin. So now, Kevin wouldn't like him back, and he wasn't going to call him Daddy anymore either, because that was babyish. He'd been the only one to get permission to let Bruno into the house, if only the basement, when it stormed. He'd bring Bruno a cookie or a biscuit or a potato when no one was looking. Tossed him a ball. Called him by name. If Kevin got another chance, no dog of his would be left outside.

He put his empty bowl in the sink, and walked out into the pine-scented twilight, crying softly, trying to whistle for his dog, hoping and praying to the night stars that Bruno would come back.

He never did.

Kevin went to bed that night hoping it was his dad who ran away next.

12

POOL

Bob's oddest purchase for the new house was an above-ground pool.

Dumb as a stump, Rita thought, living room furniture would have made more sense. She was annoyed every time she looked out the window, unless, of course, the children were happily splashing and swimming.

Bob was right this time, and whenever he dove in, he was another kid, making whirlpools and tidal waves, sweeping everyone along. Bob bought Kevin and Kitty a blue plastic boat for their May birthday. They paddled it, stood in it, turned it upside down, pretending they were under a dock. All the kids sank the boat and worked furiously to get it back up. One day, when no one was looking, Kevin got the girls to jump off the rim of the pool to torpedo the boat. They bent the rim.

The truck pulled into the driveway and a sweaty Bob got out, knocking grout off his knees as he crossed the yard. "Jeeze, this is one hot August."

He smiled at Rita but frowned when he saw the dents. Bob asked what happened, who committed this crime?

Five kids said, "Not me."

"So . . . Mr. Nobody? Mr. Nobody comes over at night to stand on our pool ledge? He must be kind of fat to crush metal. I'll have to watch out for Mr. Nobody." He balled a fist.

"Who is Mr. No-no-buddy?" Noreen paddled a duck float toward her Daddy.

"Kids. Thank your baby sister. She saved Mr. Nobody from getting a knuckle sandwich. Damn, this one is cute."

He kissed her, lifting Noreen out to Rita's waiting towel. Bob peeled off his shirt, shoes, and socks, emptied his pockets, and dove in. He surfaced like a spouting whale. Everyone laughed, even Rita.

In September, Bob started going to bars, near their store in Hartford, and money leaked out of his pockets again. He'd gamble or throw darts "to relax." Rita would yell, they'd fight, and then Bob was temperate for a few days.

October's orange and gold leaves clattered by Rita's bedroom window. She sat at the edge of her bed, breathless after getting fall jackets from the attic. She crossed into the bathroom, shut the door, and vomited. Wiping her nose and eyes, she wondered why she was sick. Rita beseeched the mirror. She was pregnant. The *last* thing she wanted was another . . . baby. She rested her arms on the sink ledge, lowered her head, and let the tears fall. No, no, not again. How naive could she be? Irish. Catholic. Poor. A stereotype. A joke.

Rita tried to put supper together, kielbasa and sauerkraut, but gagged thinking of the smells. Instead, she baked a macaroni and cheese casserole, then retreated to the den to lie on the couch. As tears slipped out of her eyes, she covered her face with an arm.

Bob whistled coming through the door, then reacted to the empty kitchen. "It smells good, but where is everybody? Rita?"

"I'm in the den."

He untied his boots, kicked them off, and walked to the couch. "Are you sick? You're never sick." He came close, the bar smells all over him.

She pulled her hand away from her face. Her red-rimmed blue eyes glistened, "I'm pregnant."

He sat on the footstool and took her hand, "How do you know? I thought we were using the rhythm method."

"We were. It didn't work. *I don't want a baby*, Bob."

"What do you want to do? We can't do anything about it . . . can we?" He seemed genuinely concerned.

"No, we can't. I guess I'll have a baby in eight months."

His thumb made circles on her hand. "*We*. We'll have a baby in eight months. You rest. I'll call the kids to eat. I'll shut this door and tell them you're a little sick. We'll get through this, Rita. I'll help you. I swear."

She faced the back of the couch, taking the bit of time and privacy he offered. *If only you would, Bob. If only you would really help me with this baby, when you've had so many opportunities, and this one I don't want at all.* An unwanted baby. She sobbed, emitting tiny moans, inhaling and exhaling in steps, then dragged her nails through her hair. *What will I do? What will I do? What will I do?*

Their parish was now St. Brigid's in Elmwood. On Sundays, Rita took the four older children to church, and Bob stayed with Noreen. This spring day, Rita counted the other large families. The Langans, five; the Keenans, Michauds, McGills: seven, eight, nine kids. The mothers looked tired. Rita felt like a blimp at 27 years old, in an ugly maternity dress, too sad to kneel or stand. She ushered her children out at the end of Mass, and Father McBride reached for her hand, noticing her huge front.

"A blessing from God." He smiled and touched the kids' heads.

"How do we make it on blessings, Father?"

"The good Lord will provide." He lowered his voice, "The nuns will bring you a food basket." He moved on.

As she stood on the church steps in the sunshine, Rita wondered, was it God's voice she listened to? Or was it man's interpretation of God, her church's rulings, her religion's rules?

Right now, Rita needed a whole lot more than a food basket.

Her older sisters helped, with hand-me-down clothing for the children or for her, or something for the house. Her sister Carolyn was back home with their father. She and her boyfriend, Mike, offered to babysit so Bob and Rita could have a nice dinner before the baby came. But as the young couple pulled into the driveway, Rita went into labor, and shock. Her due date was seven weeks away.

"Carolyn, Mike, get in here quick," Bob yelled from the front door.

Rita whispered to Carolyn, "What do I do? It's too early . . . it's too soon." She walked around the front hall without purpose, and Rita always had a purpose.

Carolyn stopped her path and buttoned a sweater around Rita's shoulders. "I'll call Dr. Klein. Is his number in your book? Rita? I'll call your doctor. Then

I'll get Aunt Rose to mind the children overnight." The children said goodbye, caught up in the excitement. The caboose, Noreen, offered her mother a fistful of pussy willows. Rita kissed Noreen, putting the catkins in her sweater pocket, as she and Bob moved out the door.

13

SHARING

Bob drummed the steering wheel driving to Hartford Hospital.

Rita, awash in guilt and dread, said shakily, "Maybe they can stop my labor." She looked out the window, hoping for a distraction. Bob put his hand on her jiggling knee, but Rita pushed it off.

"I think we have done this before," he smiled.

She swallowed, thinking how inane he was, knowing nothing about giving birth. "Not 'we,' it's just me now, Bob. It's May, the baby is due in July. I don't want to think about . . . you don't know how hard this is, how scared I . . . "

Rita stopped talking and rocked into a contraction, an electric ray that burst under her belly and moved across it, sending out ripples of pain.

"Oh, God, how could I forget this? This pain, this . . . speaking of God," Rita paused to take a few stilted breaths. "Speaking of God, why does he want me to have a baby when it's too . . . too soon? God is punishing me because I didn't want another baby. Was that wrong? But I *want* this . . . baby . . . now. I'll be a good mother . . ." Rita's voice was between a whine and a plea.

Bob said, "No, no, Rita, he wouldn't punish you. Look how well you handled all the other babies. You always manage. He knows we can do this, you and me. We can have an early baby. Say a prayer in your head."

An orderly pushed Rita in a wheelchair to the admitting desk. She was clutching her purse by her hip, as her lap was missing, and her abdomen was charging with contractions. Rita had felt naïve with Dr. Klein at her first prenatal visit, but was now willing, desperate even, to learn about birth control. This had to be their last pregnancy. Bob waited in the hall while nurses prepped

Rita with a familiar, intrusive, shave and enema. Once she dressed in a blue johnny and striped robe, Dr. Klein appeared. A quick internal exam revealed the baby was coming.

"Prepare the delivery room, start an IV drip, and tell Mr. Leonard to wait in the lounge. Let's get this going, people. Rita, you relax. We've done this before." He smiled.

Rita, now in transition, was irritated that Dr. Klein said the same stupid thing as her husband. She squinted her eyes at how little men did in the scheme of things. She was given scopolamine and morphine in the delivery room. Rita listened to the medical team, trying to concentrate on the nurses bustling around, the warm lights, the clink of instruments. Her eyes fluttered, then she plunged into sleep. Hours or minutes later, she didn't know which, she was awoken by the faint cries of an infant.

"It's a boy. Not a bad size for a preemie. Five pounds, three ounces." A nurse held a little bundle, with a red face mewling like a kitten. He was already wiped clean, suctioned, and wrapped in a white blanket before Rita could comprehend. She grappled to know what was going on. Realizing her baby was born, she was happy, but sluggish. "That's Shawn." She smiled and lifted a listless hand toward him.

Rita let her head fall back onto the pillow, and Dr. Klein turned away from between Rita's legs to peel off his rubber gloves.

"There's . . . another baby in there." Rita raised her head to get Dr. Klein to listen, but she was murmuring, thick with drugs.

"No, Rita, that's the afterbirth. We'll take care of that in a minute."

"No, Doctor," she persisted, louder now, struggling to be heard, "I know what it feels like to deliver twins. There's pressure."

Klein wheeled back around and proclaimed, "She's right. People." Out came the second tiny boy, making little sounds. The doctors and nurses were buzzing around, ignoring Rita. Twins made the room busier for everyone.

"It's another boy, Rita. He's fine. Nurse Mullins, what does this one weigh?"

"Five pounds. Even. Doctor? Doctor?" Nurse Mullins' voice signaled for his attention. She held a bluer, more lethargic twin.

Rita saw him. Tiny. Rita pushed herself onto her elbows. "What's wrong? What's the m . . . matter?"

Dr. Klein held a needle trailing black thread mid-air. "Call Neonatal. Again."

Rita saw and heard all this, her pulse quickened, and she got angry, "Dr. Klein? Dr. Klein!"

He paused. "He's fine, Rita. They'll give him oxygen. Now you rest a while."

She lay back on her pillow. Her drugged mind was too tired to form terrible possibilities, but she wanted to solve something before falling asleep, fighting the swirls of confusion between dreams and realities. What was that boy's name? She wondered. A crib. She needed another crib. Is it already July?

Rita awoke in a private room. She was usually with a few postpartum women who were lying on white iron beds, snuggling into or swimming out of anesthesia. Bob sat on the visitor's chair, mopping his forehead with his still-folded handkerchief. He was sweating, although a cool breeze ruffled the curtains.

"I'm awake," Rita, fingered the chenille bedspread. Why was she getting special treatment?

Bob leapt up to kiss her forehead. "Nice job, Rita. Oh my God, two boys. Kind of evens the family out, right? Twins again. Did you even know?" He rambled on, smiling, but his usual enthusiasm was tempered.

She took a shuddering breath, recalled the delivery room, noted this private room. "It's bad, isn't it? The little one? I never told them his name. We didn't have one . . . we didn't have a name for him . . . he needs a name . . . We should call him Kieran, after my father."

Bob sat on her bed and clasped her hand, tight. "Yes, honey, that is a perfect name. He's going to be fine, but he's gonna need a little surgery."

"Surgery?" Rita's eyes flashed.

"Well, the doctors think his intestines are blocked. They can feed him intravenously."

"Bob." Rita clutched his arm in despair, too groggy to protest.

"They called in a specialist . . . a Dr. Cook. They are going to cut out a part of his intestine, a tiny piece of the baby's intestine and fix it."

"Say his name," Rita implored.

Bob seemed unsure of what she wanted.

"Say his name, Bob, we need to give Kieran his name."

"Kieran." Bob did as he was told. "What about a middle name? Shawn's is Robert."

"They can share that middle name. Shawn Robert. Kieran Robert."

She gasped now that the names were settled. "He's too tiny. How can they work on anyone so tiny? He's . . . fragile. Can I see him? Can I see them both? Can we see our babies?"

Bob rang for a wheelchair and helped to take her to the Neonatal Intensive Care window. A nurse instructed the staff to ready the babies for viewing. One went to the incubator labeled LEONARD and lifted Shawn, gladly displaying the baby. Rita pushed to a near-standing position, beseeching Bob.

He rapped on the glass. "We have twins. Where's the other one?"

A young nurse innocently asked, "The one with the club foot?"

"What? What's a club foot?" Rita melted back into her wheelchair.

Bob stood open-mouthed. No one said a thing. He curled a loose fist to his heart then clasped Rita's shoulder. The young nurse, oblivious to her searing words, reappeared rolling Kieran's incubator toward the window. He couldn't be taken out of his incubator, as there were tubes and lines taped onto his tiny chest. He wore a wisp of a blue knit cap. He was physically near his twin, but encased in glass and metal.

Rita's mind sped. Her baby son Kieran was damaged on the inside. How could he eat? He had a physical impairment, too. How would he walk? And run and ride a bike? How would she care for her sick little Kieran, bathe him, smell him? Rita had to protect baby Kieran, but they wouldn't let her touch him. She ached to hold her baby.

Rita placed her shaking hand over Bob's, their married communication system still working. "Please take me back to my room now."

14

FIGHTER

R ita spent her mornings with Shawn, his isolette wheeled to her. She
loved to hold him, nuzzle his neck, then feed him. Walking, talking,
and singing, she celebrated every sparrow yawn, kitten stretch, and bunny-nose
wrinkle he produced.

When Shawn went back to the nursery, Rita visited Kieran in the NICU,
where she had to scrub and be masked and gowned, just to reach in to touch his
arm or stroke his leg. Draping her arm around the enclosed incubator, Rita sang
"A Mother's Love is a Blessing," the best mothering song she knew. For Kieran,
she'd coo, talk, and sing. Her voice was all she could give him. And promises
that she'd make him strong and healthy and happy. She yearned to take him
and Shawn home to be welcomed into their big family.

On the fourth day of his life, Kieran had abdominal surgery.

Bob and Rita sat in her quiet room awaiting the outcome. Hours went by.
Rita went to cuddle Shawn.

Four hours later, Dr. Cook rapped on their door. "May I come in?"

Rita stood up, pulled her robe tight, and reached back for Bob's hand.

"Your son's a fighter. We've done a resected infarcted jejunum with anasto-
mosis and gastrostomy—it's better if I draw it." He turned over the cafeteria
menu to draw roadways of ascending, transverse, and descending colons and
where the small intestine was reattached.

Rita and Bob viewed the map as Dr. Cook described the work he performed.
"He has sutures inside and out . . . he . . . Kieran will be coming out of anesthesia
soon. Would you like to see him?"

"Oh, yes." Rita rejoiced, with eyes glistening. Hope flooded her veins and warmed her face, because soon, she'd give Kieran all the promises she made.

Bob put a flat palm on his heart, and whispered, "Thank you, Dr. Cook."

They watched Kieran breathe, a cloth over his eyes, tubes and bandages, a ventilator, two nurses hovering nearby. Rita, as one who sewed, could only imagine the tiny stitches across that scrawny abdomen: a hummingbird's footprints. Bob and Rita held hands outside the NICU window and rested their foreheads on the glass. Rita whispered for Kieran's future, "Please, God. Please, God. Please, God." And because he made it through surgery, "Thank you. Thank you. Thank you."

Rita was happy back in her room that evening. From her sweater hanging on a hook, she transferred Noreen's pussy willows to her robe pocket. Rita crawled into bed, stroking the soft buds, hopeful for Kieran's recovery. The doctors said the club foot was an easy fix, a smaller surgery, not at all life-threatening.

He'd be fine.

Bob glided out of the hospital. Hell, yeah, now he could celebrate two new sons with his buddies at the Peter Pan Bar. He'd been by Rita's side whenever he wasn't working, and Aunt Rose was staying with the children.

"Hey, look who the cat dragged in."

"Line 'em up, Hank. This round's on me." Bob opened his wallet along with his mouth. "I got good news. Both my twin boys are doing great."

He stayed too long, because the night was young, until Hank handed him the bill at midnight. "I gotta start ringing out, Bobby."

Bob put his cigarette between his lips and squeezed one eye shut as he reached around for his wallet. He peeled off some mortgage money, then trudged through heavy rain to reach his truck, where he'd sit until the rain stopped. Bob snored himself awake at two a.m. and drove a wiggly line home.

Ten days after the birth, Shawn and Rita were cleared to go home. Her heart ached to leave one baby behind, but Kieran needed more care.

Shawn looked comparatively robust at almost six pounds. Rita dressed him in a tiny layette, then wrapped him in a yellow blanket, with knit booties covering his doll-like feet. He was nestled in his mother's arms for the ride.

They pulled onto Exeter Avenue on June 8, 1961. Aunt Rose watched the kids flop out of the pool to run to Rita, who was standing under a pine tree, holding their baby brother. His siblings took turns grasping Shawn's tiny fingers and feet and asking when they could hold him.

"Don't drip on the baby," Aunt Rose said as she pushed away all their wrinkled and chlorinated fingers to take Shawn.

Rita held a hand over her eyes in the bright sun, "That's strange, where's Carol? I thought for sure she'd be ready to meet this little guy."

Inside, she found Carol eating B&G Hot Peppers from the jar. Carol puckered her lips and fanned her hot exhale, "Wowie. Better than a fireball."

They both laughed. This was such an independent act. One of Rita's children was defying a rule, but not being bad or naughty, just growing up. Hmmm.

Carol turned to the counter to organize a plastic pitcher of lemonade and a stack of Dixie cups on a tray. "What about the other one? When does he come home?"

"Kieran." Rita's lips quivered, thinking how fragile Kieran looked, blue veins under translucent skin, how his chest rose and fell, while machines beeped, and nurses hovered. "Kieran. That's his name. As soon as he's well, honey. He needs to gain some weight."

It was all fragmented, with newborn Shawn at home, and newborn Kieran four miles away. Rita couldn't do this to Kieran, couldn't be happy at home without him. She couldn't do this. She needed all of her children together.

15

HEAVEN

When Rita planned to visit Kieran in the afternoon, she had to rely on friends for rides and babysitting.

Mrs. Hallenback, a mother to seven boys, came over that Saturday, bringing a tuna casserole, and a Wonder Bread bag full of peanut butter and jelly sandwiches, which was a big hit.

Rita sterilized bottles for Shawn and calculated doing double of everything when Kieran came home.

Rita forgot, during this stressful pregnancy, that no matter what went on in her life, opening a bedroom door and seeing her baby, its legs tucked under its diapered behind, all was right in the world. They would smile at her, then reach out a hand, and later, stand in a crib and call for her, their mother. She sang her love to them. Rita sang ballads, hymns, jingles, and the pop tunes on WDRC, which she left on all day. She kept singing Kieran's perfect song to him in the nursery.

On June 22, the official start of summer, Catholic nuns brought a food basket, as promised by Father McBride when Rita had rebuffed the priest's blessing at seeing her pregnant. One more man, Rita had thought, who knew nothing about giving birth and raising babies. Knew nothing about how few choices women could make about their own bodies, their own families.

Rita watched as Mother Superior pulled into the driveway in a Ford LTD station wagon. Six women in flowing black habits with clacking rosary beads piled out. Mother Superior rang the doorbell.

With Shawn in the crook of her arm, Rita ushered them into the kitchen. She presented her polished children and introduced them individually.

The Leonards got shy having celebrities in their home. Carol and Kitty poked each other and stole glances at the nuns' shoes. Rita had covered her yellow Formica table with a passable linen tablecloth and made tea, using Mother's china.

The children stood around, and the nuns did too, until Rita blurted out, "Here, Sister Helena, take this baby, while I get the sugar."

The order sat in the children's seats, giggling, eager to coo and cuddle with Shawn. As Carol, Kevin, Kitty, Teri, and Noreen hovered, the nuns drew them into conversation. The children got bolder and asked questions.

"Do you have any kids?"

"Do you have a mother and father?"

"Is there a pet in your convent?"

And Kevin made the giggling turn into laughter when he asked, "Did any of you ever run away? I would."

Rita and her children, polite and funny, walked their guests to the door, with promises to look for them in church. They then sorted the donations: a canned ham with a little key, rice, apples, jars of baby food, Cheerios, instant coffee, and oddly, on this summer day, a Claxton Holiday Fruit Cake.

After putting the last of the baby food away, Rita got a call. Kieran was not doing well. Could she and Mr. Leonard come right now? She called Carolyn to babysit, then called Bob, trying to keep the panic out of her voice.

Lately, Kieran, on the mend, had gained traces of weight and gossamer wings of color. As they raced to their son, Rita blocked bad thoughts with a litany of silent prayers. The on-staff doctor ushered them into the room, and they need not pause for cloth masks and gowns. Kieran was laboring, his stick legs still, but his tiny fists were clamped tight. He was red. Little puffs of air escaped his nose, but intake was difficult. His shoulders quaked.

He was dying.

Rita reached into the incubator to stroke Kieran's arm.

Dr. Cook quietly came in. "It's pneumonia. We didn't know. I'm so sorry."

Rita reached a hand toward the doctor, supplicating, "How long? How long have you known?"

"We . . . we thought Kieran would pull through. He's such a fighter."

Rita hadn't noticed anything yesterday when she was here. Was he more distressed? That was her job, as his mother, to notice, to see, to protect.

The nurses and doctors moved away from the incubator, knowing to step back to allow the parents in close. Rita draped her arm over the incubator's glass.

"Is he in pain?" Tears, so quiet as to not wake the sleeping baby, fell off her eyelashes.

Dr. Cook shook his head.

Kieran twitched, eyes shut, and pulled in a breath. He let it out. One more. Then, no more. His little baby hands unclenched, and he left this world.

The room went eerily still.

She would never hold him, rock him, stroke his face. Could she hold him now? Would that make it worse? Would he be cold? How could this angel be gone?

She couldn't find words to get what she wanted, to say she wanted to hold Kieran, just once.

Did time go by? Rita and Bob turned to each other in a desperate embrace. A piece of Rita was carved out, it hurt that bad. She pressed her hand to the top of the incubator, then to her heart, pushing, trying to stop the pain. Tears streamed down Rita's face.

"Our baby's gone," she murmured to Bob's ear.

He moaned low in the back of his throat, then sobbed, his shoulders moving in a rhythmic beat.

The ICU staff moved away silently on crepe-soled shoes, except for one lone nurse. Nurse Egan busied herself disconnecting Kieran from the machines. After a while, an hour . . . a day . . . which seemed like minutes to Rita . . . this brave nurse, a girl, really, touched them both, at the small of their backs, as one would little children.

"It's time to go. I will take care of Kieran now. There's a chapel on the first floor."

Rita kissed her two fingertips and touched the incubator. Without all the buzzing machines, he was a sleeping infant, peaceful.

His parents walked out the door as one. They sat close in the chapel. Praying. Crying. Breathing.

Rita and Bob knew when it was time to go home. They had done all they could, and six children were waiting for them.

In the truck, Rita spoke first, "How do we tell the kids?"

Bob blanched. "Their brother Kieran went to heaven, to be with God, an angel?" They agreed, as if it would be that easy. It wasn't.

Bob couldn't whistle the kids together, with his mouth misshapen by grief. But all the kids, except Shawn, who was sleeping in his crib, crowded into the kitchen, coming in from the neighborhood.

When Carol, Kevin, Kitty, Teri, and Noreen saw their mom and dad, and listened as he choked out that one sentence, they started to cry. It was the saddest choir Rita ever heard. Kitty clung to her mother, and Carol held her father's hand. Noreen did not understand, but Aunt Carolyn, who was carrying her, fell apart and gave Noreen to Kevin, the biggest person available. Teri hugged the cat. The weight of the room was crushing.

"Mommy?" Carol sniffed. "Kieran can only be an angel if he was baptized. Was he?"

"He was baptized right before surgery. Shawn was too." Rita wiped her nose and gave a tissue to Kitty.

Bob added, "We'll have a funeral, but not a wake. We'd like you three to be there." He dabbed at his eyes as he gazed at Carol, Kitty, and Kevin. "The little ones won't understand."

Rita took a ragged, three-part inhale, and pulled Noreen and Teri onto her lap, "How could they . . . when even I don't understand?" She kissed the tops of their heads.

That night, standing over Shawn as he slept, Bob and Rita stroked his back and held onto the crib rails for a long time.

Kieran had been alive for one month, and he'd be buried in the family plot beside his grandmother. He did not have Last Rites, as his infant soul was pure. Kieran's funeral was on June 27, 1961, attended by his sad brother, sisters, and parents. A small group of friends, neighbors, and family members came to the church, and however stoic, cried at the sight of the tiny white casket.

Rita found a poem, which gave her a measure of comfort, better than a prayer. She asked the priest to say it for her.

I, who never kissed your head,
Lay these ashes in their bed;
That which I could do have done.
Now farewell, my newborn son.
By Yvor Winters

Rita's obstetrician sent flowers. The children's principal, Miss Foley, wrote a lovely letter. Some friends and neighbors wrote congratulations cards about their new son, Shawn, but didn't mention Kieran at all.

That, and those who wouldn't, or couldn't, go to Kieran's funeral, hurt Rita most of all.

When they brought the older children home, Rita told them to take Noreen and Teri outside for fresh air.

Bob went to his basement office, while she stared out the den window, watching Kevin knot a rope swing from the maple tree's largest limb. The siblings played and fought over taking turns.

Kitty came into the house, and took Rita's hand, tapping the smooth skin. "Can you sing me Kieran's song, Mommy?"

Rita still stared out the window, and quivered, "I don't think I can, honey. Probably not today."

Kitty set her mouth to not cry, trying to help Mommy. She sat quietly with her for a long time.

Rita stopped singing.

16

WEEKEND

School ended and the Leonard kids ran through dewy lawns, made dandelion chains, and relocated worms to higher ground during rainstorms. They whipped a tetherball around a metal pole. They swam in the cool pool when Rita was done working inside.

Alone with her baby, Rita wondered: did Shawn know he was sharing his mother with a ghost? Holding him, she imagined holding her lost son, Kieran. Shawn would miss out by not having his twin.

Her first twins had bonded in the playpen, where Kevin crawled over Kitty, stole her toys, and ate her crackers. Kitty opened her mouth to stop him. Kitty was fight and Kevin was flight. They were a comedy team, friends, because twins are special.

It was so hot in the house one evening, Rita had the kids wear undershirts and underpants to bed. She turned on the attic fan and opened the windows a few inches to allow for maximum circulation, and the children fell asleep easily.

She did not. Rita sat in bed, past ten o'clock, with a book on her lap. Bob came home late, and ate leftover supper, then came into their bedroom. He gave Rita a sympathetic smile. "How was your day?"

"Hard. I miss Kieran." She closed her book.

Bob and Rita acted upbeat during the day, for the children, and saved the sad, what-if conversations for late at night. This tragedy, losing a child, united them for a time.

Rita whispered, "They've forgotten him. Carol and Kitty think all Shawn does is sleep and spit up and need a diaper change."

Bob kicked off his shoes. "Well, that's true, isn't it? But I've seen them fold a dish towel when you run out of diapers. And they can both use the duckie diaper pins on the little—"

"That's my point Bob, how would I have taken care of Kieran, too?"

Bob bent over to hug Rita, as her tears pooled and spilled. "You would have managed, Rita. You always do. Don't doubt that."

The family needed a break. Rita asked her sister Mary Alice if they could visit the beach for a few days.

The McKeon cottage was large. The attic was partitioned into rooms, sporting iron beds with saggy mattresses and flowered bedspreads. Old metal fans wheezed in every window. All the girls shared a room with their cousins Deborah and Patricia. Kevin was bunking with Brian and Bill. Rita and Bob had a small room on the first floor, and Shawn slept in a porta-crib, adorned with wooden beads, on which decades of babies had cut teeth.

Mary Alice complained about how much food the Leonard kids ate. Mac, the big-mouthed, Southern salesman, told off-color jokes and called the women *darlin'* or *doll* when they changed from their molded-cupped bathing suits into sundresses before dinner. The men sat around in their plaid trunks, with matching terry cloth-lined shirts, and wore socks with their sandals. They drank tall gin and tonics in iridescent aluminum cups.

The McKeons had stuff, and the Leonard kids, teasing, laughing, and running, wanted to play with it all: the Thumbelina doll, the crabbing pails, scooters, and Archie comic books.

In the evenings, the kids lit firecrackers and shot off cap guns, the sulfur smoke rising in a haze.

Rita spoke to Bob quietly, because the walls were thin, "We're wearing out our welcome. Our kids don't quit. They don't quit eating, telling jokes, or moving. They get sunburned on the beach, even covered up. Let's leave early tomorrow."

When Rita kissed her children goodnight in the hot attic, they were itching, blistering, and peeling all over the white sheets. But not complaining. They complained only when they had to leave.

The McKeons were relieved to see them trudge into the VW bus, crying baby and all, to return home, like a Norman Rockwell illustration.

17

CHECKS

Rita welcomed fall, as now four children attended Charter Oak School, with Teri joining in. Rita loved the routine of those first few weeks. It gave her special time with Noreen and Shawn. Kieran was gone, yet Shawn was thriving under her watchful eye.

One September evening, she brought a steaming coffee to her desk to open mail and pay bills. Rita practiced her signature on an envelope, wanting her penmanship, at least, to look middle class. Rita ripped the coupon out of the mortgage booklet and wrote a check in the exact amount to Connecticut National Bank. It was Bob's task to drop this off on his way to work, to save the five-cent postage.

Bob came in from the darkening yard, careful not to bring his muddy shoes into the living room. He peeked in from the hall. "I covered the pool for the season. I should have done it a week ago. I'm gonna get a pack of smokes. Need anything?"

She didn't look up. "Same as always, a gallon of milk and a loaf of bread. Any store open this late?"

"I can check out that deli on Prospect."

Rita tilted her head when the door closed. He was being helpful, with the pool and offering to run an errand. She sat back for a minute, enjoying the quiet, and gazed at her desk.

Bob had stripped, sanded, and varnished this desk, and polished the glass knobs. From another job, he retrieved a cane-seated chair. On Rita's birthday, right before Noreen was born, Bob handed her a tiny skeleton key. Rita, seated, looked into the mirror on the back wall of the desk. It was the only furniture gracing their living room. It was beautiful. Something nagged her as she stretched rubber bands over Bob's pile. *Ah*, she thought, *I gave Bob permission to stay out all evening, looking for an open deli, but he would find an open bar.* Rita shut her eyes and held her chin in her hands. *When will I ever learn?*

The next morning, while Rita washed Shawn's face at the sink, Kevin and Kitty got into a fight over the last of the Apple Jacks. Kitty reached to take his bowl, claiming she "called it." Kevin tapped her forehead, hard, with two fingers, snapping her head back.

Rita saw this degrading move he learned from his father.

"Kevin. Don't do that." No, she wasn't letting another generation of that behavior go on.

Kitty wailed, "I'll get you, you-big-stinking je-rk." The "jerk" came out as a two-syllable word about an octave too high. Rita made it to the table, the baby on her shoulder, and yelled at both of them.

"Why yell at me?" Kevin asked Rita. "She's the one that started it, the ugly turtle face."

"He's *stoled* my cereal." Kitty seethed with the unfairness.

"Stop fighting like barbarians. Keep your hands to yourselves."

Rita handed Shawn to Carol, "Hold him a minute." She poured some coffee, "And Kevin, what's a 'turtle face'?"

"It's her ugly mug, like this," His eyes popped open, he bucked out his top teeth, drew his lip down into a vee, and sucked in his cheeks. Rita picked up the baby and burst out laughing. So did Kevin. Kitty did too. The battle was over.

Rita helped the kids get ready for school. She drew Carol's long blonde hair into a high ponytail. Kitty and Teri's hair, fine and wispy, was held with barrettes. While buttoning the back of Teri's dress, Rita noticed Kevin's pants, light-weight chinos, ripped at both knees.

"You can't wear those to school, Kevin. Go change."

"I don't *got* nothing else."

"You don't *have anything* else," she corrected.

"I know. I said that." He was bouncing a small ball made of rubber bands.

"Stop that. Laundry basket?" Rita glanced at the clock.

"Looked." Kevin captured the ball to bring to school.

Kevin, the only schoolboy in the family, was hard on clothing. It was mid-autumn, and he was in ripped, summer-weight pants. She wondered what a stranger might think. Did Kevin look unloved? It was too late now for the magic of her needle and thread.

Kevin didn't give it a second thought. He would be running and balancing along the tops of low walls all the way to school. He'd be cold only if he stood still. Kevin tried to be first at Charter Oak, because there were monkey bars to climb and boys to race, and today, a rubber-band ball to show off.

Rita was mopping the kitchen floor when the telephone rang.

"Mrs. Leonard, please?" asked a vaguely familiar voice.

"Yes, this is she," Rita replied. She knew phone etiquette from working on a switchboard.

"This is Nurse Sherry. Congratulations on your newest baby. I see that you brought, uh, Shawn in for his four-month visit."

Rita panicked. "What's wrong?"

"Oh, nothing, I can assure you." The nurse paused. "When you came in with Shawn, just the two of you, that was nice, wasn't it?"

Rita clipped out, "Yes, it was." Get to the point.

Nurse Sherry went on. "Well, I, I mean, we, here at Dr. Saunders' office, would appreciate it if you brought one or two children at a time. For appointments."

Rita gripped the receiver a little harder. "You want me to bring in one or two children at a time, is that correct? You do realize that I have six children?" Rita asked. "What would you suggest I do with the four or five children I leave at home?"

The nurse hesitated, "Well, I . . . "

"What if most of them, say, those that I leave home, need immunizations at the same time as the ones I bring in? Do I come back another day with the remainders?"

Rita was just getting warmed up; this was a chance to tell that old biddy off. "Should I split up the twins? Would that work for you, Nurse Sherry?"

The nurse found her voice. "The doctor is busy with lots of patients. When your family comes in, they take a lot of time, and they tend to . . . "

"Tend to what, Nurse Sherry? Tend to act their ages? Tend to be ill? Tend to be well? You work for a *pediatrician*, one whom I have known for a decade. Wait a minute." Rita got louder with a new clarity. "Did Dr. Saunders request this?"

"The doctor is too busy," Nurse Sherry tried again, but Rita cut her off.

"No, he didn't. Because he's a kind, gracious human being. I *cannot* believe you have the gall, the temerity, to call me with this idea. I've got to go, Nurse Sherry, because one of my *children* is calling me. But when I make an appointment, *I* determine the number of children I bring in. Not you. And if you ever call me again, with a nonmedical issue, I will personally tell the doctor of your insubordinate actions. Good day, Nurse Sherry."

Rita's heart was pounding, but in a brave way. She defended herself and her children. That was kind of . . . exhilarating. Plus, it gave her a story to tell her bold sister Nancy.

At the little ones' nap time, Rita took boxes of handed-down boys' clothes from the attic. She laid out neat piles on the brass bed. Shirts, shoes, a Cub Scout uniform, all too big for Kevin, but she found two pairs of dungarees, some school pants, and a gray pair for church.

When the kids rushed in after school, sweeping curled yellow and red leaves into the kitchen, they raced to change into their play clothes, then rushed right back out. Rita lassoed Kevin by his tee shirt collar as he ran by her room.

"Hold on, buddy. I've got some clothes for you to try on."

"Right now?" His eyebrows shot up. "Billy and Dave are waiting for me. We're capturing squirrels."

"Is that so? Give me ten minutes." She gave him a pair of pants to put on, but he turned toward his room. "Where are you going?"

"In there." He pointed to his room. He was modest, with so many sisters.

When he returned, Rita knelt down with her tomato pincushion in hand, ready to mark the length. The pants were too long, an easy fix. "These are all your cousin Brian's pants."

"When do I have to give them back?" Kevin checked the mirror.

"Hold still," Rita said, with two pins in her mouth. "What? Oh no, these are now yours."

"Doesn't he like them anymore?" Kevin pushed his fists into the pockets.

"I think he did, but he outgrew them." Rita kept pinning.

"Wow. All these pants for me?" Now he rocked on his toes, seeing how nice he looked. He then frowned, "But do I have to try them all on? The guys are waiting."

Now, she laughed. "Nope. I can measure you once and fix them all. You are free to go trap . . . squirrels, is it? Good luck with that." Rita dusted off her knees, gathering her sewing kit and five pairs of pants. "You'll look sharp tomorrow."

He ran to his room, but with modesty forgotten in the rush to get outside, he pulled on one pant leg at a time and hopped down the hall, his Fruit of the Looms exposed. He'd die of embarrassment if he saw her laugh at his retreating butt.

While Rita was threading the machine in the den, Carol came in, ruddy from outside, smelling vaguely of dried leaves. She unzipped her jacket and dropped it on the couch.

"What're you doing?" She put her hand on her mom's back.

"I'm hemming these pants for Kevin." Rita draped a tape measure over her neck.

"Can I do that?" Carol asked, looking at the intricate machine.

"You can. Come here." Rita demonstrated how the needle thread above and the bobbin thread below came together. Her eight-year-old daughter sat still, learning the intricacies of sewing, something Rita loved.

"It's a little race and you gotta move your fingers fast." Carol's face was intense in the machine's tiny light.

"That's true . . . I never thought of it that way. Aunt Carolyn is getting married, and she wants you to be her junior bridesmaid. I said I'd make your dress. Would you help me with that?" This was perfect, for both of them.

Carol's eyes lit up. "Oh, yes. Do you have pretty material? Pink? Or blue?"

Rita finished the first pair of pants, then pulled another from the pile. "It has to be off-white. We'll need a pattern, thread, and chalk."

"Chalk, from school?"

"Well, no, it's tailor's chalk. It marks darts and tucks, so your dress fits well. We can buy sash material in blue. You'll carry a bouquet, and I'll curl your hair."

"I'll be like a little bride." Carol kissed Mommy's cheek and put on her jacket. "I'm gonna go tell Kitty. She's not in it, the wedding, is she?" Carol paused in her exit.

"No, just you. But be nice—" Rita heard the door slam, "about it." She commented to herself, "Why can't you all be a little nicer to each other?"

18

MAGIC

Rita had scrambled to get dinner made after the sewing lesson. She directed grace, then a platter of cheeseburgers and fried potato slices.

Bob came in, acting casually as he sat, but he smelled of beer and his eyes were bloodshot.

Rita rose to fill his plate, and when she put it down, he caught her wrist, and said, "Hi darling. How was your day?" He sounded like a television dad.

"Fine," she escaped his touch, and returned to her end of the table, where the pan of creamed corn sat.

He was drunk again.

Bob rubbed his nose with the back of his hand, "Cheeseburgers in October. What are these—fired? I mean fried?" He burped, keeping his mouth shut, but beer breath wafted over the table.

Kevin wrinkled his nose.

"Hey there, Noreen." Bob fiddled in his pocket, awkwardly put a quarter between two fingers and reached behind Noreen's ear. He acted surprised to find a coin there. She giggled.

"You're rich." He smiled, pleased with his trick.

Rita, reddening, continued to spoon Gerber smooshed peas into Shawn, who was happily kicking his highchair.

Kitty leaned in, "Do that to me, to my ear, Daddy."

His next coin rolled under Noreen's chair. She clambered down, picked it up, and waddled over to her sister. "Here, Kitty. You be rich." She offered the coin, generous.

"A nickel? I don't want a nickel. What can you buy with that?" Kitty scowled.

"Kitty!" Rita exploded. "Enough. Say 'thank you' to Noreen for being helpful. Noreen, sit down, honey."

Rita turned her steely blue eyes to Bob. "Could you please stop, now, with your *magic* tricks?"

Kevin and Carol watched one parent, then the other.

"Oh, and I can't have any fun with my child? My . . . children? You never want them to have any fun. They'll be —"

"Don't be ridiculous. You stopped at the bar, so you're *late* for dinner, again, and think you can—"

"LATE," he yelled back at her. "I'm LATE? I'm here, aren't I?"

He shoved his plate dangerously close to the table's edge, but Carol caught it. He scraped his chair back, standing up.

Rita stood to move toward Carol, and then Shawn cried at the yelling. Rita watched Bob, to see who she needed to protect, her oldest or youngest child.

"I'll show you late, you old . . . you old WITCH. I feel SORRY for these kids having a DRILL SERGEANT like you, like . . . I'll go where people appreciate my skills." Bob traipsed toward the door, stopped abruptly, pulled all the coins out of his pockets, and threw them on the floor.

"Keep the change," he laughed at them, at her, and at his own joke. He stomped out, and his truck peeled out of the driveway.

Rita observed each of her children and gathered Shawn in her arms. Bob, fighting in front of the kids, betrayed Rita on yet another level. A few coins were still tinkling into corners when Kevin leapt to gather them.

Rita stopped him with a sharp, "Leave it."

The children snuck glances at each other, and their mother.

"He made the mess; he can clean it up. Anybody want his cheeseburger?"

Kitty and Kevin split it.

Her heart pulsed and her hands shook, as she gave Shawn two potato slices while he sat sniffling on her lap.

That evening, Rita tidied the kitchen, leaving the money on the floor. The kids went to sleep. Rita showered and rolled her hair. Her shoulders stayed high and taut like they always did the nights he came home drunk. She moved through the house turning off lights. It was 11:39.

In bed, Rita dozed, but woke to water running in the bathroom. Minutes later, through narrowed eyes, a silhouette morphed into Bob in the dim rays of the streetlight. Bob sat on the edge of the bed to take off his shoes, pants, and shirt, with difficulty. He got in bed and threw out an arm to touch her.

"Hey, baby . . . "

Was that his feeble attempt to gauge her anger? She feigned sleep.

A more astute man would have noticed.

He tried again. "Hi, honey. Turn 'round. Maybe . . . I was . . . "

Bob was insane to think that she would turn toward him to accept his stupid apologies and attempts at . . . what? Sex? Was he completely out of his mind? The drunken, smelly fool soon fell into labored breathing, turned to face the wall, and slept, unfairly.

Furious energy coiled in her hands. How dare he? Who did he think he was? With her left hand, she bent back one finger on her right for every one of Bob's transgressions: They had no money. He came home drunk. He insulted her in front of the kids. He went back out. He smelled like a barfly and didn't even shower.

That made her the maddest of all; she wouldn't be able to sleep with this . . . slob tonight. Rita peeled off the top sheet and clutched her pillow and bedspread to make a bed on the couch. She steamed through the kitchen. The coins were in neat piles on the counter. Who did that?

Rita talked herself into methodically unclenching her shoulders, arms, and hands, to relax and fall asleep. She'd plan what to do about Bob tomorrow.

Rita woke at six, stripped her ersatz bed, made coffee, and carried a cup to her desk to start a list. She heard a door slam, then retching in the upstairs bathroom. Rita walked to the bottom step to see a white-faced Bob shift across the hall. He flopped into bed with a moan.

On her notepad, she scratched out "To talk about" and wrote, "Get through the day."

She called Big George to run the store.

Rita walked into their room and threw her wadded-up ball of bedding at Bob's head, startling him.

"Wha . . . ?" He held an arm over his eyes.

"Wake up. Bob." She shook his foot. "Bob," she got louder. "We need groceries. Do you have any money?" Rita asked, standing at the end of the bed, her arms crossed.

"Pants pocket . . ." he mumbled.

"I already looked there. Anywhere else?" She wanted to slap his sleeping, snoring, slackened face.

"Ah . . . ah." Bob waffled. He was awake and asleep at the same time.

"*Think*, Bob. Does anyone owe us money? At the store?"

She would rob Peter to pay Paul if it meant her children could eat.

Bob licked his cracked lips, "There's a check . . . from . . . some guy . . . he bought tile . . ."

Rita didn't need details. "Where? Where's the check?"

"Cash register."

After bundling Shawn and Noreen to Eleanor's house, and driving the big kids to school, Rita headed to greet George. She found the check in the register, forged Bob's signature, and drove to the bank for $67.39.

At the market, Rita filled her cart with one chicken (good for two meals), a pound of beef, oatmeal, coffee, juice, apples, two loaves of day-old bread, and dented cans of soup. Next, it was to Esso for gas. She kept $1.10 for emergencies, and with the remaining $3.50, drove to Mila Fabrics for material, a pattern, chalk, and a remnant of blue for Carol's dress.

On a regular day, Rita would let Carol choose her fabric. However, Rita didn't know when a regular day would occur, what with Bob's alcoholism and this boomerang poverty fighting her every step of the way.

Bob woke mid-morning. The house was quiet. He couldn't remember if it was a weekday or weekend. Sitting up, he noticed the balled-up bedding on the floor and remembered coming home plastered, and that Rita was livid. He hauled himself up and closed his eyes just to breathe. He pulled on his robe, as the house was chilly. He creaked down the stairs, and the creaking was coming from his knees, holding onto the railing, walking like an old man, and feeling like a dead one. Bob made his way to make instant coffee. While the tea kettle heated up, he drank about a quart of tap water, trying to quell his churning stomach. He sat down before the whistle blew, then stood shakily to stop the blast. Bob took sugar, but he'd skip it this time because his hands shook too badly to hold a spoon. Feeling a little better with the hot liquid in his stomach, he wanted a cigarette. Glancing around the kitchen for his jacket and its resident pack of smokes proved fruitless. He'd have to get up. Carrying his cup to the sink, he saw neat rows of coins on the counter beneath the windowsill. Under the quarters, Bob saw a tiny piece of paper. The note, written in beautiful script, said, "I saved these for you, Daddy, for *emerjencees.*"

It could only have been Carol, his guardian angel, always looking out for him. His lips quivered. It was two dollars and twenty cents. Now, palming the nickels, dimes, and quarters, he recalled the night before. Coming in late, he had ruined supper, fought with Rita, and thrown the change all over the floor, then stormed out.

Bob rubbed a hand over the stubble on his cheeks and chin. Again, he disgusted Rita, and himself. His resolve was strong every morning, but as the day went on, beer or vodka became his personal beacons.

Bob wandered around the first floor. He found a framed picture of himself holding four of the kids, half clinging to his back, half in his arms, all smiling.

His jacket, and his Marlboros, were on the banister. He rummaged through Rita's desk for matches, which was silly because she didn't smoke. But he did come across a letter he had written years ago when she was on a trip with her mother. He wrote the letter over many nights, telling Rita how beautiful she was, and that they should plan to live an exciting life. They should pray the Rosary to thank God for their family, and to ensure future travels together. He read on, "I feel excited about meeting your plane, the same excitement I felt on our wedding morning. I have been thinking of you, pleasant thoughts and memories. I will have to tell you myself how much I love you, and want you, and I need you. I swear to God, this past week, I had a heartache, caused by your absence."

Bob folded the letter, as delicate as tissue paper, and slid it back into its drawer. He moved from the living room into the den, where they'd hung the mosaic tile ship he made in his old garage, the nautical curtains she had sewn, and a fishnet atop the window, adorned with glass baubles, shells, and starfish she'd collected. His heart ached anew.

He eventually found matches and an ashtray, taking both to the couch. What a heel he was. Rita slept in this spot last night because he was stinking drunk.

He sat back to look up. *Please God, make me stop. Please.*

Bob's stomach settled and his head cleared as the morning marched on. At noon, Bob showered, then organized the basement, replaced a gasket on the toilet, and switched all the screens for storm windows. He zipped on a corduroy jacket to rake the backyard. Maples littered down gold, red, and orange leaves, and the pines threw down fragrant, brown, feathery clusters. The kids returned from school before Rita returned from her errands. Kevin came running into the yard, his plaid jacket streaming behind him.

"Hey, big guy, grab a rake. Wait, go change first. Hey, those are nice pants." Bob punched his shoulder.

Kevin sped off. Teri and Kitty skipped across the driveway, speaking Mootchie Gatchi Gu, their secret language. Bob gave them each a twirl, swinging them by their armpits, with their skirts and coats billowing.

When Carol walked calmly into the backyard, her father met her halfway. "Hi, princess," Bob pulled her into a hug, crushing her face into the corduroy.

"Dad. Stop." She laughed. He didn't let go. "Did you get my note?"

"Yes, I did, honey. I'll keep it for emergencies, like buying Chuckles or Neccos. You can share the candy or keep it."

Carol stepped on his shoes, circling his waist with her arms. "I'll share it only with you, Daddy."

His children still loved him and wanted to be with him.

While the kids were changing into their play clothes, Bob piled the leaves and pine needles into a mound for a someday-bonfire. He inhaled the crisp air and waited for Rita to get home with the little ones. He would apologize and make it all right again with his wife.

There was nothing he wanted more than peace with Rita.

19

ADVICE

Rita went to retrieve the little ones from Eleanor's house. It was cold enough to leave her groceries in the car, and she was happy to have coffee with a friend. Shawn and Noreen snuggled in a playpen.

Stirring her coffee, Rita said she was going to ask Bob to leave.

"Leave?" Eleanor asked. "To go where? Where would he go?" They ate Viking Bakery cookies.

"I don't care where he goes. Other people do it. Raise kids on their own."

"Not by choice. I wouldn't wish that on my worst enemy. Want sugar?" Eleanor held out a bluebird sugar bowl.

"No sugar, no cream. I'm getting fat. Back to Bob. What good is he? He's dragging me down, El. He's mean to the kids. Mean to me. Hell, excuse my language, he was even mean to our dumb dog. He's a child himself. How can he help me raise our children? His drinking—"

"Rita. Look at me." Eleanor squeezed her hand, "You can't kick him out. You can't leave him, and he can't leave you. He won't go because he loves you."

Rita flashed with anger. "But I—" She wanted Eleanor to agree that Rita would manage somehow without Bob.

"Wait a minute. Let me finish. Cut the crap. No one is going anywhere because you have six children. You have *triple* the children that we do. You work, what, ten hours a week at the hospital? That's not even grocery money. Bob won't be able to support two households. If you worked during the day, who would watch your children? Who would cook, iron, do housework, and laundry? What would you give up? *What else are you willing to give up?*"

Rita went home. She was disheartened, or heartened, she didn't know which. What else could she give up? What else did she have?

Bob's truck was in the driveway, so he hadn't gone to work.

She breathed in sharply. It was confrontation time. She was jittery from coffee and nerves, but was ready for this.

20

CHICKEN

In their backyard, the kids made outlines of living rooms and kitchens with the stuff Bob raked up, dragging it out of his pile. Noses were running, and cheeks were red in the autumn air.

As soon as he heard Rita pull in, he rested his rake against the fence, and walked fast to face the music.

Rita was unloading little kids and groceries.

"Here, let me get that." Bob took the two bags from her hands and grabbed a third.

They walked toward the house, and when Noreen saw the kids playing, peeled off to join them. As soon as they got inside, both adults started talking.

"This has got to stop." Rita plunked Shawn on the floor and unsnapped his hat. He crawled away.

"I've got to stop." Bob put the bags on the counter. "I'm sorry. I don't know why I do that. I truly don't." He started unloading the food.

"Bob, I don't care why you do it. I'd leave you now if I could."

"Don't say that honey. Look, I'm changing. Right now. I did that stuff you've been asking me to do, you know, the windows and the toilet. I've been a jerk. I know it. But don't say . . . "

She hung her coat up, came back to the kitchen, tying her apron. "I would if I could, Bob. There's not a lot I can say because I've said it all. But I'm stuck with you. C'mere."

The sun was throwing just enough light for them to see outlines of their children playing in the yard. "There is why. Them." She scooped Shawn up, before he crawled into a grocery bag. "Him, too." Rita smiled at Shawn. "I can't leave you because I can't raise them alone."

"No one is denying that, Rita." He started to approach. "I'm gonna do right by you and them. I swear to God. You deserve it. They do, too. I love you. I love you all."

She stood rigidly as this anger would last a long time. Kids started piling in.

"Mom, hi, what's for supper?" Kevin swirled around, "I'm starving."

Rita said what she always did: "You're not starving. Go hang up your coats."

Bob said, "I'm cooking supper. Mommy, give me your apron and tell me what to do. Take a break."

Rita untied the strings, shrugged, and raised her palms in a "we'll see" look to the kids, who laughed. Kevin honestly guffawed at Bob in that outfit.

"Well, there's chicken. I was going to use the pressure cooker."

"Ok, what else do I do? What do I add?" Bob ripped the butcher paper off the meat.

"You could drown it in water, and turn the heat up, put the pressure on, then that chicken will feel like I do." Rita got her jab in, and he took it.

In the living room, Carol and Rita pulled out supplies and the crinkly packet with three girls posing in various looks of the same dress. "That's your pattern. We can cut this out now, while Daddy makes supper."

Rita positioned Shawn between Kitty, Teri, and Noreen, who were playing Old Maid on the floor in the den. Kitty snatched him up. Kevin hung off the couch, looking underneath for his rubber ball.

Rita glanced at the doorway between the den and kitchen, wanting to see how Bob handled this pastoral scene when it erupted.

Carol was precise sticking the pins along the dark lines and when cutting. They were merrily whizzing along, when Rita said, "Shoot."

Carol knelt back from their place on the rug, "What's the matter, Mommy?"

"I don't have the zipper. I ran out of money. I'll try to get it, somehow." Rita wasn't usually disorganized. "We weren't going to finish this tonight anyway, but . . . "

Carol popped to her feet. "I've got an idea." She ran to the kitchen. Rita tiptoed to the hall to listen in.

"Daddy. Daddy? Are you making mashed potatoes?"

"Mm?"

"That's not how Mommy does it . . . she puts lots of milk in. And butter. Daddy?"

"What? Why are you bothering me?" Bob chuckled.

"I need that money. Your 'emerjencees' money. I need a zipper for a wedding dress."

He laughed. "You're getting married?"

"Nooo. Aunt Carolyn is, and I'm a junior bridesmaid. Mom and I are making my dress."

"Oh, sure, sure. You can have the money, but one thing. You gotta help me with these potatoes."

"Deal. I'll tell Mom and be right back."

Rita moved silently to the living room, right before Carol reeled in. "Dad needs help with the potatoes."

Rita sniffed, "I think he scorched the bottom of the pan."

"I'm gonna help him. But Mom, I got money. You can get the zipper while I'm at school. I'll see you right here, tomorrow night."

Supper was late. The chicken was wobbly-pink-underdone. The potatoes were fine with lots of milk, salt, and butter. Bob found a brick-like Claxton Fruit Cake, with bits of mysterious fruits and nuts, that they all hungrily ate. Catholic guilt had prevented Rita's tossing it when the nuns brought it in the charity basket.

That night, Rita lay far over on their bed. She didn't want Bob thinking he was forgiven. Her body hardly moved, but her mind was on a worry-go-round.

He fell asleep immediately. Why did she do all the worrying? She didn't want to worry about Bob's sobriety, about begging for money, about her children not getting enough time or attention. She was sick of fighting with Bob and tired of pretending to be getting along with him in front of the kids.

Rita wanted to be a normal housewife and mother. Was that too much to ask?

21

SOB

The children were home from school on Columbus Day, so Rita was late clearing breakfast. After moving dishes into the sink, she organized piles of bills heaped near the intercom, coming across four envelopes sent to Bob, at the store's address. They were from the bank, held together with a large, rusted paper clip, and all the envelopes were wavy and damp.

She took the pile to her desk to gather courage. Rita tore the first one open, her heart beating wildly. It was a late notice. Rita was confused. She paid the mortgage first, in full, each month. The second envelope was a late notice as well.

Bob and Rita were two months in arrears, with a late fee attached. No, no, no, no. How could this be? Whenever Rita signed that check, she was proud her name was on the deed, and on their joint checking account. Rita wound her wedding and engagement rings around her finger. Her hands shook as she opened the third envelope. It was a notice to get in touch with Connecticut Bank and Trust by October 1, to work out a payment plan. That was weeks ago.

Rita slid open the last piece from the pile. It was a foreclosure notice, a punch in the gut.

Rita rocked forward and back, until her anger banged into her heart, and barged into her brain. She could not, would not, be losing her home.

Rita scattered her kids around the neighborhood for the morning and waited for the bank to open.

Once connected by phone, she apologized profusely for the late payments and begged to work out a plan. They would hold off foreclosure measurements for now, as long as Bob and Rita made bigger installments and paid off the fees.

With a wildly shaking finger, she dialed Bob. "You son of a bitch."

"Whoa, whoa, what're you talking about?"

Rita rasped out, "The bank. The house. The mortgage. Did you really think I wouldn't find out?"

Bob coughed. "Aw, shit. I'll come home. We can talk when I get there."

"You do that, Mister Secrets. Mister Liar. I'll be here."

Home in fifteen minutes, Bob used the front door—the serious door—then placed his coat and hat on the railing. He turned into Rita, who used her five-foot-four frame and 127 pounds to slam flat palms into his chest.

"You son of a bitch. You jeopardize our family? Our *home*? For what? What else is more important than this house?"

She glowered, in the hall, under a delicate brass and glass fixture. Moving to her desk, she fanned the stack of envelopes at Bob.

"Rita, I'm sorry . . . what can I say? I have debts." Bob rubbed a shaky hand over his chin.

"Debts? I can give you plenty of debts to real people, Mr. Leahy, who provides life insurance. Dr. Saunders, who vaccinates our children. What kind of fool do you think I am, that I wouldn't notice? Besides being outraged, I'm embarrassed that I trusted you. Ever."

He interrupted her, "We can sell the house."

Her mouth dropped open. "What? This is the only thing we've got, Bob."

Rita brushed by him to get into the kitchen, knowing he would follow. She wanted the table between them. Rita, with blood pulsing in her temples, put two hands on the back of her chair, facing Bob again.

"Never."

Bob stopped trailing her when he got to his seat, and stood behind it, squaring off. He frowned. "What's that mean, 'never'? We're at the end of our rope here, Rita."

"I'll spell it out for you. If we sell this house, we will never, ever, get back to this point in our lives. We'll forever be two dumb, young Micks getting ahead of themselves. In the time it took you to get home, I figured out what to do."

He mumbled, "Of course you did."

"What? What did you say?"

"Rita. You always find a way. I'm . . . I'm . . . " Bob paused to look at the ceiling. "You always solve it, whatever 'it' is. So, what're we going to do?"

Rita pulled her chair out and sat. He seriously did not know what to do. She made a steeple of her fingers over her nose, saying, "Sit."

He sat.

There was no fear in her now. She was in control. "We're going to rent this house out and keep ownership. The apartment over the store—you'll have to kick Karen and Ray out. They can move to the third floor, which, I guess, you've been getting ready to rent out? We'll move to the second floor. It can be temporary, say, at most, a year. Longer than that, the kids would have to go to school in Hartford. I'll ask Miss Foley to let them stay at Charter Oak for now." She always got the big picture; she could save them all.

"We can't fit into that apartment. It's five rooms." Bob got up, walked to the sink, his back to her.

The pine trees bent and whooshed beyond the window.

"Bob, we've got to make this work. I'm not losing this house . . . What? . . . What?"

Turning around, he shoved his fists into his pants pockets. He licked his lips, sweat breaking out on his forehead. "We can't have Karen and Ray move around."

"They have been good tenants . . . nice kids."

"That's not . . . what . . . I mean," he grappled for words.

Rita pushed on, "We own the building, of course we can ask them to move, offering them another apartment, not as nice, but cheaper. Why not? Do they have a lease? Did you make them sign a lease?"

Bob's neck was red, and the color was creeping into his face. "No, they don't have a lease. The third floor is not empty."

Rita examined Bob's florid face. Her pulse quickened, she breathed rapidly. Was he renting the third floor without telling her? Was he pocketing that money, too?

Bob still stood against the counter, but now crossed his arms in front of his chest. "I have a lady friend living there."

"A what? 'A lady friend'?" Rita's lips trembled.

She held her abdomen as if she'd been punched, and looked away, while her heart beat in her ears. Her eyes started to run. Rita used the back of her hand to wipe her nose. Oh my God. How could he? Why would he? All this time she thought he was working, or at a bar. But this? Another woman? Could it get any worse?

"She's just a . . . waitress. I, we, and the guys, we held card parties on the third floor."

"Stop." Rita whispered.

Who was this man? Incredulous, she couldn't even process what he was saying. Rita folded her arms on the kitchen table and rested her forehead there. Her thick brown hair fell on either side of her face, creating a curtain. She heard Bob move forward to touch her, but she snapped, "Don't."

He backed up.

Whip smart. Solve it. Everything left her head, for a moment.

She rose to face Bob, barely moving her lips, "Get her out. Today. Get this house ready to rent, do every little thing I have ever put on a list. Get that apartment ready for MY family to move into. Do not cross me. Or I will find a way to kill you."

Rita unballed her fists, smoothed her dress, and walked up to their room, gently shutting the door. As the knife of betrayal pierced her heart, Rita tamped it down. She could not unravel this day. The kids would rush in for lunch soon. She paced the bedroom, trapped, hating.

If they had only three children, Rita might be able to leave him, to get a job, to find an apartment. There were so few options for women, especially mothers, except to go on assistance. She wouldn't do that, couldn't stand being judged. Leave that for the truly needy. Being on welfare was something she vowed never to do.

There was that word again: never.

Rita needed Bob's income. She needed his strength to move appliances and open jars. She needed someone to run ideas by, to drive the children to the hospital, to help her with a sick baby. He could do all that.

She would use him, keep him, to do all that.

Bob slumped at the head of the table. Ha, *head of the table*. He was such an ass. He rubbed his frown repeatedly, applying pressure to quell pounding thoughts.

Another man did all those things, committed those crimes.

Bob's sinuses flooded, as he choked back a sob.

He had to get out of the house, go back to the shop to determine the work he needed to do. Get Lynette out. He met her at a bar and let her rent the place. When she ran out of money, the lazy drunk, Lynette offered no-strings sex instead. Bob hadn't planned on it, it had just happened. He held poker games in her apartment, and she waited on the guys.

He called out, as a courtesy, or a habit, "I'm heading to the store. I'll see you later."

Big George was at the store, opening boxes of paint. Bob told him, "I gotta go fix Karen's sink. Then I'm gonna ask them to move to the third floor. Back in a few."

He was ready to start solving some of his problems. After fifteen minutes on the second floor, Bob went to assess the third floor. He shouldered the stuck door open. The place was dark, and it stunk.

What an ass, what a fool he'd been, to take advantage of Rita, to hurt Rita, for this dump and a trashy woman.

Bob shook his head, taking in the nubby couch, stuffing poking out at the seams. An ashtray overflowed with cigarettes. Beer cans and whiskey bottles drew flies to the trash barrel in the kitchen. The toilet had a disgusting black line of mold at the water line.

He hadn't noticed any of this when he was here drinking, flirting, and betting. Bob was a louse and an idiot when he was drunk, a whole other shitty guy.

His sober self felt like throwing up, but the bile hung in the back of his throat.

Back at the store level, Bob thought about how to sheetrock off part of the store to create more living space. "What do you say, George? Want to help me fix this place up? My family is moving in."

George put a big hand on Bob's shoulder. "The Missus found out?"

Bob pinched the bridge of his nose to keep from crying. "Yes. Everything. I gotta make it right. For her. For Rita."

At his desk, Bob drew and erased, drew and erased, until he had a plan: he'd make a living room/bedroom, and half bath on the first floor, improve the kitchen on the second, and make all the other spaces into bedrooms. It would be a sort of upside-down house, but it worked. Bob was pleased he could solve problems, too, even the ones he created. He called Rita with the plan.

She said it was the stupidest thing she'd ever heard. Bob banged the phone down, instantly fuming, yelling to George, "Leaving."

He headed to the Peter Pan Bar, where Hank was bagging lunchtime trash.

"Bob. You never come in this early. First beer is free."

Bob moved to the farthest seat of the empty bar. The place smelled of wet wood and ashtrays. Hank expertly slid a beer down. Bob aimed one finger and made a clicking noise as a thank-you.

"Self-serving old biddy," Bob mumbled. "Stupid songstress. Sanctimonious. Is that a word? Something she'd say."

Hank was pushing a broom around the dining area. "Who're you talking about?"

Bob swiveled. "What? Oh, my wife. Goddamn know-it-all." He turned his stool back, catching Hank's reflection in the mirror.

"What's your problem with her?"

"She wants us to move out of our house." Bob made it casual.

"So. Lots of ladies do that, get a bigger house, that's normal, especially with more kids."

"Well, actually, the bank wants to foreclose." Bob blew out a breath, saying it out loud. "Rita wants us to move into the apartment above our store."

"What the hell, Bob? That ain't normal. What happened? What the hell, you got a good business, right?"

"Yes. No. Rita's been putting money aside all along for the mortgage. But I blew it."

"You're lucky she doesn't throw you out." Hank moved back to the business side of the bar. He turned his attention to the coffee machine and handed Bob a cup.

"What's this?" Bob pulled back, suspicious.

"It's a coffee, you moron. My wife left me four years ago. I send them all my money, and they all hate me. I miss them, my kids, my ex-wife. Go home, Bob. You're sober right now, and you gotta work this out with your wife. Apologize. Often."

Bob knew Hank was right.

But knowing and doing are two different things.

22

LIONHEART

Rita retreated to their room for five evenings, after the children's bedtime rush.

Bob stopped apologizing after four days. He slept in the cellar, his new lair.

Tonight, sitting on the edge of their bed, Rita was miserable. Who could she confide in? She waited until late night to call her sister Carolyn, shutting the door, not wanting any child waking to their parents' marital disaster. She told Carolyn all the sordid details. There. It was out, and Rita felt a little better, knowing she could tell Carolyn everything. Rita's head ached when she got off the phone.

Now she allowed the tears to flow, and her red blood cells gathered, making her whole face hurt. Her reflection in the bathroom mirror was a puffy, moist mess. From the linen drawer, Rita dampened a washcloth to soothe her face, noticing the brass lion-head pulls that she had chosen, because "Leonard" means lion heart. Back in bed, Rita stared at the ceiling.

Exeter Avenue to Park Street, house to apartment, suburb to city. Everyone would know they couldn't afford their home.

Rita's head was swarming with ideas, like bees, with all the moving plans.

She slept until birds chirped and light slimmed in beneath the window shades. Noreen climbed on the bed, and got under the quilt, with teary brown eyes.

Rita reached out, "What's the matter, honey?"

"I had a nightmare. In the *darktime*." Noreen framed Rita's face with two warm hands. "Somebody was crying in the *darktime*."

Rita's crying was a self-indulgent luxury; she wouldn't cry like that again. "Well, I'm here, and it's daytime. Your dreams will be better now."

"Good." Noreen played with Rita's hair. "Where's Daddy?"

"Let's go find out." Rita helped her daughter off the bed, and to the dreaded kitchen, where Bob was reading the paper.

"There's Daddy." Rita made her voice sweet, slitting her eyes at Bob.

After a breakfast of her mediocre acting, Rita shooed the kids out the door, and Bob left for work.

Rita cleaned out the refrigerator, then made a meatloaf that Bob could heat later. She had to work on the switchboard that night, and wanted the house organized. Her mind never stopped whirling. She had to rent the house. Change utilities. Alert the school.

Later that morning, Rita paused for a cup of tea and a phone call to Nancy. "Got a minute to talk?"

Nancy was good at a number of things. She had excellent taste, was well-organized, and she expected her husband to do her bidding. She would help Rita stand up to Bob.

"Now, don't go crazy on me, but Bob lost almost all our money and we have to move."

Nancy ranted and raved and called Bob names and told Rita to divorce Bob, get it over with. "You tell that good-for-nothing bum, you'll dump his ass so fast, his head will spin."

This is exactly what Rita expected, and was even a tiny bit amused. "No. I've solved this one. We're moving, temporarily, to our building on Park Street. For a year. I know you think it's nuts, but I'm not getting divorced. I just need your organizational skills. Can you help me shoehorn a house-worth of stuff into a five-room apartment?"

Nancy said that Hartford was dangerous, the schools were horrible, and the streets were dirty.

"I know. I'm not asking for your opinions, I'm asking for your help, your expertise. Can you come over and help me decide what to bring? Please, Nancy?"

Nancy boxed chafing dishes, out-of-season clothes, sporting equipment. Yes, to the pressure cooker, no to the green glass-footed bowl. She stood up, rubbing her back. "I'm not used to physical labor. Hey, let's keep the attic for your storage, and leave the basement rooms for the tenants."

"That's what I was thinking. Bob can put a lock on the attic door."

Nancy folded sheets while Rita thought aloud, "Where do I do laundry, and hang out wash? Can I cook decent meals on that ancient stove? Where will the children play?"

"Listen, I don't know. This whole idea is cockamamy. I've got to go, but I'll shut up."

Rita smirked. "No, you won't." They both laughed, knowing that was true.

Carol, Kevin, Kitty, and Teri straggled into the kitchen, home from school. "Surprise. We're moving," Rita greeted them as they registered the mess.

"Why? Why are we moving? Didn't we just move in last year?" Carol curled her lip.

"Oh, it'll be an adventure. We're going to live over Daddy's store. He's making it cute right now."

Kevin razzed, "*Cute*. That spider cave? Have you seen that basement over there? Worse than our hatchway. Mwa-ha-ha-hah," he snarled, curling his hands into monster claws.

Rita kept upbeat. "It'll be fine. It'll be fun. We'll be back here in a year. Go see what you want to pack, and what can stay in the attic."

Rita contacted a rental agent who suggested a businessman's month-to-month lease with taxes and insurance included, and the tenants maintain the property.

She asked her friends Eleanor and Marie over for coffee to explain their having to move, angry and embarrassed, blaming Bob's actions. They cried, and Rita teared up. "I'll be lonely without you both."

The following Monday, Rita dressed neatly, then put Shawn and Noreen in the carriage to walk to the school. Rita had made pineapple upside-down cakes for the PTA for years. Today, she had an appointment to meet with the principal.

Miss Foley was matronly in her navy blue dress, sensible shoes, and tight hairdo. She opened her office door and swept Mrs. Leonard and the youngest two in with a big smile. She asked to take Shawn out of the carriage. The little ones were settled with wooden alphabet blocks.

Miss Foley took a seat at her desk. Rita sat forward on a cushioned chair, with her legs crossed at the ankles. Her intention was to politely ask if Carol, Kevin, Kitty, and Teri could stay at Charter Oak School, being temporarily out of the district. As she spoke, Rita started to shake. Her heartbeat ratcheted and her palms slicked with perspiration. Blood rushed into her ears, pulsed: failing, failing, failing. "We are . . . we are in bad shape."

The story unfolded of money misspent, gambling, lying, cheating, drinking, all the layers of a trashy and bleak existence, more than she planned to tell, more than she told anyone else. "Can they please stay?"

Miss Foley handed Rita a tissue. She brought a chair over. It was a child-sized chair, silly, really, but she moved close to Rita, who was gazing out the window.

"Mrs. Leonard. You remind me of someone brave, who said, 'Do something every day that scares you.' You're doing that now. It's scary to move, to try to keep your marriage, to hang onto your house."

Rita stared down at her lap, nodding.

"You are fiercely protective of your children. My God. 'The Sunshine Twins?' Carol, so smart, and Teri, the dog artist. Your children are always smiling. If you own a home in town, your children are welcome here."

When Rita regained composure, she asked, "Who said that, about being brave?"

"Eleanor Roosevelt. You'll recognize her as a woman who lives her beliefs."

Rita pushed the carriage fast on the way home, trying to beat the rain. "I must be brave, kids. I must be brave, like Eleanor Roosevelt said."

The lion-head pulls were a good omen.

23

REFRIGERATOR

B ob and Big George were rushing to finish the third-floor apartment for Karen and Ray. This hurried and hot work was Bob's penance, but only part of it.

It would be a long time before Rita was civil to him again.

"George, help me." Bob was sweating, trying to get the kitchen shelving into place.

George laughed, "I always do."

Rita wanted nothing to do with this floor: no cleaning, no painting, no feeding the guys.

Bob mumbled, "This place was the devil's spot, the den of iniquity."

George snorted, "What's that mean?"

Bob swept dirt, sawdust, nails, and a crushed Hires soda can into a dustpan. "It means a place where no one needs morals to go, only degenerates go there. It's from the Bible, I think. I'm more like a mo*ron*."

His heart was a stone, and telling small jokes made Bob smile briefly.

He painted all the walls off-white, to take the dirty feel and stink out of the place. Now, if he could whitewash his soul, or erase the last six months, he might not despise himself as much. In the daytime, he was sober, a family man, a working stiff. At night, he was a drunk who hurt everyone he loved. Bob was ashamed, and shame is a tough emotion to haul around. It was hard to revisit the third floor, but it was also difficult to revisit it in his mind. He blushed, thinking back to his actions. But this time, by moving into the second-floor apartment that he and Rita could afford, he would be a better man.

She still wouldn't look at him.

The week after, Bob worked on their apartment by updating the kitchen with new cabinets and a splatter-painted linoleum floor, which he waxed until it shined. He used green asbestos tiles for the bathroom floor. Rita chose a paint called "Sunflower" for the kitchen. Bob smoothed all the wooden floors, with his heavy and loud sander, his arm muscles bulging under his white tee shirt. When the dust settled, Rita came over with the children to check on his progress.

Bob put Kevin to work. "Help sweep up, then you can sit on the floor buffer."

Kevin rode the buffer like a cowboy, but when trying to operate the powerful machine, it scarred the floor in half-moons before Bob yanked it back. "Okay, okay, let go, for Christ's sake. Tell Mommy you gotta leave soon, because I'm going to varnish, and that stench will kill you."

Days later, when the smells subsided, Rita was organizing the first floor behind the store. It was their new bedroom/living room, made from storage space.

For an old house, it was starting to look good, Bob thought. He was doing his damnedest to make it, and them, work.

Rita was putting sheets on the pull-out couch, their now marital bed.

Bob stood holding his toolbox in the doorway, drawing a blank about his task, being in the same room with Rita.

"Can I work in here?" He asked. "You know . . . the radiators." He jingled the coins in his left pocket, awaiting permission.

Rita didn't stop moving as she unfurled the top sheet. "Yes." She watched Bob cross the room. "I'm trying to let my anger go, Bob. It's exhausting. This move is to get my children back home to Exeter Avenue in a year, you understand that?"

By now Bob was kneeling on the floor, bleeding a radiator. "Yes, I know." A blast of steam burnt his hand, turning it a wet red. "We will . . . Yeeow. Oh, Jesus, Mary, and Joseph. Yikes."

"Oh no, I'll get some ice." It was the best sentence Bob had heard in a long time, and he widened his eyes as she brushed by. He shook his burnt hand and dared to smile.

Rita was talking to him again.

Kevin skulked out of the brown house on Exeter Avenue. It was a nippy, sunny Saturday morning, and the neighborhood kids were making a wagon train with Radio Flyers tied to bikes. He was held back from the fun, to help load stuff.

Kevin called out to Dad, "I got friends here. Who am I going to play with in creepy Hartford?"

Bob didn't pause. "There's kids in Hartford."

His parents were pretending it was an adventure to move, but Kevin wasn't buying it. "Is there a brook, or pond? Is there a playground?" He slung boxes into the back of his dad's truck.

"Yup. I'm sure there is. You'll have to find them. Help me load Mommy's desk and quit whining. You can play with Little George today. You're both the same age. Seven, is it?"

"I'm eight." Jeesh, his father didn't even know how old he was. "Kitty is too. We're twins. Remember?"

"That's enough out of you, wise guy."

Big George brought his Dodge Power Wagon, filled with furniture, to the new place.

Kevin, Carol, Kitty, Teri, and Little George ran through empty rooms, yelling out echoes. They clomped down into the basement of rocks and mortar walls, an uneven floor, and a big metal drain in the center. It smelled of spilled oil. Spiders lived in every corner, dangling from webs. Two bare lightbulbs hung listlessly from joists. The ceiling was an open collection of crisscross beams, with light from the floor above squeaking through. Frayed electrical wires were crushed against the dried wood with bent and rusted nails.

Kevin and Little George met behind the ancient furnace, the darkest spot. "Let's lock the girls in this dungeon," Kevin said. "When I say go, hit the stairs." Kevin added to the terror with a stage whisper, "Look, George, *a rat*. Go."

The boys banged up the stairs and Kevin slammed the cellar door. They hid behind a tower of moving boxes.

When the latch clunked down, Carol, Kitty, and Teri ran up, hammered on the door, screaming about rats and spiders.

Dad and Big George had just strapped a newer refrigerator to an appliance dolly. They parked it long enough for Dad to jerk open the door.

"Knock it off." Dad yelled at his three quaking daughters.

"It's Kevin's fault . . . he locked us down there and turned off the . . . " Kitty started to talk back.

Their father wielded a yardstick, a silent threat.

Kevin, backpedaling the next flight, whispered, "Please shut up, Kitty. He'll hit you if you don't be quiet."

Miraculously, she did, and the girls squeezed by the men, then angrily ran after the boys, who found a closet and pulled the door shut.

Carol's saddle shoes pounded the stairs, and Kevin's heart pulsed in his throat when she tore the door open. "You turd." Carol was sinking her nails into the back of his neck, pulling him forward.

"Yeah, bird turd." Kitty lunged at him, pulling his hair, but he squirmed away, yelling, "Run."

When Little George crashed into Teri, they all heard an ear-splitting whistle. *HOO-whit!* Caught.

Get in front of Dad, double-time, and don't lie, don't talk back, and don't move.

Georgie got its meaning from the reactions of the Leonards.

Kevin was wary of that whistle, afraid to be first within reach. He was halfway down the staircase when Dad lifted him over four or five steps by his shirt front. Kevin giant-stepped back once he hit the floor, and pulled Little George behind him, protective.

Dad had two large straps in his hand. "You all stand over there."

His eyebrows were mean and low. He pointed toward the front door, slapping one of the straps in his palm.

Kevin kept his hands down, knowing if they moved, the whack would be worse.

The girls and Little George stood stock still behind Kevin.

Dad and Big George returned to getting the refrigerator to the upstairs kitchen. Dad put one strap around his forehead, attached it to the top end of the fridge, and Big George put the other around Dad's middle and tightened the cinch, at the lower end. Dad carried that Philco on his back, sweating, and groaning, up the rounded staircase, and into the kitchen, with Big George behind him, pushing. Finally, Dad let the appliance down with a bang and a loud, "God damn" and "Yes, ma'am." The men laughed and coughed.

Kevin, safe for now, hoped Dad forgot who'd locked the door.

"Wow. Daddy's strong," Carol proclaimed, and gaped at Kitty, who nudged Teri.

Kevin added in wonder and relief, "God damn."

His sisters gushed laughter, surprised that Kevin said bad words. They saw Dad's true strength *and* had gotten away without being hit. All Kevin had to do was to avoid Dad when he was mad.

Sometimes Kevin just had to outrun Dad. Or outthink him.

24

BLIZZARD

That night the children squished into their upstairs bedrooms. Everyone helped put the beds together, like giant Tinker Toys. Rita read *The Poky Little Puppy* to Shawn and Noreen.

After the older kids' nighttime routine, Rita hung clothes in the narrow closets, stalling, staying nearby. When Rita thought everyone was asleep, she stood peering into what used to be a living room, a dining room, and a bedroom. Wide arches connected all the rooms, offering no privacy.

Except for the traffic on the street, it was quiet.

"Mom? What are you doing?" Carol sat up in bed, noticing her mother standing in the hall.

Rita snapped out of her reverie, "Um, I don't want to go downstairs. I feel like I'm leaving you all in your own apartment. As if I'm a neighbor, just checking in."

Carol nodded, and Rita stepped over boxes to sit on her bed.

"My kitchen is upstairs, and my bedroom is down. I don't know where to go." Rita gave a small laugh.

"Are you scared?" Carol asked.

"What? No, I . . . just . . . " Rita realized how deep that question was, and then, how scared she was, indeed. Of living in the city. Of not being near her children while they slept. Of trying to find a way to live peacefully with Bob.

Rita asked Carol. "Are *you* scared?"

Carol bunched her covers around her. "No, I'm scared of you standing in the hall, being a ghost. All of this is odd, but it will be alright. I'll get you if anyone needs you in the night. But quit hanging around like some ghoul."

While Carol fell asleep, Rita scrubbed the kitchen extra hard, to stay on their floor longer. Then she headed downstairs to watch TV with Bob. Rita knit, listening to hear if anyone needed her, while Bob laughed at *The Dick Van Dyke Show*.

The next Monday was the first time Bob drove the older kids to school.

Rita readied the little ones for their day of playing, and then collected laundry. Her old wringer washing machine made it to the second-floor kitchen. But without a dryer, Rita waited for Bob's return before she could hang out laundry in the miserable little yard one floor down. God, she missed her home.

One month after the school year started, on a Saturday, Rita let Noreen and Shawn play in the backyard while she unpegged crisp, dry sheets and folded them into a basket. Noreen was eating the last of the mulberries off the only bush in the yard. Rita scanned the hard-dirt plot. Shawn was missing. His blue dump truck, full of sand, was left behind. Rita spun around, responding to a scraping sound, "Shawn? Shawn?"

Leaves hid in the corners of the yard, but no Shawn. Nineteen-month-old Shawn must have gone through the "gate," which was two garbage cans blocking the opening in the falling-down fence.

Rita, seeing Kitty coming off the back porch, halted her. "Go get the kids. Shawn's missing," Kitty thundered the steps to scream the alarm. They all came running.

"Shawn's missing." Rita whirled around. "Spread out and find him."

They ran to the street.

Rita hauled Noreen into her arms, slowing her down, but the other children fanned out on the busy sidewalk. Carol and Kevin turned left, and Kitty and Teri headed right.

Rita shielded her eyes with one hand. Shawn made it to Liggett's Drug Store, where cars honked, pedestrians whisked by, and traffic lights blinked. He stopped to look at something on the sidewalk, then started toddling toward the curb, where a blue dump truck lumbered close.

No driver could have seen the little boy in a striped jacket, red pants, white socks, and baby shoes.

Rita screamed, "Somebody stop him, somebody help him!"

Kitty scurried to snatch Shawn by his red bottom and whisked him toward Rita.

Shawn was crying, "My *fruck*. My *fruck*."

Rita knelt on the sidewalk, holding Noreen, with one arm outstretched to embrace Shawn. She closed her eyes, and shook her head, stopping long enough to breathe in Shawn's scent. Rita ran out of arms, but Kitty hugged her mother's neck, and rubbed Rita's back gently.

"Here he is, Mommy. Safe and sound. Here are all your kids, Mom." Kitty helped her up.

The rest returned to Rita and Shawn and patted his head.

Rita could lose her home, her mother, even Bob. But she couldn't lose another child, especially Kieran's twin. Eventually, as they walked back to the yard, her heartbeat returned to normal.

In early January. Rita woke at 5:30, her nose, hands, and feet cold.

"Bob." She pushed into her husband. "Is it cold in here?"

"Hmm?" He rolled over to her. "What? Cold?"

Rita answered, "Yes, I'm freezing." She cocooned in the quilt, pulled it tight, shivering. Her eyes popped open, then her feet hit the cold floor as she grabbed his robe. "Bob, get up. I don't think we have heat."

Bob came awake fast. "Oh, my God, you're right. Go check the kids, I'll check the gauge on the oil tank." He pulled on pants and a holey sweater.

The predicted blizzard had arrived, dumping not inches, but feet, of snow. It was piled on cars, softening edges of buildings and mailboxes.

Rita hit the stairs, two at a time, and checked the boys' room. Cold. Carol and Kitty's room. Cold. The little girls' room. Cold.

In the kitchen, Rita lit the gas oven, blowing on her fingers to strike a match. She lit two burners, got water from the sink—so cold the pipes could freeze—and put the pans on for oatmeal, and hot cocoa. She returned to their room for their quilt and socks to wear with her threadbare slippers.

"Damn it. The oil gauge is at zero. I can't believe I didn't check it." He flicked off the flashlight. "At least we have electricity and cooking gas. We should be fine."

Rita was collecting coats. "Bob, get hats and mittens."

She and Bob jostled their bundles on the stairs. The kitchen was warming up. Rita stirred the cocoa, a thin film already forming on it.

She grabbed Bob's arm. "You call the oil company; we'll pay our bill as soon as we can. Tell them we have a baby."

She pushed kitchen chairs into a half circle in front of the opened oven door. The first rays of winter sun might have poked through the windows, but the flurry of flakes blocked even weak light. Rita went to wake the children.

"Kevin," she shook his shoulder, "Kevin, get up. We're out of heat. The kitchen is warm, and you can take the blankets off your bed." Rita guided a sleep-walking Kevin to a wooden chair. He sat, wrapped in wool, and stayed asleep.

Bob was on the phone, raising his voice, "I know it's a blizzard, pal, but we've got little kids. I need an oil delivery *right now*." He punched the wall.

Rita woke Carol and Kitty, and told them to get Teri and Noreen, and have everyone bring their blankets to the kitchen.

Shawn was wearing thick flannel pajamas, but his diaper was wet. Rita couldn't undress him in this frigid room, so she took the pad from his changing table, then laid it on two chairs in the kitchen, making him warm, clean, and dry. Rita handed him to Carol, who enclosed Shawn in her blanket.

Everyone huddled around the stove, as the blue and yellow flames danced and made a cozy little parlor. Carol and Kitty awakened more easily than the others. Teri and Noreen cuddled together. Bob and Rita handed out bowls of oatmeal and cups of hot cocoa.

As they waited for the oil delivery, the girls took turns running to the bathroom, the toilet seat a block of ice on the back of their legs. They skittered back to the warmth of the circle and giggled about it.

Kevin woke amid the heat and the food smells, his family cozying around the stove, draped with blankets and bedspreads. "Well, I never saw this on *Leave It to Beaver*."

Oil was delivered. The apartment thawed, the oven was turned off, beds remade, and school was canceled. The weather report on WTIC stressed staying inside due to low temperatures and high winds.

Bob shoveled, but the snow whipped right back, stinging his face. Before he went to work in the store, he warned Rita, "Don't let those kids out. It's too darn cold."

Rita always wanted the children to play outside, but today that would be dangerous. She told them to play in their rooms. Carol and Kitty came back to the kitchen.

Carol asked. "We're bored. Can we play outside?"

Rita was scouring out the oatmeal pan. "No."

"Mom. Mom." Kitty slid into a kitchen chair. Rita was sweeping up. "Yes, what, Kitty? Move that chair to the table." Kitty scootched the chair over.

"Can we go outside?" Kitty tilted her head.

"What? Outside? It's a blizzard. Didn't you hear Bob Steele on the radio? No."

Kevin was tying Teri to his bed with a jump rope. "You can't be a cowboy or *a Indian* if you can't escape. That's all they do, catch each other and escape. Think of Roy Rogers and Dale Evans. You tie me, and I'll show you."

Teri, age six, couldn't even tie her shoes.

Kevin escaped in no time. "This is dumb. You're dumb. I'm going outside." He coiled the rope on the bedpost and left to get snow pants on.

Mom stopped him at the top of the stairs. "No one is going anywhere. It's 20 degrees outside, snow and ice, and wind," Mom piled it on.

"What am I supposed to do in here? I can't even play in my room if Shawn is napping."

"Yeah." Teri followed him into the hall.

"Oh, you too? You want to go out in this?" Mom pushed these two to look outside.

"It looks like a glittery landscape." Kevin knew Mom liked big words.

Carol and Kitty joined them and turned their widened eyes toward her.

"Yes." Kitty perked up. "Let us out. We love snow. You know we do."

Carol added her two cents. "Please, Mom?"

Noreen came around the corner holding a stuffed rabbit, "I want to go." She didn't even know what they were talking about.

"Daddy said no. He's been out there, and even he didn't last."

"Mom. We don't have *no* place to play. The living room is downstairs, the kitchen is up, we haven't got a basement except that dungeon down there, probably freezing . . . " Kevin was pleading his case, the whole group's case, to get out of this prison.

Rita caved. "Jeesh. Okay. I give up. Don't let Daddy know. Play where he can't see you, on the side by the shoe store." She made them promise to go to the bathroom first. "I'm not putting you in all these clothes, so you come right back in."

Kevin got in line for the bathroom, and then put on long johns, a sweater, and extra socks. His sisters were doing the same. At the front door they pulled on snow pants, hats, boots, and mittens. Rita helped zip, buckle, lace, tie, and snap. After a half hour of readying, Kevin led four siblings to tumble into the Arctic. And tumble they did.

He ate icicles and licked chunks of snow off his mittens. They made a snowman, and a snow cave, with piles of cannonballs, stacked in pyramids. Kevin pummeled them, until Kitty and Carol lobbed back, two against one.

Their cheeks were rosy and glowing. Noreen was the first one to bang on the door. No answer.

"My fingers are burning up," Teri yelled as she joined Noreen on the steps. She tried to turn the doorknob. It was stuck.

Kitty complained, "I c-can't feel my toes."

Carol and Kevin came to the steps when their mouths froze, and their noses leaked into their scarves. Kevin, being the bravest, hammered the door, and kicked it. Mom wasn't answering.

"She sh-should be there. It's fr-frozen shut. Knock harder." Kevin couldn't believe it. His teeth hurt, his lips cracked, his cheeks chapped, his boots leaked, and his mittens were sodden.

Rita finally opened the door. They fell in a heap, then began clambering to the cast iron radiator, struggling to get the smelly wet wool, and metal buckles, away from their skin.

"Mom. W-why w-would you do that?" Kevin had trouble speaking. "W-what are we, mush d-dogs?"

"I was distracting Dad with coffee because you were playing, and I didn't want him to catch you outside. Then Shawn and I watched the store, while Dad checked the third-floor tenants. I *told* you it was a blizzard. I got here as soon as I could. The door must have frozen shut. Do you know what the temperature is?"

He snarled at her. Who cared? His fingers were red, painful, and probably frostbitten.

She laughed at his reaction, "Kevin, all of you, it was fifteen degrees out there, and then there was the wind. I knew you wouldn't last . . . "

Carol shook off a small avalanche. "We lasted. We were out there for what, about an hour?"

"You lasted nineteen minutes. I kept checking my watch."

Carol was smart in her response. "Oh?" She cocked one eyebrow. "Then how did we get so much done? The snowman, the fort?"

"The same way you got out there in the first place: sheer determination. And that's how you got stuff built: determination. Oh. And sheer numbers. You ganged up on me."

Back in the kitchen, Mom served tea and toast. Like Oz's Tin Man with the oil can, as Kevin got lubricated, his jaw began to work. He scratched his neck and thought about his day.

"I guess it's kind of funny, us being outside, for nineteen minutes. We thought it was hours. But, man, my feet and hands froze."

Rita poured more tea. "A blizzard is a big deal. So, you were very hardy to stay out as long as you did."

"That's cool." He and his sisters survived outside in the great blizzard of 1963.

Kevin, dead serious, asked, "Can I go back out?"

25

HOLIDAYS

I n June 1963, happily, skittishly, Rita directed packing the apartment for the family's return home. They'd saved money by renting out their home for a year, covering the overdue mortgage payments.

Back at Exeter Avenue, the children dropped boxes in their new/old rooms and blasted into the neighborhood to reclaim friends.

Rita and Bob hosted a cookout the first weekend of summer. As families arrived, Rita covered the picnic table with a flowered sheet. She paused by Bob under the pine tree, heading toward their friends.

"Can you get that grill going, or is it too rusted?"

"Nah, I lined it with tin foil. It'll last at least through today."

He poured lighter fluid on the charcoal heaped in the grill. He told the hastily assembled boy cousins to stand back, then tossed a match and watched it BOOF! into happy combustion. The children oohed and ahhed before scattering.

The women carried plates of a wiggly green Jell-O mold, coleslaw, potato salad, and State Line Potato Chips to a serving area made of plywood over two sawhorses. The ladies sipped chianti as Rita surveyed the yard, which was looking good with the picnic table and family and friends.

The pool bubbled with kids.

When the coals turned white with bits of red licking their corners, Bob loaded on hamburgers and Grote & Weigel hot dogs. The men sat on metal lawn chairs, drinking beers from the cooler. Bob whistled the kids out of the water for the meal. They filled plates and sat on towels, shivering, and eating.

Rita loved being back in the mix, with the moms coaxing ketchup onto their kids' burgers and settling squabbles. Rita got tipsy and rolled Carol's bike from under a tree. Rita hunched over the handlebars laughing, "Come on, Carolyn. We'll ride double, like when we were kids."

Carolyn slid off when Rita couldn't manage the pedals. The sisters fell into a heap laughing, and Rita wet her pants. Seeing that, Ceil and Pat fell apart and toppled onto the pile.

That evening, Rita winked at herself in the mirror as she brushed her teeth, "Everything is going to be fine." She was happy *not* being in control for once, not managing Bob or the children.

The following morning, the party's euphoria lingered. She was home. It had been a few tough years, but now it was going to work out. She started singing "Ramblin' Rose" that morning as she did the post-party cleanup.

On Monday, Rita invited Eleanor and Marie for coffee. Shawn played nearby with Lincoln Logs. Rita felt empowered by what she, she and Bob, overcame. She was glowing with happiness and wanted to share some of her success.

Eleanor complimented her, "I don't know how you survived, Rita. Look at you now, home sweet home. Is everything back on track?"

Marie coughed into her fist, "And Bob. How's he?"

Rita smiled, "Yes, he's doing well. Coming home after work, helping with the kids."

Financial issues, family issues, sobriety issues. She would never boast, but oh, she wanted to. Rita wanted to tell the world that she saved Bob, her children, and her home.

Rita read the *Hartford Courant* to search for cheap summer activities. They got Faxon library cards with tiny metal plaques and took out books. Next, Rita drove her family to Beachland Park to sign up for the swimming lessons the town offered.

"We gotta take swimming lessons? We know how to swim." Kevin complained.

"It's a life skill that I never learned. Instruction for form and safety."

"What's the matter with my form? I don't even know what that means."

Rita clung to the pool fence to watch them take tests.

Kevin was insulted to be placed in advanced beginners with Kitty. On the walk to the car, Kevin snapped his wet towel at her, "Don't embarrass me, don't even talk to me in that class."

"Fine." She kicked him instead.

They began going to the park early, then back for afternoon swims, their still-wet suits rolled in their damp towels. They joined the Beachland swim team.

Kevin, barefoot, reclaimed the paths to Trout Brook with Billy and Dave. He climbed down the ten-foot cliff backward, hanging onto outcroppings and bulging tree roots. To cross the brook, Kevin flew from rock to rock. Billy didn't have Kevin's fearlessness and Dave didn't have his agility. They took some plunges.

The first time Kevin went through the woods, he got to the pool twenty minutes before his sisters. Kitty wanted to use his paths too.

"No. It's not for girls." Kevin took off running, but they followed him to the park side of Trout Brook. Kitty was scared when critters rustled in the woods, but Carol was the most vocal in her attempt to follow. Teri just went along. They stopped at the water's edge.

"Where'd he go? We don't know how to cross." Kitty jumped when an acorn hit her.

Kevin was perched in an oak tree. "Whaddya doing here? I told you, it's too scary for girls."

Carol held a hand over her eyes. "What're you doing up there?"

"Studying the forest. The squirrels. They are so . . . fearless." He chucked a stick at Carol.

"Quit it. Show us the way across. Once. Then we won't bother you."

Kevin crashed out of the tree, then dusted his shorts off, knocking leaves and bark to the ground. "I love this place. Don't ruin it by screaming and whining and all that junk."

Teri frowned. "We won't."

Kitty was not quiet following Kevin's leaps across. "Is it cold? Are there animals that bite? Is that slippery?" She stopped on teetering rocks, trying to balance with a towel under one arm, waving the other.

Kevin came back and held out a hand, but he expected his sisters to keep up, shut up, or go the long way. He didn't have time for cowards. He was at peace in the woods and took pride in his ability to capture animals, to be awed or amused by them, and then let them go.

Kevin didn't need any noisy, screaming girls around to ruin his piece of heaven.

Sometimes, he came here to get away from his mom or dad. Or them.

Bob liked closing shop on Saturday afternoons when Rita worked. They had a sitter, so didn't have to rush home. They were getting better financially. Plus, it was her birthday.

He held some cash aloft, "Rita, I believe this goes to you for groceries and gas. And, for your birthday," he wiggled his eyebrows, *"silk stockings."*

"No one buys silk stockings anymore, Bob." Rita walked behind the counter, dragging her hand around his waist.

He kissed her and slipped the money into her dress pocket.

Between kisses, she asked, "Do you owe this to a supplier?"

"Nope."

"Do you owe this to anybody on the seedy side of life?" Rita pulled away to challenge him.

He laughed. "No, no one. That money is free and clear. What about you? You been paying the mortgage, utilities, the stuck-up oil companies?"

Rita climbed on a packing crate to playfully sit on the counter. "All the big ones, yes. I owe a few little medical bills and the kids need—"

"Yeah, yeah, they're fine." Bob kissed Rita's neck. "This, *this*, is the reward I get for quitting the booze and bars, guys, gambling. All I ever wanted: *you*." He slipped his hand under the hem of her dress to where Rita's garters held up her stockings. He unclipped one.

"Not silk?"

"That's nylon."

"Nylon is just fine."

Leaning over the cash register, Rita turned off the store lights.

That September, the children walked to school.

Bob's new freedom from duties, being alone, made him feel buoyant. He decided to stop at The Lighthouse Bar, driving home from work. It would be one quick beer. Bob loved watching the beer's white foam settle to a clear amber. He loved the smell of it. His pulse quickened at the first sip. Ahhh. He was a man's man again. Some things Rita didn't get. He'd keep this a secret.

After a different quick beer, and a shot, later in the week, Bob came into the kitchen with a large paper bag from The Toy Chest. He whistled, and the children came running, even Dave Gabriele. He was kneeling on the floor, pulling out squirt guns for everyone. "Here, Dave, you take Shawn's. He's probably too small for a squirt gun."

The kids rushed to sinks to fill them. Then Bob pulled out a big, black, plastic Tommy Gun. "There's one rule: outside only. Go hide." Bob filled his water gun and herded them out. The kids squirted each other, rolled, dove behind trees, and yelled, "gotcha" all over the lawn. Bob ran around the corner to pummel them with streams of water. They were laughing, screaming, running. Carol brought out a bucket of water to fill their guns faster.

He loved horsing around with his kids. Bob couldn't outrun some of them, but he could out-gun them. Ha. He went into the house to reload, took a flask out of his pocket, and reloaded himself. The booze would keep the fun going. The whiskey ran down his throat, and the vapors stung his eyes. Kevin dashed up the hatchway as Bob put the flask away, and through the open window, squirted his dad in the face. Bob grasped the kitchen sink sprayer and nailed

Kevin right back. Finally, darkness fell, and Bob whistled them back together, waving his white handkerchief in surrender on the back steps.

David had to get home, as it was dark. "Thanks, Mr. Leonard."

Bob punched his shoulder. "You bet, kid." *His* dad never came out to play. Yeesh.

In early October, Bob came home late for dinner more often. But tonight, he was on time. He sat at the head of the table, smirking. Rita was passing around baked pork chops and warm applesauce.

Kevin stared at his dad. Bob put his finger to his lips. The inside of Bob's jacket was moving. He winked at Carol. A tiny sound emerged.

"What that noise?" Shawn piped up. Noreen sprang out of her seat. A tiny calico kitten's head popped out of Bob's jacket, climbing his chest with stiletto claws, mewing with plaintive cries. Noreen, the fuzz-loving pipsqueak, climbed into her daddy's lap. She petted it gingerly and squealed.

They all cooed and said, "So cute."

Bob brought home a pet without discussing it, but this gamble paid off.

Rita put down a dish of milk, as a smile brightened her face. "I'm glad it's not a dog."

They named her Patches, and she slept in the dish towel drawer.

Rita commented to Bob about being late for supper, but he always had a reason: to wait for a supplier, or to replace the fluorescent lighting in the display area.

One blustery night, the children were at the table, scraping the last bits of vanilla pudding from bowls, when Bob decided to get the Halloween season started by scratching at the side door. Rita had been sewing costumes all month, but none of them were scary. Bob donned a green rubber Frankenstein mask, pulled his jacket on backward, unlaced his work boots, and rang the doorbell.

Kitty opened the door and screamed into the living room. Kevin, registering the stranger, tried to shut the door with a yelp. Bob's big arms, ending in stiff electricians' gloves, grasped the door. Frankenstein stalked in, arms outstretched, menacing, with his huge green head, dark gray coat, and big, heavy footsteps. The children laughed or cried or shook, depending on their ages.

Rita grabbed a wooden spoon and held it aloft, got in front of the kids, ready to use it.

Then she recognized his eyes.

"Bob, stop. You're scaring the children." Rita yelled. "Stop it. This isn't funny!"

She gathered Shawn and Noreen to her.

Bob did not break character, roaring into the front hall, and kids scattered and screamed. He lumbered up the stairs. He whistled, not as loud as usual, after all, they were playing inside the house. His posse assembled. "Hmmm, let's play hide and seek . . . hmmm. . . one rule . . . no lights."

Bob's audience roared approval, flicked off lights, and spread out through the four bedrooms, sliding under beds, slipping into closets, and squatting beside bureaus. Bob warned them in his monster voice, "Don't be found first, hmmm, but worst is being found last."

The screaming, running, and laughing ended when Rita, sick of the noise, stomped to the second floor and turned on the lights, "Enough, Bob. That's enough fun for one night."

By Thanksgiving, Bob was drinking beer in the house.

He always had an excuse: a weekend, a football game, or company, and he held it in check on these occasions. But Bob noticed his behavior changing, like his parking. It was a little skewed. He bent to tie a shoe and missed making the knot, left cigarettes burning in ashtrays, and made fart jokes, which he knew Rita hated.

She asked him what was going on.

"Ah. It's nothing. I stop for one beer, not like the drunks on this street, sitting at Delmonico's. Be glad I come happily home to you, my dear." Bob smiled, brown eyes warm, acting like that made him better.

"Do you want to go there?" Rita rubbed her arms.

"I go there because . . . they have a cigarette machine. If I'm out. Of cigarettes." Smooth recovery, he felt.

"Watch it doesn't get out of hand, Bob."

That Christmas was a fine holiday, with gifts, a decent tree, and kids' art all over the house, the Santas, and paper chains smelling of white paste. Bob took pictures of his dressed-up children, in front of the tree. One snapshot was blurred when fuzzy Patches strolled by.

By January, the bills were accumulating again. Rita got a call from Hartford Hospital. In two years, they still hadn't paid Kieran's surgery bills. Rita listened to the harsh voice at the other end. "Yes, I will. I don't know when." Her voice caught in her throat. The woman went on and on. "My baby died," Rita murmured mournfully.

The bill collector stopped talking, then gently said, "I'm sorry. Take your time," and hung up.

Rita worked that night. It was snowing, but she looked forward to talking with her co-workers, eating their late supper together. Rita never called out sick or missed a shift because of the weather. She was a switchboard operator at the hospital; the work was important, and they needed the money.

At ten p.m. Rita got a call from home. "Yes, Bob?"

In a whisper, Carol answered, "It's me, Mom. I woke up and looked for Daddy and he's not here."

Rita was calm. "He's probably in the basement watching television."

"I looked. And I checked your room. Then I looked out the window."

"What? Then what?" Rita held one hand to her headset, blocking out the busy office.

Carol started to cry. "I saw him back out from the driveway."

Her voice dropped, but Rita told her to go on, knowing how hard it was for Carol to tell on her father.

"I saw him drive away. He left us all alone. At night. In this storm."

Rita waved the supervisor over. "Carol, I'll come right home. Hang up, but stay awake until I get there."

She drove home slowly because of the storm, tense, strangling the steering wheel with gloved hands, thinking of the big things that could go wrong: a fire, an electrical blackout, a break-in. And the little things: a nightmare, an upset stomach, a fall out of bed.

Take your time, the bill collector had said. But Rita was out of time. Bob's time was up, and Rita vowed to get him away from her children. There was nowhere she could take six children, not for longer than a night or two.

It was Bob.

She had to get Bob out of their home.

Chapter 26
Time

R ita got in at eleven o'clock to no Bob and no note on the table. Carol was sitting on her bed, holding a book, which she wasn't reading in the dim light, waiting for a parent to come home.

Rita hugged her daughter. "I'm sorry this happened. Maybe Daddy has a reason. You can go to sleep now, I'm home."

"He'll be angry at me. For telling. Because Mom, you always yell at Daddy. I'm his friend in this house." Carol wiped a tear away. "Can you be nice to Daddy when he gets home?"

Rita pulled the bedspread around her. While choking down her rage, Rita whispered, "I'll try."

Rita waited for Bob to make an appearance, tight as a coil. He slipped into bed in the wee hours, too late to take him on.

At six the next morning, Rita showered, wrapped her hair in a towel, walked into their room, and shut the door.

Bob was sitting on the edge of their bed, hungover, head in hands, like before.

Her voice was low. "You endanger our children for a beer? Or a highball or ten beers, I don't know—what's your magic number? It's bad enough you started drinking at home, but now you went out? I could call the police on you, that's a crime, abandonment or endangerment. Where was it you went? Where did you have to go in the middle of the night?"

"I ran out . . . of cigarettes." He looked sheepish and disheveled.

"Then find a butt in an ashtray," she spit out, louder.

"Rita, I needed a drink. It's a disease." Bob's voice was a rasp.

"I don't care. People with diseases get better. You don't. I don't care what you do until it affects my children." She pulled the towel off and angrily ran a brush through her hair.

A knock rang through their bedroom door. Kevin asked tentatively, "Mom?"

Rita barked at him, "Not now, Kevin. Get ready for school. I'll be down in a minute."

Rita hardened. "I'm going to take care of my children now, Bob. When they leave for school, Bob, and if you can get up, we can talk then, Bob."

She slammed the bedroom door and stomped down the stairs as well as she could in a housecoat and slippers. In the kitchen, Rita dared anyone to speak to her while she made Cream of Wheat, rage emanating from her shoulders. She wasn't letting him stay, not any longer. She needed a plan to force Bob out.

The children ate quietly, then put their bowls in the sink. Carol fed Shawn in his highchair. In the hall, Kitty gave Teri an order to move it.

Rita didn't have the energy to address the children right then. She made lunches and filled thermoses with milk. When the kids reappeared, en masse, she was sitting, not reading the paper, just staring into her coffee. Kitty rinsed the breakfast things, then walked over to hug Shawn and her mom.

Kevin didn't steal anyone's fruit or knock anyone over in his haste to escape, but he paused at the door to call out, "Bye, Mom. I hope you feel a little better."

The children left for school. Shawn sat on his mother's lap and played with two spoons and a sugar bowl. He was a sweet kid, blue-eyed, pale-skinned, easy, funny. Rita smiled at him.

Last night had been the straw that broke the camel's back. She tried hard and long, not always consciously, to keep Bob's alcoholism from family and friends, but most importantly, from their children. They thought he was a fun guy when he wasn't mean. He played, brought them toys, and thrilled them with suspense. In their eyes, she was the curmudgeon, the rulemaker.

Bob was the rulebreaker, and a fun, lousy example to the kids. The last straw? What a joke. There were dozens, hundreds of last straws.

Rita was sick of being a camel. Today, she would call a priest. And a lawyer. The knot in Rita's stomach grew anticipating Bob coming down the stairs. Her mind darted. Rita would have to quit her job. She didn't want to, because it kept them from being really poor.

Leaving her children with Bob at night was not an option.

Rita put Shawn on the floor and opened the cupboard. She sat there with him, pulling out pots and pans and a wooden spoon.

"Do you want to play drums?" she asked.

He often repeated phrases. "No. No. Let's cook. What to cook? What to cook?"

"Oh, let me see, how about spaghetti? You like spaghetti."

"*Pagetti*. Pagetti. I make it. I make it." Rita and Shawn giggled. She felt calmer playing with her youngest.

Bob walked into the kitchen, showered and shaved, but his eyes were bloodshot, his skin blotchy. He didn't speak, until his gaze moved to Shawn. "I, uh. Hey, what're you doing? Cooking?"

"Yep," he went back to stirring.

Rita pulled herself off the floor. "I'll get you coffee, because I've got two things to say."

"No, just say it." Bob stood there, his arms hanging limp.

"One, I've got to quit my job, to be home at night." She paused, then wiped up the sugar Shawn spilled.

"Okay. I get it. That will help me."

Why did Bob think it was always about him?

Rita threw the sugar in the sink and rinsed the dishcloth. "It's not to help you, Bob, you can help yourself. You're an adult." She dried her hands, then took her seat. "Here's the second thing. Think about where you want to live."

Bob's face blanched. "Nowhere. Here. I'm not moving out. These are my children, you're my wife . . . I love you all . . . "

Rita's heart was drumming, she was going to say what she had planned many, many times. "It's time for us to separate, Bob." Rita's eyes misted and she bit her bottom lip to keep herself together. "You should find a room or a little efficiency."

"No." Now he sat down. "No. No. No. No."

"What do you mean, 'no'? I'm asking you to leave. It's about the children's safety. It's about you being drunk and out of control and mean and . . ." Rita was trying to stay calm, for Shawn's sake. She glanced at him, but he was busy, with his head in the big pot. It echoed with his singing.

Bob took her cue and lowered his voice. "Do you not love me anymore? Is that it?"

Rita tilted her head, shut her eyes for a moment, then held her forehead. "No, I never said that. I do . . . love you. Always have. That's been my downfall, Bob, but it can't be our children's."

Bob responded to the first part, "And I love you. Two people who love each other, who . . . who've been together . . . I'll be a better man. I'll be a better father. Rita, please, I'm begging you."

His eyes bounced all over the room, looking for one of his distractions: a coffee, a cigarette, a beer. Carol had asked Rita to be nice to him. She'd try, hoping to keep Bob still long enough to finish this conversation. Rita brought him coffee, and then sat across from him.

"I'm going to try to get a meeting with Father McBride. We can't divorce, the church won't let us . . . but maybe a legal separation? I don't know what Catholics do in this situation. We've got to make plans, Bob, because this is not working."

Bob looked her in the eye, and whispered, "I'm not going anywhere."

Heat bloomed on her neck, but Rita knew to be quiet. She swallowed, then raised her eyebrows to let Bob know she heard him. "Let me go get this guy dressed." Rita took Shawn, leaving Bob alone. She had said her piece.

Rita was able to see the priest that afternoon. It was a blustery day, but she put Shawn in the stroller and made the walk to the rectory in Elmwood Center. She needed the air and exercise.

The Father was a young guy and the principal of St. Brigid's new school. They knew each other a little because she was a regular at nine o'clock mass, and the children went to catechism on Saturdays.

Rita was nervous to be in the rectory, as she'd never asked to be alone with a priest, to seek counsel. McBride's housekeeper suggested tea and whisked off to make it. The Father was in black slacks and a gray turtleneck. Rita thought it too trendy for a priest, looking younger than he did on Sundays. She pulled Shawn onto her lap and offered a toy ambulance. He squirmed, getting down to walk around, exploring.

Father McBride raised his chin to Rita. "He's fine, he can run around here. I'll put this vase higher."

Rita smiled. People without children couldn't see all the lures and dangers a room like this presented to someone as curious as Shawn. She'd keep an eye on him. "I don't know if you remember my last pregnancy. One day after church, you and I spoke. We were out of money, and you offered, um, a food basket, and ah, some prayers. And, of course, you know that his," she pointed to Shawn, "his twin died."

"I do. I do. All sad circumstances. I'm sorry for your loss."

The housekeeper set the tea tray on the table, giving Shawn a cookie.

"Yes, well, yes, thank you. We had two difficult years after that. Bob, my husband, has a drinking problem." Rita took a breath, took a sip of tea, then moved Shawn away from a glass candy dish. "We aren't getting along. But that's the symptom. It's his . . . alcoholism . . . that's the issue. He can't, or won't, stop drinking. I want him to leave, leave our home, and leave our marriage."

Father McBride stood, suddenly angry. "Well, now. Hold on there a minute. You took vows. You both took vows, 'For Better or Worse', do you remember that part of your wedding? 'In Sickness and in Health.' This is the hard part: *this* is where your faith comes in."

Rita was surprised at his response, but also ready for this fight, "I know, and I do remember. But I don't remember a vow that said, 'Keep him even if he is a danger to your children or if he can't feed them or put a roof over their heads.'"

McBride sat back down, seeming to remember his role. "You cannot, as a Catholic, get divorced."

Rita nodded. "I know. I'm not looking for a divorce. How can I get him out, legally, if I have to? I need some advice on how to move on . . . without him."

"How do you propose to do that? How will you support your children? Who will guide them on their spiritual journey, if not their parents?" He was sputtering, red-faced.

"I will. I'll support them, I'll ask Bob for help, financially, but I'll get a job. I'll be sure that they go to church, have milk with their supper, sleep soundly at night, knowing I am there for them." Rita raised her voice, "*I will*. Do you think that without a man I can't take care of my children? I will find a way."

Rita's face was hot, and she was sweating in the stuffy room. She dabbed her lip with a tissue. Shawn, alerted, tiptoed over to climb into Rita's lap.

"Well . . . I can tell you that you need a lawyer for a legal separation. You might have to sell your house and split the profits. Do you know how hard this will be? Raising six children without a father. I'm begging you, reconsider. I'll waive tuition at St. Brigid's School if that's what you want, I'll send more food. We, the church, do not want to see *you* do this to your family."

"Father, I thank you for your time, your tea, and your advice." She put on her sweater and took Shawn's hand. Rita strode to the stroller parked by the front door. The priest hurried to catch up. Rita thought he might apologize for his harsh words.

Father McBride opened the door, looked down at her, and said, "Mrs. Leonard, you will never make it alone."

"We'll see about that, Father."

27

BOXES

She pushed Shawn home fast, incensed at McBride's naive and shallow view of married life. Rita pointed out various trucks to Shawn as they rumbled by until he dozed off. It was folly for Rita to take advice from someone who chose a vow of celibacy and poverty. That tea service didn't exactly scream poverty.

That her and Bob's wedding vows were sacred was a joke. Why was it the women had to abide by commandments, and men got to interpret them at will? Bob could spend his paycheck in a bar, and his children could go hungry. The audacity of that prig demanding that she needed Bob, that she'd never make it without him. It was her religion that eschewed birth control, to force Catholic women all over the world to have too many children. And then to become ever more dependent on their men. She was infuriated at Father McBride for his blind devotion and at his taking Bob's side. Every man's side.

Rita needed to tell Aunt Rose and her sisters, and her friends Eleanor and Marie, that she was ending this marriage; she wouldn't shield Bob anymore.

Shawn was hungry when they got home, so Rita opened the refrigerator and said, "Let's cook, buddy." Her irate energy went into chopping off celery tops and bottoms and smearing two crackers with peanut butter for Shawn. While he ate in his highchair, Rita attacked the carrots, onions, and potatoes for Shepherd's pie, being careful not to slice her thumb off.

When the kitchen was back in order, Rita walked Shawn to the den to roll his train around, then retrieved her wedding album, needing to remember how she felt that day. Though just 18, she was excited to marry someone she truly loved. The vows had meaning, and she welcomed exchanging them with Bob. Her heart fluttered that day, but today it pounded, her stomach a little sick.

That evening Rita and Bob acted as if they were in a polite dance. She tried to keep their fighting from the children, but with the tension of their parents' clipped conversations, they knew something was up. When Bob walked into the kitchen for supper, Carol slid her chair over to be near him. Rita needed to get Bob alone.

Saturday morning, Rita walked into the bathroom while Bob was shaving, shutting the door behind her. "Bob. Think where you could live for a while. With your mom and stepfather?"

"Uh, no. I'm not living with my parents. I have a house, and a family." He dragged the razor through shaving lather and flicked the excess water into the filled sink, "I, uh, believe I built both."

Her mouth dropped open, "Built both? This house? You built this family? What have I been doing these last twelve years? I *made* you save money; I *gave* birth to the children; I *helped design* this house, I—"

He coughed, then wiped the remaining foam off his cheeks and chin with a towel. Bob viewed her in the mirror. "I'm not done in here, in the bathroom. If you'd open that door, I'd appreciate that."

His condescending tone amazed her as much as his statements.

Rita's arms clutched her ribs. "You want me to get out? Is that what you want?"

Bob started to clip his fingernails. "Yes. I do."

Rita pitched a tube of lipstick at his brow and said, "That's *exactly* what I want: *you* to get out."

While grocery shopping that Saturday afternoon, Rita was consumed with Bob's stubbornness. She made poor choices, picking the 33-cent loaf of bread instead of the 35-cent one, which had five more slices. Kevin and Kitty snuck Marshmallow Fluff into the cart, taking advantage of her distractedness.

When she unloaded the groceries, Bob helped.

Rita said, "I can show you how to cut coupons and use a shopping list."

Bob paused as he slid canned goods across the counter. "Rita, let's stop this nonsense. I *am* changing. Haven't you seen that? I'm here with you now, unloading groceries, for Christ's sake. Haven't had a drink in days."

Holding a can of peas, she envisioned throwing it at his smug face, but took satisfaction at the little cut on his brow.

They all went to church on Sunday. Rita chose an early Mass when Father McBride wasn't preaching, that pious punk. The Leonards stopped at Elmwood Bakery for doughnuts and pumpernickel bread. She made a roast chicken dinner.

Bob and Rita slept in the same bed, her to keep the illusion for the children, him because he wanted to be with her. Rita didn't kiss Bob anymore. Sometimes, during the night, he reached for her hand, and in her sleepiness, she gave it. She'd miss that small gesture.

Before breakfast Monday morning, Rita asked Bob what furniture he'd like to take. Rita tensed when Bob didn't look up from the paper.

"None of it. I'm not going anywhere, for God's sake. So, drop it, or I'm gonna get pissed off."

"I thought you'd want the footstool." She'd be generous.

Bob bolted up, punching a cupboard door, splitting it with such force and noise, that Rita ducked. She covered her head and huddled with her back to Bob, then slowly turned to stare at his face.

Bob shook his fingers out, as if his hand hurt because of her.

"I *said* drop it."

Rita took deep breaths. No, not like this. He can't be allowed to hit stuff, or me or the kids. She wasn't done with her mission, but Rita needed a better plan than badgering Bob to death.

On St. Patrick's Day, Rita made corned beef and cabbage, baked Irish soda bread, and graced the table with two Belleek shamrock teacups. She switched the radio to WTIC, to sing along with Irish ballads all day.

Bob left for work in his khakis, zip jacket, and Irish wool cap, saying, "See you at six," as he pulled the door shut.

Rita thought, "Please, God. Let him come home sober." After six o'clock was a dangerous time for an Irishman on St. Patrick's Day in Hartford.

At six-thirty Bob wasn't home yet. Rita passed the food out. The children especially wanted the sweet soda bread. During the blessing, Bob's truck announced his arrival. Rita was glad. She stood taller and breathed easier.

Then she wasn't glad.

Bob careened into the kitchen with a bottle of Jameson Irish Whiskey, half empty.

"Top o' the morning, ladies, I mean *laddies, lassies*. Got a big '*sprise* for you." He giggled like a girl. "Whoops. A *schmall 'sprise*. I brought home a leprechaun. A real one . . . you be nice, and I'll, ssh. I'll get him."

Bob moved to the door, held open the storm door, and yelled, "Sal. Sol. Whatever yer name is, get in here. Oh, Pat, I mean."

A very short man with a full black beard on a large face came through the side door. He tipped a floppy green hat at the table. He wore a costume of knickers, a green vest, and a large bow tie.

Carol cocked her head. "You're a real leprechaun? I thought that was a fairy tale."

"Nooo." Patrick giggled, "I'm real as rain."

Kevin laughed, "I hope you got a pot of gold, cuz we could use it."

Rita held a hand up to stop her children's bad manners. This was a guest in their home. She said hello.

The children were tittering at this small, colorful man at their house, leaning on their elbows for a better view. He didn't look Irish, but he sounded it.

"Ah, but isn't it the family down to a *loovely* repast? Don't mind me if I just sit wi' ya for a small bite and a wee drop."

"Pa . . . Patrick. I'll get you a s-seat." Bob banged around, coming back with Rita's antique desk chair.

She stood to give Patrick her usual seat. "Take mine. Yes, join us for supper."

The children sat wide-eyed and open-mouthed. She shook her head at them subtly. Rita moved to get their guest a plate, then served the two men.

Bob reached across Carol and grabbed the delicate teacups and poured two drinks. "Pass th . . . this down. Oh, Rita, you wanna *drjinnk*?"

She didn't answer.

Patrick dug in, then the kids did too, sneaking glances at his little fingers, and his big head. They searched Rita's blank face.

Patrick broke the silence. "Now see, where I come from on the auld sod, we had only the one giant ear of corn. Me Pa would throw it on the *taybul*. The wee ones gathered 'round, would gnaw on a row of corn, then Pa would yell, 'Turn,' and all the lads and lassies would roll that big cob to the next level to start in anew. Now, then, I am so small, as ye can see, because they pushed me out: the runt of the litter."

Bob hurled out a laugh, and a hunk of corned beef plopped onto his plate.

The kids laughed too and asked Mr. Patrick all sorts of things. Was he magic? How old was he? Could he run?

He answered in the most ridiculous ways and in the most wavering brogue Rita ever heard.

She was angry because Bob was stinking drunk, and he was taking advantage of this stranger. Rita squeezed her eyes shut for a moment, eager for this meal to end.

When she cleared the dishes, she touched Patrick's shoulder.

"How about I call you a cab?"

He hooted, "That would be fine, Miss." He probably was done with this farce, drunk or not.

Rita made them coffee and noticed the additional whiskey Bob laced into the men's cups. She directed the children to the basement and turned on an Irish Step-Dancing contest on TV.

When the taxi driver beeped, Rita saw Bob give Patrick some cash, then waltzed him to the front door. Bob called out, "Going Up" to an imaginary elevator operator, clunking upstairs singing "Danny Boy."

Rita followed to give him a piece of her mind, but he fell onto the bed, making the footboard and headboard rattle. Fuming, Rita stomped back down, noticing her lovely wallpaper. It kept repeating, repeating, repeating the same scenes. Just like Rita's life with Bob.

Tomorrow, she'd get her paltry finances in order, then find an attorney.

Rita awoke from the couch, made coffee, then opened her desk to make a list of people to call. Her insurance agent, Mr. Leahy, and a lawyer. Her bank, to check on their mortgage and savings. Rita and the children wouldn't, and couldn't, go back to their building on Park Street.

Bob had mortgaged that property and it had lost much of its value. He was leasing his own store from the new owner. He was lying and stealing from her all along. Bob's disease, if she called it that, which she didn't, affected the quality of his work, where he spent his days, and who he avoided in town. Hadn't her own mother said Bob would ruin her family?

Answers to her questions were almost too raw to bear. The attorney would charge Rita in advance for the paperwork. Bob had to be kept out of their home and out of her bed to prove they weren't cohabitating. Rita could cover the mortgage for two months, if she emptied every account, and borrowed the seventeen dollars in each child's school banking program. Real estate taxes and homeowner's insurance fees were due in July. They owed the utility companies. The lights were shut off more than once recently.

She needed a job, now, to get a temporary apartment, because she couldn't afford this house alone. Her attorney had a family who needed a lease, but by the end of May. Five children were in school until late June, so it would be difficult to be out by then. Rita's mind was ticking, day and night. In mid-April, the gas was shut off. Rita heated big pans of water on the electric stove and carried them up for the kids' baths. The baths were quick, and shallow, like her breathing.

One late April Tuesday, Bob was on a remodeling job with his cousin Fran, so his truck was home. While Shawn napped, Rita filled three boxes to help Bob move out. Into the first box, she put coffee cups, saucepans, a can opener, cutlery, potholders, plates, and a baking dish. The second box held two blankets, odd sheets and towels, and Bob's clothes. The third box contained toiletries, three books, a shoehorn, ashtrays, matches, stamps, envelopes, and paper. Rita found a framed photograph from last Father's Day, 1962, when the children gave their daddy breakfast in bed. She would have added his penny collection, but the bean pot was too heavy. Rita put everything neatly into his truck, sure he'd see his belongings on the front seats.

Bob came home sober and work-dirty. "What's going on in my truck, Rita?"

Washing his hands at the kitchen sink, he saw the children playing outside. She was stirring beef stew. Bob tossed his cap on the counter, rubbed his hands on a dish towel, and looked at his seat. His spot was empty.

"I'm helping you move out." She finished setting the table.

"Now? Today? What the hell . . . we didn't even talk about this."

Rita didn't pause in her work. "That's *all* we've talked about."

"No, that's all *you've* talked about."

As she put spoons out, he yanked her arm, to stop her movements.

"I'm being fair, here, Bob. I . . . I keep asking you to find a place."

He held on. "Just like that? I'm out? Like some old dog? Like Bruno, just disappear?"

Bob used his grip to move her toward the corner, between the oven and sink, trapping her. Bob dropped his grasp of her arm, but slid his hand under her chin, forcing her mouth shut. Then he moved his hand down to her neck and squeezed.

"You're hurting me," Rita wheezed out.

"I mean to hurt you. Like you're hurting me."

Bob was pressing Rita's back into the metal edge of the counter, then used two fingers to snap her forehead back. He seemed to like the panic in her eyes, his power over her.

Rita could hear children grinding the stones as they approached the door. Bob dropped his hands, and Rita turned to lean on the counter, to face the wall, to catch her breath.

Kevin burst into the kitchen and ran through the hall, to the stairs. Kitty was right on his heels, arms outstretched, clawing the air, "Give it back, you jerk. It's mine."

Bob smirked. "How you gonna handle that, huh? These kids when I'm gone?" He put his hands in his pockets and looked around again, then walked over to the decorative spice rack on the far wall. He violently snatched the wooden frame from its hooks, and the twelve hand-painted ceramic jars rattled, and cinnamon and cardamom crashed to the floor.

"I'll need this, you know, for my new place." Bob then stormed out.

28

NAILS

Bob sat in his truck, sober. Where could he go? He pounded the steering wheel with his calloused hands. Those hands. He never wanted to harm Rita, but his ugly temper flared, making him a monster. Bob relived the kitchen scene, choking her, breaking things. This was new, this meanness when he was sober. What the hell? Bob drove to the airport, parked on the perimeter road, watched planes take off and land, and wished he had somewhere, anywhere, to go.

He returned to his driveway late. By the streetlight, he rifled through the boxes to find sheets and blankets to sleep in the back of the truck. He prayed sleep would come, because awake, he tortured himself thinking of what to possibly say to Rita.

At daylight, Bob went to the side door, hesitated, then knocked.

Kitty cracked open the door, "Hiya, Dad."

The screen door separated them. "Kitty, go get Mommy."

Rita knew he slept in his truck. She scowled through the screen. "Yes?"

Bob held his toothbrush, "May I?"

Rita rolled her eyes, crossed her arms, and spit out, "No, you may not."

"Rita . . ." he pleaded, "can we talk? When can we talk?"

"Do I need to get a . . . a bodyguard?" There wasn't one soft thing about her this morning.

Bob was crawling out of his skin, sweating, "No. I'm better. Today. I'm sorry."

"Ugh. Okay. Come by after work. And Bob? Come sober or don't come at all."

Rita pushed the door open, blocking him, as kids started streaming out between them, going to school, not knowing a crisis was coming to a head. Four girls and one boy called out variations of "Bye, Mom. See ya, Dad."

"I could give them a ride to school," Bob suggested, hopeful.

"No. Let them go." She began to shut the door, "See you around six."

Bob climbed into his truck, balled the sheets into their box, and pushed his night away into a dark corner.

He drove slowly past his children, who smiled and waved. All day, as he worked in the tile store, he was haunted by Rita's simple words: Let them go. Let them go. Let them go.

Rita now knew why the lawyer advised changing the locks to keep Bob out of her house and out of her bed. His mean streak was widening. Bob was stronger than she, and angrier.

No, not angrier. Her anger was fuel to keep her going, to get him out. What she would do next to raise the children, she had no idea.

Hartford Lock and Key installed a deadbolt and a chain lock on the side door. She asked Aunt Rose to sleep over, in Rita's bed, to convince Bob he no longer lived here.

Rita expected Bob to show up by six that evening.

He didn't.

By seven o'clock, the littlest ones, Shawn and Noreen, were in bed. The other children were horseback racing, carrying each other through the circuit of kitchen, den, and living room, spurring their own horse/sibling on. When Kevin stopped his horse by throwing both arms out at door jambs to trip the other kid's horse, someone fell off, laughing.

Rita was washing dishes, with Rose drying. Rita's head swiveled when the truck pulled in. She flung an arm out to stop the whirling horse race. Kids piled up in the den; she gave the quiet sign.

Bob walked to the side door. They saw him through the sheer curtains, as he twisted the knob. Nothing. Then he tried his key. Bob knocked on the door, and banged on it, then rang the doorbell, repeatedly, creating a maniacal musical urgency.

Carol moved forward, but Rita stopped her. "Don't get it. Anyone."

Rose stepped closer to Rita and the children, away from the door.

"I know you're in there, Rita. Open up," Bob roared. He waited a beat or two, then stomped away, and his truck door creaked open. A pause, a slam, and the rubble of the stones as Bob moved toward the house. He crashed something heavy into the door's lower windowpane. Glass exploded.

Carol, Kevin, Kitty, Teri, and the women screamed or gasped.

Bob reached in and unlocked the door, but as he opened it, the new chain held fast.

Rita found her voice, "Bob. Stop it. Stop."

He lowered his shoulder, and with the whole power of his arms and back, ripped off the door's oak molding, tore half the chain from its bracket, with the remaining links swinging from the splintered door, as glass bits and broken nails rained down. Bob let the rag-wrapped wrench clank to the floor.

Rita, Rose, the four children, froze.

Bob bent to retrieve his hat, turned to shut what was left of the door, and walked nearer to them. All instinctively drew back.

He took the teakettle from the stove, filled it at the sink, then turned on a burner. He busied himself getting a cup, a Tetley tea bag, sugar, and a spoon. When the kettle whistled, Bob made a cup of tea, and sat in his chair. He seemed comfortable, as if to say, what, a man can't have a cup of tea in his own kitchen?

Rose murmured, "Well, saints preserve us."

Kitty held her mother's hand. Kevin moved to the front of the pack. Rita didn't know if Bob would remain calm or lash out at them. She squeezed Kitty's hand, and with the other, Rita pressed her thudding heart.

Rose was on. "Bobby, Bobby, you leave now. You're scaring Rita. You're scaring the children. Go on with yourself." She moved her burly body closer to Bob, looking brave.

Bob put on his hat, placed his cup in the sink, pushed in his chair. He was leaving, but then paused. He glared at Rita, "This is *my* house."

Rita stood firm, not thinking before she blurted, "Not anymore."

He was around the table and across the room in three long strides, his hat falling to the floor. Bob grabbed Rita's shirt front and yanked her close, making her rise on tiptoes, rasped at her ear, "Who the hell do you think you're talking to?"

Rita was able to screw her head around, "Rose, take the kids upstairs."

"I'll stay here, Rita." Rose dug in.

Kevin brushed between the women. "Quit it Dad, stop hurting us."

Bob held Rita fast but used his left hand to punch Kevin in the chest, causing him to bend over and sputter. Carol clamped both hands to her mouth. Kitty retreated into the den, still watching, but pulled Teri along. Kevin gathered air, ready to pounce, but Carol yanked him back.

"Not them, Bob, not the kids." Rita jerked Bob's grip from her collar. She whipped around to push Carol and Kevin back, commanding, "Go. Call the police."

The children ran through the den to the living room, and across the hall in seconds.

Bob shoved some chairs out of his way. "You and your old biddy of an aunt. A bunch of brats. What're you all gonna do, Rita? Gonna hurt me? I'll crush each and every one of you."

As Bob approached her again, Rita warned, "Don't touch my kids."

Rose eyeballed Rita and yelled, "Run."

Rita ran through the living room.

At the stairs, the kids had escaped, but Bob cut Rita off in the hall, pulling out a fistful of her hair. Rita twisted under his arm, and by now Rose was ripping at his shirt, her nails digging into his back.

Bob, a monster, raged, "Get OFFA me," but Rose dug her talons in, giving Rita the break to bolt up the steps.

In their parents' bedroom, the girls huddled, sniffling. Rita locked the door. Her immediate concern was Kevin, who was pacing, a caged animal, fists balled, a sneer where his ready smile belonged. She asked Kevin to raise his shirt.

There was a mid-size red spot in the center of his chest.

"Are you alright?"

"Except for getting him back? I shoulda punched him, kicked him. I'm gonna. Some night—"

Rita tried to slow his path. "Don't. He'll take it out on me. He won't be living here anymore. But are you alright?"

He shrugged, giving his always-reply, "A little better."

Carol broke from the sisters, "Daddy won't live here? Where's he going?"

Rita slowly shook her head. "I don't know."

Carol's lips trembled.

Aunt Rose came up to report when Bob was gone. "Bob walked back to the kitchen. I followed him. 'I got no beef with you, Rose,' he said, then took his hat and knocked the splinters of glass from its rim. Blood ran down his arm." Rose was shaking. "I said, 'You get out, Bobby. Leave Rita be.' He calmly walked out the door, just as you please, and drove away."

Rita hugged her aunt, then turned to Carol. "Did you call the police? Where are they?"

Carol's lips struggled on her face, as she wiped a tear. "I couldn't. Not on Daddy. I called Uncle Mike instead, I said, 'Come quick. My dad's hitting my mom.'"

"Ah, ya don't want the police. Isn't Mike about the biggest man you know?" Rose offered.

Rita grinned yes, and asked her to let Uncle Mike in.

They heard Mike banging nails, securing the door, bringing a temporary feeling of safety. She walked around her bed, then sat. She stood. Sat back down and massaged the back of her skull where Bob had ripped her hair out.

Kitty slid over the quilt. "I'll do that."

Rita twisted her mouth. "Do what, Kitty?"

"Rub your neck where he hurt you. Why did Daddy hurt you?" Kitty kneeled behind Rita and rubbed the tender area.

"He's mad at me."

Rita was breaking down. She was losing her soul. Her belief system. Her idea that if you were a good person, good would be returned to you. That someone loving you meant they cared for you, helped you, protected you.

Carol sat on the bed, and Kevin and Teri came on from the other side.

Rita angled her arm over the brass-knobbed footboard, turned away from her children, so they didn't see their rock crumble.

"Why's he mad, Mommy?" Teri asked, "Is he mad at us, too?"

Rita laid her left cheek in the vee of her arm, eyes on the floor. "No. No. Not you kids . . . only me."

With a huge sigh, she rubbed Kitty's arm to tell her to stop. "Please all go to bed now." She whisper-whined, knowing she could say no more. Her anger wasn't strong enough to keep Bob away. Rita needed something else to fight with. She needed to get over this grief. This shock. This betrayal.

Rita, 29-year-old mother of six, needed courage she never dreamed existed.

But she sure as hell was going to find it.

29

SEPARATING

B ob disappeared after the door-smashing incident.

Rita filed her nails in the darkening kitchen, waiting for tea water to boil. While sadness, fear, and anger all tripped over themselves vying for Rita's attention, she still needed to find Bob, to get their children settled elsewhere. Now she was worrying about him too. She called the store. Although it was evening, Big George was working late because Bob hadn't shown up. Cousin Fran didn't know where he was but promised to look around.

Two more days passed when Rita got a late-night call.

Aunt Rose was already asleep.

Bob spoke softly, "Rita, I'm sorry. This is all new to me . . . it's hard. I'd like to come by and fix the door. And everything else . . . "

This conversation was expected, but still, her pulse quickened, and her breathing was off. She skipped broken-heart-how-could-you-do-this-to-me mode and went right into defense mode.

"That was five days ago, Bob, it's done," she said. Curt. Cold. Anger was winning. "Mike fixed it that night. What if you wanted to come smashing in here again? You can't . . . I mean . . . you don't live here anymore. It's not safe for me or the kids. You *punched* Kevin. Do you remember that? He does. He twisted Kitty's arm the other day. Thought nothing of it. You got that? You're not teaching these kids that violence is something people do . . . to . . . to . . . make a point. Ever."

"I know. I was wrong. I'm sorry. I was just, I didn't mean to hurt anybody. Tell him. Oh, God."

Rita could hear him exhale, in jabs, over traffic. "No, you tell Kevin. He won't even talk about it."

A car backfired.

"Where are you?"

"A phone booth. Outside of Stebens' Automotive on Park."

She knew exactly where he was. She visualized him shutting his eyes, leaning his head on the glass of the phone booth, fiddling with pocket change, hating himself. He could use some self-loathing. It would take the burden off her.

"Did you have something else you wanted to . . . fix?" Rita sneered.

"No, no. I've been driving around trying to get the courage to call you," Bob admitted. "I've got some cash to give you. I finally sold the VW bus that's been parked at the store for months. I found a little apartment, right over the Hartford line, so I'll need a few things. They're putting in a phone early tomorrow. I could swing around after that."

Rita was glad he was taking this separation seriously, finally listening. Thank God. Now Rita could move on to the next phase of her plan. But she needed to trust him.

"So, can I come by?"

"Bob, the last two times you were here, you were Dr. Jekyll and Mr. Hyde. You flipped a switch. Do I need someone with me if you come over tomorrow? Be honest. Are you in control right now? Of your anger, or alcohol, or whatever it is?" She twisted the phone cord.

"I haven't had a drink in four days. I'll be fine, I promise. Let's talk."

She inhaled. "After the bigger kids go to school, come tomorrow. I'll tell Eleanor to watch out her window, and be ready to call the police, to keep Shawn and me safe."

"You don't need to do that. I'm sober, I'll be fine, and you will be, too. I want this to go better. I'll be there around ten. And Rita? Thanks."

After the kids left for school, Rita dropped Rose at work, then returned home to set Shawn in the den with a burlap bag of blocks. Patches the cat twisted through Rita's legs as she called Eleanor to say Bob was expected.

With sweaty palms, Rita made coffee.

Bob came to the side door and respectfully knocked. They both kept their distance as he walked into the kitchen. He peeked at Shawn in the den.

"May I? Can I go see him?" Bob was polite. The way he used to be.

Rita nodded and poured their coffee, hearing Bob crouch down, and say, "Hi ya, tiger."

"Hi Daddy. I'm building a park *grage*." Shawn played with his mismatched trucks.

Bob laughed, rubbed Shawn's arm. "Looks good, buddy. What kind of truck is this?"

"I think a *sment* mixer." Shawn pushed it on the rug, making revving sounds.

Bob's knees cracked as he stood, "Good job. Keep playing. I'm going to talk to Mommy." Bob walked into the kitchen, and sat in his seat.

Rita wondered, was it still his chair? When did it stop being his? Two mugs of scalding hot coffee were on the table, with the sugar bowl near him.

Rita positioned herself near the phone. "Let's try to be civil. Before you forget, what did you need for your new place?"

He looked at his work boots and noticed a dusting of dirt he brought in. "You got a doormat of some sort that I can have?"

Rita cut him off, "I thought *I* was your doormat."

"Never my intention, hon."

Hon? When did that stop, the small intimacies that couples shared? "Go on, what else?" Rita was tired of keeping her anger high on her small frame, with her forearm muscles tensed and her neck creaking.

"I could use some curtains, it's only one room and a bathroom. Also, my Philipps screwdriver, a crowbar, a flashlight, and some batteries." Bob swallowed the hot liquid. "Yeeow. That's some hot coffee." He waved his hand over red lips.

Rita smiled that he never learned. "Sure. I'll find those things and you can grab your tools before you leave. You want an English muffin?"

Now it was his turn to smile. She always fed people.

Rita moved with an economy of motion.

Bob rested his right ankle on his left knee, then blew on his coffee.

"I know how rough life with me has been. I saw the same look on my mother about my father. It breaks my heart that I'm like him," Bob paused and took the English muffin from Rita, but just stared at the swirl of strawberry jam. "I know you have given me more chances than I . . . than anyone . . . deserves."

Rita held her cup in two hands, and kept her voice low, "Do you? Do you know how difficult life is with you? Never knowing when you'd be home, and if you'd be sober." She sipped, looking over the rim at him.

"You're right to kick me out." Bob sat back and breathed in and out, heavily. "I need to be alone, to, to work on 'my crutch.' It's gotten worse in the last three years."

"Bob, if we had any money in reserve, if, I don't know, if you didn't expect children to take care of themselves . . . I think we'd still make it. But Noreen? She has not known the nice dad that you were. Kevin doesn't know if you are going to hug him or hit him. Teri has nightmares. Carol wants to protect you, and Kitty wants to protect me. That's not their job. It's our job to protect them." It calmed Rita to explain this to Bob, the things they fought about, for ages now. Her shoulders settled.

"Rita, you're like a lioness, protecting your cubs with a fierceness I can't fight. Since they were babies, you've protected them. Driving them in a blizzard when I was too drunk. You took on Nurse Sherry, begged the principal to let them stay at school, and told off the electric company. Kept them clean and fed, even when we were dirt poor." Bob finished, "I'll do whatever you ask."

Rita was stunned at all Bob remembered. They were quiet. Nibbled at their muffins. Rita attempted to drink her coffee, but it was tepid.

"I intend to . . . keep them safe." She needed to disclose her plan slowly. "We all need to move because I rented the house out again. That's why I want a legal separation, so I won't be responsible for your debts, and to be able to sign forms for the children's field trips or medical care."

"The house is in both our names," Bob pointed out, "I'm not willing to get off the deed." He rubbed his thumb across his bottom lip.

Rita let that one lie. "I know. But I'll need child support, every week. What do you say to $100 every Friday?"

"I don't make that much." Bob's face whitened.

Rita's jawline set, "The least we can live on, Bob, is $95 a week. Contribute that and be on time. I want to still do family Sunday drives, you to still be their father. If you are drunk, hungover, or just plain mean, I'll limit these visitations."

Bob agreed, then edged a cigarette out of its pack. He opened the junk drawer for matches and peeked in on Shawn playing. Lighting his cigarette, he sat down. "I'll mow the lawn until the tenants move in. I can fix the loose gutter, and your car could use a little tune-up." Bob was magnanimous in his offerings, chagrined at his failings. He rolled the cigarette between his thumb and forefinger, "My hope is someday, when I dry out, get cleaned up, and grow up, we get back together. I desperately want to take your hand right now, but I won't. I have to respect your decisions, Rita."

She was not offering anything else so put her hands in her lap. A knife was twisting somewhere inside, the pain visceral, of explaining her next decision. "I do have something you can help me with," Rita said. It was a big one. "I've decided to split the kids up . . . to finish the school year . . ."

He stood, rubbed his stomach, then leaned against the stove. "No, I thought you'd get a little apartment . . . don't do that . . . no, they need you, they can't be without both of us. Both parents."

"We're going to leave Exeter Avenue. Again. Really, Bob, no one's going to take me and my six kids in. This is for a few weeks. I'll get a job, then an apartment, but until then, they need to finish the school year. I'll stay with Aunt Rose. Help me decide who to ask, who of our family or friends can take one of our kids."

"You've thought about this? You made up your mind? Jesus," he muttered. "Jesus. What about foster care, a family that can take a few together?"

Rita's mouth dropped. "No. I'm not sending our babies to strangers. No, family or friends only. People we love and trust." She was shocked he would even think that. "I've started a list in my head, but I'll get a pen and paper, and address book from my desk."

Rita shakily walked to the living room, taking a minute to wipe her eyes. That was the first time she had said her plan aloud.

To be without her husband was sad.

To be without her children would be torture.

30

LISTS

E leanor answered on the first ring. "Are you safe? Is Bob still there?"

Rita talked fast to keep the pain out of her voice. "I'm fine. He's here and he's behaving. I have a huge favor to ask. You know I've rented the house out for June first? Can you take Kevin, you know, for a few weeks, until the end of the school year?"

"Well, I . . . I . . . sure, sure, Rita. What else? What else can I do?" Eleanor was a calm, sensible friend.

"Yes. Please don't be so kind. That will be my undoing."

Both ladies gave small sorrow-laughs.

Eleanor's son Billy and Kevin were best friends. "I'll send over his clothes, a few toys, his lunchbox. He'd love it if I strapped a knapsack to his back or let him pull everything over in a covered wagon. Eleanor, thank you. Oh. We'll see you on Field Day."

The ladies hung up. Rita took a jagged breath, looking at Bob. "One down, five to go."

"If Kevin gets to the brook, he'll be happy."

The rest of the morning, Bob and Rita made a list of possibilities for their children. They had gathered good friends over the years, and the closest knew about Bob and Rita's struggles. Placing Carol was next, and Rita relied on her sister Carolyn. Carol loved being around her young aunt. Rita was jealous, and this timing was all wrong, as Carol was livid at Rita for forcing Daddy out of the house.

Rita wadded her tissue and threw it at the table, eking out, "I told Carol about our moving. She can't wait to leave me. Why?"

Bob answered, "She's angry. You're tough on her, being the oldest. Rita . . . you . . . your opinions . . . you set them out as laws. She sees how we fight, but doesn't know what I do to set you off."

The blood drained from Rita's face. Did I gloss over Bob's issues so much that now Carol loves only him? She barked at Bob, "Well, don't hold back. I was looking for one reason, not ten." Rita held her head in her hands and shook it back and forth. "I'm not the bad guy here, Bob."

Her heart would break if she crammed one more emotion into this day.

He flicked his cigarette lighter. "Sorry. I shouldn't have said that. She loves you, but she loves me, too. Carol is scared and angry. *I* was her job. She's losing her father and her job."

When she stopped sniveling, Rita told Bob she was calling the Zambrellos for Kitty.

"It's just a few weeks, right? Nice family." Bob padded to the den, to sit with Shawn on the rug while Rita talked to her friend.

"Marie, are you sure you can take Kitty?" Rita felt like she was selling a prized pet. She cried into the phone, "Sorry." Then she blew her nose.

Marie listened. "Rita? Would you do this for me? Would you take in my Bobby or Patty or Albert?"

"Yes."

"Well there you go. I'll call you tomorrow."

Bob walked in from the den, "I'm getting Shawn a snack. What? What's wrong?"

Rita flushed from her neck to her forehead, "Those were our closest friends, and they had offered to help. Who else is in the school district?"

"So, not my mother and stepfather?" Bob offered. He delivered Shawn's cut-up apple, then took a seat.

Rita smiled warily, "No, they don't live in town, and I want to keep them as good grandparents. The Concannons or Hallenbecks? No, they have too many children." Rita wrote, then scratched off names.

"My brother Joe and his wife Pat? Out-of-towners. How about your sister Nancy?" Bob was trying to contribute.

"No, her house is too white, too clean, too serene." Nancy had suggested not relying on Bob and had a ridiculous solution: "Go on welfare. Get an apartment and buy all the kids slippers. That way, they'll be quiet."

They paged through their address book. Former neighbors, the Leahys had always been kind to them. Their daughter, Trisha, was a year older than Teri. Rita needed courage for this call. He was their insurance agent, for God's sake. Battling humiliation, Rita dialed with a pencil, as her hand was too shaky, hoping they didn't remember Bob falling off their porch that time. Inya, a gentle, soft-spoken woman, listened to Rita's quickly told story. "Oh, Rita, we're sorry to hear of your split, and we will light a candle and pray for you."

Rita felt like a charity case, thinking Inya was saying no, "I'm sorry to have bothered you."

"Of course, Mr. Leahy and I will take Teri. She can sleep on a cot in Trisha's room. They can walk to school together. We'll be sure she gets to church on Sundays."

"Thank you, thank you." Rita tried to stop gushing.

Bob handed her a glass of water when she hung up. "Ah, we're now placing my Chocolate Girl. Who are you thinking of for Noreen?"

Rita ran her fingers through her hair, making it messy. "I'm thinking the Klunes?"

"No, not Edith. She's nuts, and she smokes."

"You smoke, how's that different?"

"She's a chain smoker and a Nervous Nellie. I don't want Noreen there."

"She's *not* nuts, but *is* nervous, so what? Then, who, Bob? One of your barfly friends? Some old gambling buddies? You're not helping here."

Bob had no one.

Noreen was going to the Klunes' house. Edith was kind, promising to drive Noreen to kindergarten, and offered to take Patches, the family cat. Rita explained Noreen, "Edith, she's a lefty, loves little spaces to hide in. She's a picky eater. Noreen likes her hair brushed, being read to . . . "

Edith chirped, "Oh, don't you worry. She's like a little mouse, cute as a button. I'll get her some doll clothes, and we'll dress the baby dolls together."

Rita bit her trembling lip at Edith's simple solution. When she replaced the receiver and looked up, Bob's hand was splayed across his chest.

"What?" Rita asked.

He shut his eyes and tilted his head back, a strategy she recognized. Keep your eyes shut, and nothing will leak out. Rita turned on a television show for Shawn and closed the double doors to the den. Little Shawn didn't need to hear talking about sending him away.

"Can he go with you to Aunt Rose's?" Bob was serious.

"No, Bob. I'll be sleeping on her back porch. She takes in boarders to make ends meet. That's no place for a baby."

Rita laced arms over her abdomen and rocked, taking three deep breaths, "When I went into labor with my babies, the nurses said, 'Breathe slowly,' but they didn't tell me how to breathe while giving those babies away." She moved toward the bathroom, for a full-sit-on-the-floor cry that she didn't want Shawn to hear. When she stole by, Bob reached out and touched her hand.

What more are you willing to give up? Eleanor had asked her. She was giving up Bob. Giving up mourning Kieran together, getting strength from being part of a couple, being held, and being called *hon*. Giving up all the positives that Bob had ever been and done. But he was no longer that man. And, for a short while, she would give her children up too.

Coming out fifteen minutes later, she hoped Shawn wouldn't see her tear-streaked face. Bob set out steaming cups of coffee.

"I'm going to ask my sister Mary Alice, and Mac. They'll leave for the beach house soon. Shawn would like that. Mac is on the road a lot, maybe Mary Alice would like our cute little boy."

Rita rang her sister to ask if she had room for one more, along with her four children.

"You're really doing this?" Mary Alice snapped.

Rita held her hand over the mouthpiece and asked Bob to go take Shawn to the potty.

"Yes." Rita spoke softly, facing the kitchen corner, like a small child herself.

"You can't talk with him there?"

"He went into the other room. He's a wreck, we both are."

"He should be a wreck. So, you're splitting up? Are you out of your mind? All of us put up with crap. Our husbands will be threatened by you, your decisions. We *don't* leave our husbands."

Rita had to get her support. "I'm tired, Mary Alice. So tired. I'm tired of waiting for the hurt to end." She begged, "Please help me."

Shawn could stay with them at the cottage.

"Thank you. I'll always be grateful."

Rita arched her back. The day was fraught with emotion. Bob and Rita's morning-long session littered the table with the rental lease, separation papers, help wanted ads, and lists. While Bob got his tools off the pegboard in the basement, she rolled curtains and a small, braided rug into a paper bag.

Bob asked Rita, "Can I have that picture of Shawn?"

"Yes, I'll get it."

In a photo album, tacked in with small black triangles, was a great picture of Shawn, newly two, wearing a camel hair coat, short pants, and knee socks, like a little prince. Beautiful. Rita slipped it into an envelope, and wrote, "Shawn Robert Leonard." Bob slid the envelope into his top pocket and patted it twice.

Noreen sauntered in from kindergarten at noon. Rita and Bob ate grilled cheese sandwiches with their youngest children. Then it was nap time.

Bob hugged Noreen and whispered, "Sweet dreams my Chocolate Girl."

Shawn pitched out of Rita's arms, hugged his Daddy's neck hard, and said, "See ya later, *algator*."

Rita gently said, "It's time, buddy, let Daddy go."

As they left the room, Bob unfolded his handkerchief, wiped his eyes, and blew his nose.

Moments later, Bob and Rita tidied the kitchen. He put a stack of cash on the counter by the stove, then turned toward her. She opened her arms for a hug, and he stepped into it. He smelled like her man. Her long hair brushed his neck. Rita vowed she'd never hold Bob like this again.

They stood together for a long, long time. Crying. Breathing. Letting go of their fifteen years together, years that started strong and pure, then slowly splintered into pain. By one o'clock, Bob was gone, and the house was in order, but Rita was not. She phoned Eleanor.

"Are you okay?"

"Nope. Not yet. Not anytime soon. But I will be."

31

DANCES

Teri waited after school for her second-grade teacher to take her yellowed dog art from the bulletin board. She was timid about asking, but wanted to show Mommy. It had been up for weeks. She skipped it home.

Kitty stood on the porch railing, taking in laundry. She gave Teri the hurry-up sign, then stepped onto the milk box and hopped down.

"Mootchi Gatchi Gu." Kitty loved to gossip in their secret language.

"What? Tell me."

"Mommy told Daddy to get an apartment, cuz he won't be living here."

Teri smiled, a little glad that Daddy was leaving, but pressed her lips shut, thinking it wasn't the right response. She kicked the milk box with her shoe. "Does Mommy mean it?"

Kitty put a folded towel in the basket. "Yup. Mommy canceled Kevin's Cub Scout meeting here today."

"Then it's bad." Teri put her dog picture on the top step.

"Mommy couldn't act all happy today, she said, because her world is falling apart, and we all *hafta* move out of this house for a while."

Something fluttered in Teri's chest. "Where is everybody? Carol?"

"She's inside. Carol yelled it was Mommy's fault that Daddy was sad, and she hated her. Mommy slapped Carol, sending her to her room. If you go in there, you'll get a chore, or hit, too. You should stay here and help me fold clothes."

Kitty was a good organizer, Teri thought, while she gathered clothespins. Carol yelled at Mommy. No one yelled at Mommy, well, except Daddy. "Where's Kevin?"

"Oh, yeah, that's the second part. Kevin is packing for Billy's house. He's bringing his bow and arrows. Mommy told me we're all going to friends' houses until the end of school. I'm going to Patty Zambrello's. You're going to, um," Kitty bit her upper lip, "I think the Leahys' house."

Teri made a face. "Whose? Whose house am I going to?" She made the clothespins bite each other. How could she go anywhere without Mommy, or speak Mootchi Gatchi Gu without Kitty?

Kitty shrugged. "They have a girl in my class. She's nice. That's all I know. But don't bother Mommy right now. Noreen broke a bottle of perfume all over the stairs. She got a spanking, too. Now Mommy's cleaning everything and yelling at everybody. Plus, it stinks in there."

"What about everyone else?" Teri raised her eyebrows. "Where's Mommy going to live?"

"Mommy is going to Aunt Rose's old-person house."

"Can anyone go with her?" Teri's insides sparked with the possibility.

"Uh-unh. There's no room, even Mommy's gotta sleep on the back porch."

Teri balled her art, carried it into the house, and threw it away. There was a lot of noise upstairs, but the kitchen was empty.

She sat in Mommy's seat and wondered how long she'd be lonely.

Rita was sweeping the kitchen, getting the house spick-and-span for the new renters.

She planned to explain things at supper. Scrambled eggs, bacon, toast, tea. No kid would balk at that. Rita's heart was pounding, thinking how she might fail them, as each child came to the table. Their father was never going to live with them again, ever.

The older kids accepted the move to friends' homes, for a few weeks, while she, Mommy, got a job and an apartment. Noreen and Shawn, who couldn't understand this split, were going to the more distant homes. Rita put as much of a positive spin on the placements as she could. The cat going with Noreen was good, as she needed the softness. There weren't enough buffers in this world for her youngest daughter.

"Shawn, my little man, you're going to a beach house with big kids who want to play with you. Won't that be fun?" Rita's breathing hitched. How would she know if he'd be happy?

Teri sat staring down at her plate, nibbling her toast, pushing the eggs around. "You, Teri, are going to stay with some nice friends of mine. They have a daughter one year older than you. The Leahys." Rita couldn't think of anything else to entice Teri. They were an older couple in a crowded house, with college-age sons. She would be shy without her siblings, who gave her strength and made her laugh. Teri blushed. Rita reached under the table to take her hand, swinging it gently. This fragile connection to her daughter, if broken, would make Teri disappear. Rita swallowed hard. This tenderness didn't last, couldn't last, because every child needed something from Rita at that moment.

Kitty asked a million questions, Carol glared, Kevin just ate more bacon.

That night, Rita orchestrated their packing on the upstairs hall floor. The children went through laundry baskets to collect underwear, socks, shorts, and shirts. Kevin snapped a pair of his briefs at Kitty. "Ooh, you're gonna hafta pick through strange boys' unders at your new home. Carol, you gonna hafta rinse poop out of diapers."

Carol shot back, "Oh, grow up."

Kevin stood with his pile, "Make me."

He hopped over the remaining basket, but Carol caught his leg, making him fall. While his neatly folded laundry fluttered around him, Carol, Kitty, and Teri attacked his prone position, and Kitty laughed, "Pig Pile." They peppered him with jabs, tickles, and kicks, until Kevin yelled, "Uncle."

Rita was matching socks. "Why don't you all stop? Can't you just enjoy your time together?"

"What are you talking about?" Kevin dusted himself off and gathered his clothes. "We just did." He twisted a shirt around his head like a pharaoh and patted her shoulder, "We just did, *Mummy*."

Rita giggled, and returned to ironing school clothes, stroking each item tenderly.

Each day, there was less essence of them at 23 Exeter Avenue. Their bedrooms echoed as Rita and her children deconstructed bed frames. The kids sprang between mattresses, proclaiming the floor was hot lava, and Kevin and Kitty struggled mightily to throw each other in.

Each child, in some way, let Rita know what he or she was feeling. Carol told Rita she couldn't wait to go. Kevin was a cowboy leaving town. Kitty rubbed Rita's arm and scratched her own. The next day, the teacher called to say Teri cried in class but couldn't say why. Noreen clung to small, fuzzy things. Shawn followed Rita around the house, the only one not radiating hurt, too young to know what was coming.

The work of leaving went on. Packing away crosses and a statue of the Virgin Mary was cathartic. None of those items had helped Rita, despite her years of prayers.

Rita clung to normalcy until the last evening in the house. The radio intercom was on as they started wrapping up the kitchen. The twins, supposedly bagging canned goods, fought about the words to "Runaround Sue" until Carol yelled at them.

"Who cares? Dion? He's square. What about Elvis? or The Shirelles? Or, I know, Ike and Tina Turner."

Kevin stopped sticking his finger in the peanut butter jar, "Who? I mean, I know about Elvis, but who is Ikeena Turner?"

Carol was smug in her musical knowledge, "They are Negroes. Much better than Caucasians. Better singers. Better dancers. Much cooler."

"Cooler than Elvis? How?" He was eating a pile of Ritz crackers.

Rita joined in, "How do you know they're Negroes?"

"I saw them on *American Bandstand* with Aunt Carolyn. We danced all over her rec room."

Rita sighed, visualizing that. "Well, let us know if they come on the radio."

"Everything's changing. The 1960s, yeah, music is getting cooler," Carol said.

Just then Chubby Checker's "The Twist" bopped out of the intercom speakers throughout the house. Kevin jumped up and mugged, "Cooler than this?"

He twisted like it was his invention. Carol sprung off the floor, blasted the volume, and twisted, her ponytail swishing her shoulders. Rita stopped wrapping glasses in newspaper, joining in. Teri whooped into the kitchen, and shimmied onto a chair, pulling Kitty next to her. Noreen and Shawn quit playing Legos to join the craziness. They showed some newly discovered moves. The impromptu dancing went on with "Chain Gang," "Wipe Out," and "He's So Fine."

This—this dance party—this was what Rita wanted them to remember.

When WDRC broadcast news, the spinning stopped. They had to finish packing.

Rita enticed them with a picnic on the kitchen floor. Broiled hot dogs, canned brown bread, steamed warm, and baked beans served on paper plates. Rita tried to keep the mood light, but she saw and felt her children quiet down. Rita reclined her back against the wall, legs out straight, so Noreen could crawl on to whisper in Rita's ear, "Will you come see me?"

Rita could only nod her head and give Noreen a butterfly kiss. This one, who asked so little, would have the hardest time being apart.

When Rita got a job, in three or four weeks, she'd scoop them together somehow.

And never let them go.

32

KISSES

Kevin loved Field Day.

He loved the gym teacher, Miss Mona Duquette, who made the end of the school year a big deal. She was competitive and encouraged the same in Kevin. While Carol, Kitty, Noreen, and Teri had fun in contests of broad jump, discus throwing, and sack races, Kevin went from one sweaty event to the next, not always winning, but always trying to win. He pushed himself so hard, he puked behind a garbage can, but recovered in minutes.

Mom being there to say goodbye to him was a distraction. Dad being there was just a joke. At the end, they waved him over. Kevin wasn't about to stand around and make his parents' separation a federal case. He looked for his escape route.

"You're all sweaty." Mom tried to get a hug. "Kevin, you alright? You need some water?"

Kevin kissed her cheek, punched Billy on the arm, and waved bye to Dad. He ran backward, yelled, "Nah, I'm a little better." Kevin was going to a fun place for three or four weeks. "Let's go."

Billy's mom Eleanor spoke only to Rita because she hated Bob. "Kevin will miss you, but I'll take good care of him. What you're doing today is tragic. Tragic. I'm so sorry." Eleanor followed the boys off the field.

Bob was dropping Carol off at Aunt Carolyn's. When they crossed the school grounds, Carol's back was straight, but then she twisted to give her mother a big wave. Rita's heart fluttered with gratitude at her daughter's gesture.

"Oh . . . my."

Kitty was going to the Zambrellos', Teri to the Leahys', and Noreen to the Klunes'. Rita hugged the adults. The receiving mothers and fathers watched planes flying overhead while the giving parent hugged her daughters too tight, and murmured vague plans as they left with other families.

Rita tried to be brave. Her Field Day prize was just one little boy.

She strapped Shawn into his plaid canvas car seat, where he could see out the window. She was bringing the most stuff for him, including sheets and a rubber mat in case he wet his bed, but that rarely happened anymore.

"See that bird? Mommy, do you like ice cream? Ice cream?" He tried to get Rita to look at him.

Reviewing her dismal day of dispensing her children, chirps pulsed from her heart. Louder grindings were coming from the engine. It was an old car, but it needed to last.

"I'll come visit you on Sundays, with everyone, and Wednesday nights. Will that be good?"

"Always, Mommy," he cheered.

Rita's heart now drummed, thinking, it won't be "Always, Mommy" for three or four weeks. So long for a two-year-old. And for a 29-year-old.

When Rita arrived, Mary Alice came out, followed by Deborah and Patricia. They made such a fuss over Shawn that she felt encouraged.

Rita took him into the small bedroom, to watch her make the bed, fill the dresser with clothes, and line toys along the far wall. Shawn giggled when his Mommy made his bear dance.

Later, Shawn sat on her lap on a lawn chair. Mac held a drink in his hand. Did he always have a cocktail close by? Mary Alice urged her to get on the road before dark. Rita mentioned that Shawn was toilet trained, but needed to be reminded to go to the bathroom, especially if he was playing.

Rita pulled Shawn to her, and she put on lipstick, so when she kissed his cheek, her love showed on his sweet face. "Be good. I love you."

When she made to walk away, Shawn grabbed her legs, crying.

"No. No. Mommy stay *wid* me. Stay *wid* me."

Rita picked him up, and her face crumpled as she brought Shawn to Mary Alice. "Please take him, before I change my mind."

She pictured him in footed pajamas, his smiling face, blonde hair, and translucent skin, on her dark ride to town. Her long day ended with lugging suitcases into Aunt Rose's city house. Rose's boarders were Timothy and Jack. With all rooms taken, Rita got the second-level sleeping porch.

She had ironed a brown pin-dot dress the day before, and once on the hanger, draped it with a cream-colored sweater. This, paired with the alligator high heels, all borrowed from Nancy, would be her job interview outfit. She'd wear Mother's pearl necklace, too.

Her room had a sagging cot, a pole lamp, a plant stand, and a straight-backed chair. Rita failed to fall asleep, watching the curtains sighing rhythmically across the windowsills. They seemed to whisper *empty* as they brushed in, and *alone* as they brushed out.

Rita scoured the "Help Wanted, Female" ads, circling anything that she could do, and some she had no skills to justify applying for. She had interviews, but lack of experience thwarted her. Rose did the dusting and "marketing." Rita offered to help, to cook, to clean. Rose let her work in the yard, or "Hoover" the rugs, but there was no real demand, no immediacy.

Rita telephoned one child every day, visited another each evening, and wrote them letters.

A week went by. She walked blocks of Park Street looking for work. At night, her empty arms ached.

On Sunday, Bob and Rita gathered their kids. They kissed and tickled Shawn as he crawled over them in the backseat on the way to Hammonasset Beach. At the end of the afternoon, the dropping off was reversed, children calling out, "See you next time."

Wednesday was Shawn's night. Rita drove to the beach, played with him, stayed for supper, gave him a bath, and tucked him in. He cried for her not to leave. Beyond the obvious pain of being away from her children, Rita had a niggling thought about Shawn, but she couldn't identify it. For his third birthday, she brought Noreen to take the two of them for ice cream.

When they got back to the beach house, Mary Alice ran out to get Shawn, but also encouraged Rita and Noreen to be on their way. Through the open kitchen windows, Rita could hear Mac ranting at someone. His words were slurred.

A second week went by, Rita still without a job or income.

She worked a few nights with Aunt Rose at the Town and County Club, where they served canapes to wealthy ladies, of whom Rita was jealous. Her empty arms still ached.

Rita mowed Rose's lawn with a push mower. She painted the pantry. At night, she sat on the edge of her bed and swayed in pain. No child needed holding or carrying or hugging. No one needed her to take out a splinter or fix a scooter. No one applauded her cooking, sewing, or singing.

With Bob's child support money, she made sure the children got what they needed, then chipped down debts with the utility companies, dentists, doctors, and a plumber, one dollar at a time.

One night Rita got a call. Her sister Carolyn, upset after visiting Mary Alice, found out that Shawn cried, kicked, screamed, and threw his toys on Sundays.

"On Sundays? One day a week? Why?" Rita asked, amazed that sweet Shawn would act that way.

"It's after you all leave. You drop off Shawn first, and he thinks he is the only child you leave behind. Every week." Carolyn paused, "I'm sorry to have to tell you this."

Rita put the phone down to cover her face with her hands, crying, "Oh my God. Oh my God." How insensitive could she have been? How heartless? That poor baby. She had to fix this. This she could do, just not fast enough. Rita *had* to get him first, on the first available day, which was a Saturday in June.

Rita encouraged Bob to drive to Shawn as fast as possible. He would be first this time. Rita had to show him they all were separated.

"Where is all the kids?" Shawn asked from his car seat.

Bob answered, "Oh, they're coming. It's your turn to be picked up first today, tiger."

"But . . . where is every kid? All the kids?" Shawn was perplexed, looking at the empty seats. It was an expression no child his age should own.

Rita turned from the front seat to smile at him, "Who should we get second, Shawn? They live in different houses, but *all* the kids want to see you," Rita offered. "How about Noreen?"

"She doesn't *lib* with you?" he asked. "With you?"

"No, not right now. We are going to live together again, but not right now. Let's get Noreen, shall we?" Rita did not say "we all." Bob would not be moving in with them, wherever she and the children landed.

"Noreen. I like Noreen." He laughed and kicked his foot, which Rita was happy to catch, and rub.

They made the rounds, Shawn watching his siblings running out of houses, other adults waving in doorways, a brother and four sisters sliding across the Fairlane's ripped seats and greeting each other, squishing shoulders. He clapped his hands with each addition, as Rita said their names, which Shawn repeated. Rita was giddy, drumming her fingernails on the seat back, watching him at every pickup. Her plan was working. He was seeing that the family came together after being apart all week.

At the end of the day at a petting zoo, Rita and Bob returned the children to their other homes. Shawn watched each of them kiss and hug their parents goodbye. He was the last one in the car with his mommy and daddy.

After a long while, Shawn bent forward, "But where is all the kids?"

Rita knelt on the front seat. Had her plan made Shawn even more confused? "We live apart, honey, for now. But I'll come and get you real soon. For good."

She wiped a tear with her hand, then extended it to grasp his.

"Mommy. Mommy. I like *all* them kids." He drifted off to sleep for the rest of the one-hour drive, which gave Rita a chance to silently cry in the dark, continuing to hold his foot.

Shawn's outbursts lessened after the reversed visits, according to Mary Alice.

33

SCHOOL

Those last weeks at Charter Oak School, Teri looked for Carol, Kevin, Kitty, and Noreen every day. They snuck across the cafeteria during lunch. Teri or Kitty held Noreen's hand at recess. Each morning, they huddled at the school gates to make fun of their new lives, to amuse each other. Teri's roommate had a glow-in-the-dark Jesus statue. Kevin's house had a pipe-smoking father, so he mimicked the sounds of *mup, mup, mup*. Kitty's family's mother didn't sing while doing housework. The Leonards compared bedtimes and bath times, games, TV shows, chores. Everyone complained about new foods.

Kevin snorted, "How about borscht? With sour cream. Disgusting."

Carol laughed, shoved him, and called him a liar. "You do not get borscht."

"I heard it on *Rocky and Bullwinkle* cartoons."

Everyone missed Mommy.

Only Carol and Noreen missed Daddy too. They wanted to go home to Exeter Avenue.

Teri did not draw one picture while at the Leahys'. She didn't feel like it.

On the last day of school, Kevin raced Billy home, Kitty skipped away with Patty, Carol and Noreen got rides in cars, and Teri wandered the halls, not seeing Trisha Leahy leave the building.

Teri walked by Miss Rosetta's kindergarten, and the nurse's office, where she'd barfed on the nurse's shoe in first grade. She felt lonely, knowing she had no real home to go to. For three years, she had been surrounded by siblings and teachers who knew her. Now they were all gone.

By the big window at the end of the hall, silhouetted by afternoon light, stood Principal Foley, with arms open and a red lipstick smile visible as Teri got closer. That giant pillow of a woman smelled of talcum powder and roses, and gently swayed Teri, back and forth, cooing, "Have a good summer. We'll miss you. You come back to us someday, yes?" Miss Foley pulled a tissue from her pocket for Teri. "Better?"

Yes, she was better, being held. It wasn't Mommy, but Teri got hope or strength, she didn't know which, and she was fine. Miss Foley held her hand as they walked to the door. Teri could get to the Leahys now, all by herself. Mommy said this was only until the end of June.

They would be back together in a few days. Teri could manage until then.

34

RE-PLACEMENT

R ita had begged her friends to keep her children until the end of the school
year, but not indefinitely. She couldn't take advantage of their kindness,
so began asking her out-of-town friends to help out. Carol and Kitty moved
to their summer placement with the Davins in South Windsor. Rob and Ceil
Davin were good family friends, although Rob had stopped drinking two years
earlier and had steered clear of Bob since then. Kitty started bickering with
Carol in the truck.

"I wanted to go with Teri. She's my better friend. And you're not even my
twin like Kevin."

"You're no prize. I'd rather be with Kevin, too. We could ride double on my
bike. Or he'd pedal really fast, and I'd be whipped along on my roller skates."

Kitty quietly offered, "I could do that."

Carol swung her foot. "Not on your best day. You're too chicken."

As Bob drove on the highway, Rita asked Kitty why she was tearing up. "I
thought you missed each other these last few weeks."

Kitty scratched her elbow. "Well, first, how did I get stuck with Carol, the
bossy one? And not play with my twin, Kevin? It's better when we're all
together. And who will take care of you, Mommy? I'll still be missing you."

"I'll come every week, to see you both. I'll write letters and call you on the
telephone."

"But I won't have a Mommy," Kitty added, "every night."

Rita looked out the window, afraid to see Kitty's little face. She was dramatic, and a worrier, but they were going to a nice home. Kevin, Rita wasn't so sure of.

"Carol," Rita swiveled back to them, "you told me you got along at school. Please, do this for me. I don't want to worry about you big girls."

Kitty called Rita in the morning to report their lucky break, "Our bedroom is really the playroom, and we can talk all night, well, not all night, because Aunt Ceil won't give us ice cream money if we don't sleep."

Rita held the phone tight to her ear, as this was as precious as a long-distance call. "Kitty, are you getting along with Carol?"

"Carol's my almost-best sister now." The spark of light from that call, her older daughters happy, gave Rita a glimmer of hope that she was doing the right thing.

Someday, this will be a distant memory when we're under the same roof.

She hoped Teri and Noreen would fare as well in East Hartford.

Teri sat on the steps of the Leahy house waiting for Mommy to come. Mrs. Leahy had ironed the pink dress with a lace collar Mommy suggested. Her shoes were neat, with white socks peeking out. She felt a little sick, wanting to talk to just Mommy, not Noreen or Daddy.

In a few minutes, Daddy's truck pulled up. Mrs. Leahy and Trisha waved goodbye as Teri climbed in. Noreen, an elfin five-year-old, sat on a crate, her feet not touching the floor, wearing an identical outfit. Teri was out of place in a pink dress in the dark cavern, sitting on jumbled boxes. After a loud and bumpy ride, Daddy held his door open, and motioned the girls into a brand-new neighborhood. Noreen took his hand, skipping up the driveway. Teri grasped her mother's hand, uneasiness rising.

"It will be good. Being here will be nice for you, Teri." Mommy led her toward the house.

Teri stopped walking. "You said we would go home when school got out. I behaved. I listened at Leahys'. Why am I being sent away again?"

Mommy tilted her head. "Oh, no, honey. This has nothing to do with it. I know you were perfect. But . . . but I don't have a . . . a home for you yet."

The door swung open. Daddy greeted his brother and sister-in-law.

Two boy cousins stared at the quiet, pink girls. Jimmy held out a stuffed monkey that wore sneakers, enticing Noreen to run off to play. Teri was intrigued, but needed to be with Mommy.

She stood still to stop being left this time. "I can stay with you at Aunt Rose's. I'll be very quiet. I'll just draw, quietly." She stared at her shoes.

Mommy knelt to hold her hands. "Oh, Teri. I can't take you to Rose's. There's no room for a smart artist like you. There are no kids there. Come on, let's just say 'hi.'"

Teri sat on the couch between her parents, leaning on Mommy. Her heart was thumping too fast. This was a new house, nice, but small. She snuck looks at the neat room, with its flowered rug and books on the built-in shelves. The big uncle, the skinny aunt. Teri knew they were nice, from holidays and family visits, but she didn't want to learn new rules and try new foods. The thing that kept her whole was Mommy.

They drank iced tea and Aunt Pat asked if she wanted to play. She shook her head, a fake smile on her lips. Teri knew she was being left again, shrinking, melting into a very small person. She shivered despite the warmth of the day, which seeped in through the picture window.

"Well, let's get that furniture," Daddy said. He and Uncle Joe carried two bed frames, dressers, and mattresses up the stairs.

Mommy offered, "Come out with me, Teri, while I get your clothes."

Teri looked for birds in the sky. There weren't any because there were no trees. Mommy took a pillowcase of sheets out of the truck, and was reaching for a suitcase, when Teri pulled her arm back.

"Don't leave me here," Teri squeaked out. "Don't leave me here without . . . you."

Her mother pulled her close. "You've got Noreen. I'm leaving Noreen with you."

Teri twisted her dress sash. "No."

"I need you to watch her. She's little." Mommy's voice waffled, "I need you to be the big sister."

"No. I can't do that. Carol or Kitty is the big sister. Besides, Noreen sleeps a lot."

Mommy smiled as she stood but left her hand on Teri's small shoulder. Keeping her sad face down, she wondered, what if Mommy never got a job? What if the pain inside got bigger? And she got smaller?

"Aunt Pat needs your help. She's never had girls before. Can you help her out?"

Teri said the smallest "yes" of her life. They went back inside.

Pat looked from daughter to mother. "C'mon, Teri, let me show you the room." It was as if someone made the stairs pretty, and then forgot to finish the room at the top. There wasn't a closet, or doors or walls. It was stifling hot, a bare attic with wooden planks for a floor. Teri's heart sank a little more.

"We need to make these beds. I put some curtains up, and here's a lamp and a fan. I was happy to buy you pink things. Isn't that silly?"

Teri smiled to be polite.

Downstairs, Mommy picked up her purse, and everyone walked outside. Noreen was on Daddy's shoulders. He kissed her face, swinging her down.

He held his hand out to Joe. "Take care of my Chocolate Girl."

Joe gave a quizzical look. "Chocolate?"

"Only Kevin and Noreen got my brown eyes. And take care of that one, too. Teri's pretty special."

After quick kisses goodbye, Mommy and Daddy got into the truck.

"Shall we watch them drive away?" Aunt Pat offered.

Them? She wasn't special to Daddy, being green-eyed, and that was fine with Teri. But with her mother moving on, she could only nod through her tears. They walked from the driveway to the front steps. Teri got as close to her aunt as possible, then Aunt Pat pulled her closer. "I've known you since you were a baby. I'll take good care of you. Mommy will telephone you, and your whole family will have outings on Sundays."

Maybe she could trust that promise, that they'd be together on Sundays.

Cousins Mike and Jimmy played baseball at a local park, where Aunt Pat pushed the girls on swings. She took her nieces to Kresge's to buy 88-cent polka-dot playsuits.

Mommy called at night. Teri whispered that Noreen spilled her milk at supper, and she'd gotten scolded. Teri didn't want to tattle on Aunt Pat, but Noreen cried.

"Ask Aunt Pat to put Noreen's glass on the left side of her dish. You remember how we did it at home?"

When Noreen's spill rate went down, Teri didn't have to worry about her as much. In bed a few days later, Teri noticed the pine sap oozing out of the rafters, and wondered where her family was at that moment.

Noreen climbed into Teri's bed, and despite the cloying heat, promptly fell asleep.

Teri was a good big sister. She'd tell Mommy when she called again.

On the way to Somers, Dad drove fast to make Kevin laugh, hitting all the swoops on Mountain Road, getting his truck airborne.

Mom's old friend had a son, so he was being dumped with them.

When Kevin met the family and scanned the countryside, he almost ran after Dad's retreating truck. Even being with Dad was better than this.

Kevin and Danny sat in lawn chairs overlooking the quiet road below. Because Danny had a broken leg, he couldn't run, climb trees, ride a bike, or swim. Kevin was assigned Danny's chores, like mowing the giant lawn and checking the rural mailbox. They had a barn, with no animals. A fake farm. Kevin could have thrown dirt bombs at passing trucks, but not one rolled by. He asked Danny what he did for fun.

"We go fishing. Ride bikes. Play tag. But the neighbors are on vacation."

No kids around? At home, Kevin challenged his buddies and sisters to do daring feats. He'd hoist them onto garage roofs and climb up drainpipes. Built dams in brooks at Beachland Park, made leaf boats, and then torpedoed them with acorns. He'd dare Billy and Dave to crawl through sewer pipes to pop out at the dump.

"Let's roll down this hill," Kevin suggested to Danny.

"I have a broken leg. Remember?" The kid pointed to his cast.

"Do it like this." Kevin lay down on the rough grass, crossed his arms at his chest, twisted his legs together, and flung himself down the hill.

Danny was getting down to try when his mother yelled from the porch, "Danny. You can't do that. Go practice piano. Kevin, go sweep the barn."

At the bottom of the hill, Kevin ignored Mrs. Mavis.

This place stunk. Not like his fun June with Billy, in their neighborhood. Here, there was no pool, no park, no place to ride a bike. He followed a dirt path toward rushing water. The trail was barely visible, with leaf litter, broken branches, steep drops that he slid down, and hills etched with tree roots. His favorite type of path: secret.

He missed Mom. She let him eat two or three sandwiches on a Saturday. She was funny because she tried to hit him when he was bad but laughed when he dodged away. He liked Carol because she was a fast skater and swimmer, and always fought back. Kitty and Teri were adventurous enough to cross the brook in winter. Kevin persuaded Noreen to change the TV channel. Shawn was still a baby. Kevin might give him another year or two before he took him on secret agent missions. Kevin cried that day, tears streaming, his eyes crinkled, his head in hands, sitting on a riverside rock. And then he stopped. He brushed dirt from his dungarees and took off running, inhaling the balm of the woods.

Mom visited the first Friday of his stay. The Mavis family sat on the porch fanning themselves with newspapers. Kevin watched from a tree, as he'd rather sit with the squirrels than the squares. When Mom got out of the car, he shadowed her. She waved a paper bag to Mrs. Mavis, climbing the steps. Mom never arrived anywhere empty-handed. "I hope you don't mind, but I brought meatball grinders for everyone. And chips, and lemonade."

Mrs. Mavis looked surprised, "Oh, you didn't have to, but, thanks, I don't like to cook in this heat."

While the mothers were jawing it up, Kevin snuck onto the porch steps and slid his hands over Mom's eyes. "Guess who?"

Mom giggled, caught one of his hands, "Kevin?"

He accepted a quick hug, "Yup. Let's take a hike." Kevin jabbed a thumb toward the sideyard, hopping from one bare foot to the other.

"Listen, Pauline, would you mind if Kevin and I took ours on a little picnic? I'd like to see what he does in this beautiful country."

Pauline's face reddened, "Sure, good luck. That boy shows up for meals, but other than that, he's outside. We hardly see him."

Oh, now the old bag was gonna rat Kevin out.

"Come on, Mom. I want to show you something." He grabbed her hand to thread down the skinny path into the woods. Kevin took the food from her, hopping to flat rocks to place their meal on a huge boulder in the middle of the river. "It's beautiful here, at the water," he yelled. He came back for her, widening his eyes and making an O of his mouth. It was his dare stare. "Give me your hand."

"I can't cross this river, Kevin." She hesitated, smiling. "I might fall in."

He leapt to the first stone. "Take your shoes off. Trust me. And so what if you get wet? You remember fun, *dontcha*?"

Mom dared to jump, laughing as she made it, cold water splashing. He held out his hand to her each time. They ate supper sitting on the boulder.

"Are you okay here Kevin?" She asked when they got settled.

"Okay? Yeah, sort of. But Danny is bor-ring. His parents want me here to do his work. Like, what's his name? Oliver, in that orphan movie."

"Oliver Twist? I don't think that's true. Aren't they nice to you?" Rita squinted at Kevin.

"Nice enough, Mom. But really, I've got no sisters or brother, no mother, no father, and no friends. Can I go back to West Hartford? Somewhere a kid can have fun and laugh, crack jokes that people get?"

"I've got nowhere to keep you, Kevin. I would if I could. But I'll tell you a secret. I had a really nice job interview today. Keep your fingers crossed, because if I get it, I can start saving for an apartment. Can you last a few weeks? I'll call you, and oh, I have letters from Carol and Kitty. Will that make it a little better?"

Kevin swirled a stick in the river, "Yeah, a little better, but can I live out here? In the woods, like in a tent?"

"You need to be inside at night." Mom indicated his body's bruises, scratches, bites, and stings.

"Mom. This is nothing. I've been dive-bombed, chased, cornered, sprayed, and sunburned."

Mom balked. "Did you show Mrs. Mavis? All your rashes and injuries? Doesn't she take care of you?"

"She would if I showed her." He was too proud for that. "But that Danny never did *nothing* outside, so she doesn't know what it's like to have a real kid. She doesn't know what I do all day, out here by myself."

"I want you taken care of, Kevin. To get help when you need it. And when did you start calling me Mom?"

"I'm ten. I'm too old to go running to someone else's mommy for help. In our house, only a gushing wound would get you a Band-Aid," he snorted a laugh, "you didn't baby us. So, we are tougher than other kids. Don't say nothing to her either, I'm better off on my own."

They hiked the path toward the house. Mom turned to Kevin, squeezed his shoulder, and asked what he wanted. He looked off to the horizon, purple dusk pushing against an orange sunset.

"Want? I want Carol to swim across that river with me. Kitty or Teri to ride my Tarzan swing. I want adventures, Mom. But I don't always wanna do them alone." He flung a rock into the darkness, "I want to be home with all the kids and you, Mom, somewhere, anywhere. Go get that job."

Mom rubbed his sweaty crew cut. "I know. Out on the river, you know what you said to me? 'Trust me.' Well, you *trust me* now, and keep your fingers crossed about that job."

35

RESCUED

"Rita, telephone for you." Rose stood at the bottom of the stairs, holding the receiver to her ample bosom.

Rita, in from visiting Kevin in Somers, was hanging up her good clothes, so skipped down in a bathrobe. The front window was open; the porch sitters were eager to eavesdrop.

"Yes, this is she." She was cautiously polite. "Oh, yes. No, no problem at all."

"This is Mrs. Hatch, from The Children's Village. You interviewed with us today." Rita's hands shook. She pulled out the chair to sit, but instead stood behind it for support.

"We know you worked in a hospital, but this is more like a community."

Rita spoke up, "Oh, I thought it was lovely. I was impressed by your grounds and your programs."

While Mrs. Hatch went over the details, Rita's mind raced. Is she or is she not offering the job? If yes, her life was about to change. If no—this jackhammer of a heart was about to break.

"Your eagerness to be helpful starts the minute you greet clients at the front desk. The salary is modest to start, but we offer health benefits to your family and paid holidays. I know it's tight notice, but would you be able to start training on Monday?"

Rita sat down, and clutched her bathrobe tight, answering in a dazed murmur. "Yes, I'll see you on Monday. Thank you." She walked onto the porch.

Rose stood up, playing, "What is it? A bill collector? Did Bobby go to jail?"

Rita broke into a real-Rita smile, as she pulled her aunt into a spirited jig. "I got the job. I got the job!"

"That's my girl. You done it, Rita. Glory be."

Breathless, Rita pronounced the benefits, "I'll get paid and have insurance for my kids and paid *sick* days, Rose. Paid *holidays*." Rita stopped twirling, gasping. "I need more clothes. I can't start a full work week with one dress."

"Ah, don't you know, I've got a closet full of things from Mrs. Peck's daughter." Rose's other job was cleaning houses, and wealthy clients gave her their unwanted items. "Have a peek in there. High quality stuff, from the Lucy Baltzell Shop, or Lord & Taylor. Hand-me-*ups*, you might say." Rose bent over, laughing at her own joke.

While they were selecting dresses, Rita told Rose about the position as the switchboard operator at The Children's Village in Hartford. It had beautiful grounds, with old oak trees along a curving driveway. The children's cottages were in a wooded area. Originally built in 1925 as an orphanage, it now served emotionally disturbed children. The pay was $1.35 an hour, ten cents more than minimum wage, and the hours were solid, Monday through Friday. It was nearby, and classy. Rita was thrilled.

A bit later Rita was in Rose's room, holding a rust-colored dress with a matching belt. These were beautiful clothes that Rita could not afford. She was deciding what to hem when the phone rang again.

"Rita." Rose again held the phone against her body, "It's for you. Grand Central it is around here."

It was her sister Carolyn, just returning from the beach, where Shawn was staying. It was evening. "Rita, I don't want you to panic . . . but . . . you need to get Shawn out of there."

"Why? What happened?" Rita went on high alert, ready to crawl through the telephone wire. "Was Shawn hurt? Was he by the shore?" Her mind raced through sunburn, shark bites, and drowning.

"It's Mac. He's as bad as Bob. He was drinking a lot and said really terrible things to Shawn, about Bob. And . . . about you."

"Like what?" That bad feeling was growing in her stomach. This was not fear, it was anger.

Carolyn hesitated. "We went for an overnight visit at the cottage. Mike and Mac were drinking beer all day, and switched to whiskey while grilling supper, Mac complained about feeding someone's bastard and why the hell didn't Bob take care of his own kids?"

"You heard that?" Rita asked, standing straighter.

"Yes. I don't think Shawn did. He was sitting at the kids' picnic table. Then Mac said you were a bitch and who did you think you were, leaving your man, giving all our wives ideas."

"What did you say? To Mac?"

"Nothing, Mike told him to shut up, and he did for a minute. Then when Shawn got his hotdog, a bee was on it and he tried to get away, and Mac swiped his plate and tossed all Shawn's food across the yard and called him a little shit."

Rita's heart was pounding in her ears, and a headache came roaring in. "Who . . . who helped Shawn?"

"I did. I said, 'No, no, you don't talk to Rita's son like that. He's been through enough.' Then, Shawn was standing on the grass, crying, and wet his pants. He was so scared."

"How could anyone treat a child like that, Carolyn? He's three years old, for God's sake. Please tell me you picked him up. Please . . . " Rita and Carolyn were both crying.

"Of course I did. I scooped Shawn up, while Mary Alice stood frozen, in shock or fear, I couldn't tell. I told her I was taking Shawn back to town. But she said, no, she would keep him safe from Mac tonight. Rita, I don't know what's going on there—"

"I'm going to get him. Right now," Rita declared. "You call Mary Alice to pack Shawn's things."

"I will, then I'm coming with you. Pick me up; after that, you can leave Shawn with me."

"Carolyn, you have two babies. That's a handful. And you took in Carol. No, I'll think of something."

She called her friend Ceil and asked if Shawn could stay with them for one night. Ceil didn't hesitate. "Bring him here. You stay tonight too. God, Rita what, you've been through—"

Rita cut her off, "Ceil, I've got to be strong for about three more hours."

Rita swung her old clunker into Carolyn's driveway ten minutes later. The sisters drove to the beach in record time. Mary Alice was rocking a sleeping Shawn on the porch. Rita tossed the car door so wide it chipped the mailbox. She dashed inside, grabbed him from Mary Alice, kissed Shawn's neck until he stirred.

He smiled and clung to her, "Mommy. Shit. Hi, Mommy."

"*What*?" She whispered, "What baby?" She glared at her sister in the low light. Why was he saying this? No one she knew spoke like this. Under his pajamas, she could feel a diaper. Was he a totally different boy?

"Where is all the kids?" He asked.

"I'm here for *you* this time, Shawn." Rita turned to Carolyn, "Can you please strap him in, while I talk to Mary Alice?"

Rita demanded, "Where is he? Where's Mac? I'd like to tear his head off."

"I thought it best he wasn't here, knowing how upset you'd be. He took our kids for a late ice cream. My girls will be sad with Shawn gone. Rita, look, I'm . . . I didn't know that it would go like this . . . I can't even keep my own kids safe." Mary Alice didn't apologize. She was in the same crappy space as Rita. She stood, offering a paper bag, "It's sandwiches, a thermos of coffee, Styrofoam cups, and Twinkies for Shawn."

Rita gathered his things. "Never think I don't appreciate all that you did do. Thank you. Thank you for trying. I'll talk to you soon. But you tell Mac to go to hell. I'll pray for that."

Rita whisked into the car. Shawn fell back asleep.

Carolyn peeled the waxed paper from a ham and Swiss on rye, kept half, and handed the rest to Rita, who took a greedy bite. Knowing Shawn was out of harm's way, she got drowsy on the ride back to town, so Carolyn poured her a coffee. Rita took Carolyn home, thanked her, and said, "Don't worry."

Carolyn put a hand on Rita's arm. She knew the deal: don't be too nice.

"Oh. On the plus side, I got a job. I start Monday."

Rita put the car in reverse, yet could still hear Carolyn yell out, "Of course you did!"

36

VISITOR

R ob and Ceil greeted Rita and Shawn at their door. Ceil whispered, "Come in. All five kids are sleeping. But your girls gave us grief when we told them to sleep in our room."

Rita's chin dipped. "You didn't have to do that, move them, for us."

"Oh, yes, we did. Those girls will go crazy with Shawn. They'll wake our boys, then none of us will sleep tonight."

"Let's sneak up quietly," Rob whispered.

Rita, piggybacking Shawn, tiptoed to the second level. Shawn tightened his arms around Rita's neck.

The bedroom was dark, except for the angle of light that yawned across the bed when Rob opened the door. Rita made out Carol's sleeping form. The lump next to her was Kitty.

"Shawn," Rita whispered, "some kids are here for you. Can you find them?" She lowered him to the bed.

The adults stood silent in the dark. Rita swallowed hard, reached out a hand to draw him back, then stopped because she trusted her daughters' feelings for their little brother too.

Carol woke first. A small ball of warmth, energy, and sweetness was crawling this way and that, climbing on the jumble of blankets on the big bed.

Carol pulled him to her. "Oh, my goodness. Shawn? My little Shawn? Oh, you're here, you're here." Carol kissed and squeezed him.

Shawn's voice happily rose. "I am here. You are here. Is all the kids here?"

Carol, wiping tears on the hem of her nightgown, considered his question. "Oh, no, not everyone . . . but Kitty is. Look."

She shook Kitty's curled back. Kitty tousled on the bed, murmured dreaming about Shawn, then walked on her knees to Carol's pillow, "Is this a dream?"

"No. Wake up, you dodo bird. It's really Shawn."

Kitty surrounded Shawn with her arms, kissed his head, over and over, then pulled him onto her lap, "Shawn, Shawn, the leprechaun. We missed you." When Kitty hitched a gulp of air, the exhale and tears mingled in a tight little squeak. "Our baby."

All the adults were now crying, too.

Rita whispered to her friends, "You don't know how much this means to me. I *failed* to protect him. He's been through so much, and . . . and this welcome is what he needs to know how loved he is."

In the semi-darkness, the sisters petted their brother, stroked his cheeks, traced his legs, and squished him to their chests. He giggled, talked, and looked from one to the other. Then he crawled crazily all over the bed. Shawn came back to their adulations, their praise, their embraces, and said, "Here is good kids."

Ceil nudged Rita. "Go to them."

She sat on the bed to hug her three children, smoothing her girls' hair, patting Shawn's back as Carol held him tight. He yawned. It was the cutest yawn Rita ever saw. "Shawn and I are staying tonight, so we'll see you ladies at breakfast. Won't that be nice to wake up with Shawn and Mommy in the same house?"

Kitty cut her off, "Let him sleep with us. We'll put him between us, and he won't fall out of bed."

Carol backed her up. "Yeah, and we'll take him to the bathroom in the middle of the night. Wait. Is it already the middle of the night?"

Rita said it was, it was midnight. Ceil and Rob stepped out. Rita was torn leaving her baby with her daughters. She wanted him all to herself. But Carol and Kitty missed him, too.

She smiled mischievously. "Show me what you three will look like when you're sleeping."

Kitty shut her eyes but sprung them open when Rita softly laughed. Shawn was trying to pull Carol's eyelids up, who laughed too, and coaxed him, "Shawn, play you're napping, or Mommy won't let you sleep with us. Shh."

Rita stood by the bed, and spoke to Mr. Nobody, "Oh look, my children are dreaming. I will leave now, but hope they visit me on the couch first thing in the morning."

The girls suppressed giggles, so Shawn faked some, too. Rita kissed each actress and actor. She pressed her palm to her eye as she pulled their door shut.

Taking her shoes off, she headed downstairs. There, Rita paced on the carpet, anger emanating from her tense body. Moving, moving, moving, like a shark.

She whined to Ceil and Rob about "that demon, Mac" and the things he said to Shawn. "My Shawn. Did you see that little boy we watched five minutes ago, laughing, crawling, happy? Who says mean things to a child, yells at him when he's scared? How could I have left him with them?" She was shredding a Kleenex. "If I'd needed an abusive alcoholic in our lives, I would have kept my husband."

Rob teared up and cupped his twisted mouth. "We know . . . what that's like. I was so bad to my family when I was drinking. The harm I caused . . . "

Ceil patted his arm. "Not now, Rob. Let Rita rest. We'll talk in the morning."

In the morning, Carol stood holding Shawn. "Go wake Mommy."

Rita was awake, but now she played napping, with her eyes squinched shut, breathing a little too loudly. She kept her hands clasped above the sheet.

Kitty placed Shawn near Rita's feet, and he scootched to her face. He held it in two hands, squishing her lips like a fish. "Wake up, Mommy."

Her eyes flew open, and she swallowed him up and patted the space for the girls to join them.

At a noisy family breakfast, with the three Davin boys and three Leonard kids, Ceil convinced Rita to let Shawn stay with them. "Rob feels it's our duty, as old friends. Just until you get on your feet."

Rita spilled her coffee. "My feet? I'm landing on my feet soon. I forgot to tell you last night. I got a *job*."

Ceil and Rob handed out congratulations along with plates of bacon and pancakes.

"First, I'll have to save money for an apartment and find one that fits us all. It might take a few paychecks." Rita was smiling at her children, explaining her goal, proving she could do this, "Just you wait and see. We're getting our own apartment. Soon."

Rita drove home that Saturday, her mind wandering to all the negative people who thwarted her plans. Nope. No. She had to be more positive now. Rita felt a smile move into her eyes, which she checked in the rearview mirror. The smile moved onto the rest of her face, as she thought of all the angels helping her. The miracle of the Davins. Her sisters and generous friends. Mrs. Hatch because she gave Rita a job.

Things were looking up. Things were definitely getting better.

37

PORCH

R ita hadn't slept alone for twelve years but was now without Bob for two and a half months. She traded in the whispery breathings of her sleeping children for those of Aunt Rose's two whiskered boarders, who hacked and snored in nearby rooms. Rose fell asleep during baseball games, with the television buzzing long after the last inning.

Aunt Rose's cot was the size of a pool float. Rita was lying on a wafer-thin mattress, supported by flat metal struts held by coils that sproinged when she turned over. One strut snapped, leaving her butt sinking lower than the rest of her body. This July night, she was going to ignore this discomfort and block out the sounds of the house and the city.

Tonight, she was happy. She had a job, her children were safe, and Shawn was with his adoring sisters. Rita set her alarm for six a.m., and started to doze, but her eyes sprang open. All of her energy had been usurped with gathering courage to split from Bob, placing her children in good homes, and trying to keep ownership of the house, their safety net, even if she—they—couldn't live there anytime soon.

Rita thought about Bob.

When Bob was out, she had listened for the gravel spewing from tires, him traipsing up the stairs, stomping around the bathroom, and banging into their bedroom.

As the children had gotten older, and there were more of them, Bob yelled at them to shut up, or get to bed, and smacked anyone who left a bike outside. He'd find a ruler to crack on the back of someone's leg for leaving a dish on the table. Rita was constantly pulling his arm, or pushing a child away, whispering, "Go." It occurred again and again.

It was good that he was gone. Rita's thoughts continued to stray.

Married at 18, she curved into Bob each night with the longest lengths of their bodies touching, arms and legs entwined. She was his shy girlfriend, then his ardent lover. Rita learned things that no Catholic schoolgirl ever spoke about. Creative times and places to have sex, like on a docked boat down by the shore. They joked at what prudes their friends were. Bob and Rita didn't care when she got pregnant once they were secretly engaged. They couldn't wait to get married because they were in love, love, love. She missed the comfort, strength, and warmth of Bob's shoulders, arms, and back. She missed his earlier kindness and humor. Their antique brass bed had been their altar of love. Now, it was in boxes in Rose's garage.

Rita eventually slept well, until the alarm did its job. She dressed in a 'hand-me-up' pleated navy dress with embroidered daisies along the hem, screwed on tiny yellow earrings, and skipped downstairs to twirl in front of Aunt Rose, who wolf-whistled. The women giggled.

Rita was at The Children's Village early.

The janitor, Art Keyser, opened the door to the reception area, her office. He offered to get Rita coffee. Oh, coffee, yes. She was sick of tea. It was a simple act, but the kindness caught her off-guard. She demurred. It was too presumptuous to be drinking coffee before her boss came in.

Rita looked out over a covered porch, peppered with matching blue wooden chairs and benches, and a few potted plants. Inside, this beautiful room had a desk, a PBX console, file cabinets, a fireplace, and a Seth Thomas clock, its pendulum swaying gently. She uncovered the typewriter and began rummaging in a drawer for a steno pad when she was startled by a short, blustery, and delightful middle-aged woman.

"Oh, how rude," she drawled. "I'm sorry to be late for your first day. I'm training you and here I am frazzled, and you lookin' all pert and *purty*. Oh, my stars, we met before when you dropped off your application. I remember you. Your smile. There it is. I'm Ruth Watkins."

Ruth spoke with a southern accent, in no particular hurry, but she talked a lot. Her eyes twinkled blue, with traces of dimples in smooth skin. She was stocky without being fat, her face soft. "Let me put my things down. Then we'll get you a cuppa coffee. You can't start your day without that, nor would one want to. When we get back from that huge undertaking," here Ruth cracked a grin, "we'll light up this switchboard."

The rich smell of coffee wafted down the hall, and Rita's shoulders relaxed. She grinned. It wasn't just the aroma. It was meeting Ruth and Art and looking out to a front porch with potted plants. It was an antique clock over a beautiful fireplace. Rita felt welcomed, appreciated, and hadn't yet done any work.

Coworkers breezed in throughout the day to introduce themselves. She was greeted by her boss, Elizabeth Hatch, an elegant lady. Clients of social workers, psychologists, or caseworkers did not breeze in, but approached the front office with hope, and patience, and a child or two. Rita, missing her own children, welcomed these boys and girls. She found them little items to play with: the stamp dispenser, or the typewriter eraser, a round rubber wheel with black whiskers. It was a cat if you looked hard enough.

The switchboard buzzed all day. When she answered a phone line, if Rita didn't know an answer, Ruth scribbled it on the steno pad. Once or twice, Rita covered the mouthpiece as Ruth stuck out her tongue at some silly request, and they tried not to snicker. They accepted mail, directed visitors to the children's cottages, and delivered notes to staff mailboxes. The ladies lunched in the dining hall, another beautiful room with floor-to-ceiling windows. The cook, Miss Janey, made an aromatic Chicken Marsala. Staff could buy food there, but it was frequently for important lunch meetings for the "big cheeses," as Ruth called them.

Rita had brought a deviled ham sandwich, an apple, and a crossword puzzle, the last of which never came out of her bag, as co-workers stopped by to say hello.

The only hard part, the difficult part, was lying to these lovely people. When they asked about her, Rita replied that yes, she lived in West Hartford with her husband and six children. Meet Mrs. Rita Leonard, liar. She hadn't planned on lying, but she wanted her life to seem as run-of-the-mill as everyone else's.

Being single, she'd be deemed a divorcee. Any woman who couldn't hang onto her man was scoffed at. A mother not raising her children was socially exiled. Being Catholic only made her more guilty, but lying would get her children home sooner. God would understand.

The clock ticked languidly, but Ruth pointed at it. "Look at that time. Oh, my stars, you're a natural, talking to people. Some of these young parents are uncomfortable asking for help. All of us need help now and then. Well, put your feet up when you get home and tell your hubby to cook for you. You deserve it. I'll be here tomorrow, on time, I promise. Don't you worry a lick about that. Bye-bye, y'all."

Walking out of work, Rita swung her purse. She hadn't been this happy in, how very long? She started her car and said, "Oh, my stars."

Rita planned on visiting one or two children every other day, beginning after her first workday.

During supper with Rose, Jack, and Timothy, Rita blabbed on and on, until Rose cut her off. "Hold your horses now, Rita, take a breath and take a bite. Now, can't Bobby visit a child or two tomorrow?" Rose sipped her warm beer.

Rita puckered her mouth. "He could. He's supposed to see Kevin, while I go to East Hartford. Did he call here today? I haven't heard from him since Friday." Rita polled the table. The men shook their heads, shoveling mashed potatoes in. They hardly ever answered the phone. Or spoke.

Rose defended Bob, "Well, he's probably working hard. There's no harm in that."

"I need money from him. For the kids, and you, for groceries. I need money until . . . until I get paid." Rita bantered, "*Paid*. I like the sound of that. But he's still got to give child support. I'll call him . . . again."

Rita sat at Rose's big desk to call Bob's apartment, then the store, where he was now just an employee, no longer the owner.

The next morning, Rita had toast and tea in the sunny kitchen and packed lunch and a small suitcase for her visit with Noreen and Teri. She was excited about her workday and, after that, being a mother.

But without the money Bob was supposed to give her, she couldn't take her daughters out for much-needed sneakers.

Why wasn't he calling? She wanted to tell him about the job. And what about her car? It started to shimmy, which Bob could probably fix.

If only he'd call.

38

MEN

The following Thursday morning, Rita was hurrying to get to work. She yanked the Fairlane's door open, tossed her bags onto the ripped bench seat, and slid in. She turned the key, the engine started, and she shifted into reverse. It didn't move.

Rita put the car into forward, and it rolled fine in that direction. She'd drive forward over lawns, but backyards were sectioned off with rusting chain-link fences.

Needing to back out of the driveway, Rita tried R again, talking sweetly to her ten-year-old clunker. "Come on, baby." Rita patted the dashboard. "You cannot do this to me. I am a responsible person. I have a job."

The car didn't listen. Rita laid her head on the steering wheel and hummed a high-pitched whine. There was no time for this.

She bounded into the house to get Jack, a tinkerer. He thumped outside wearing leather slippers and a plaid bathrobe. Sitting behind the wheel, he fiddled around, turned the key, and played with the gear shift.

"Nah," he croaked, stroking the whiskers decorating his neck and chin.

"Nah?" Rita bent over to watch him.

"Look, it goes forward, ayah?" He demonstrated the car's forward crawl. She took steps to keep up with the open door, not needing someone to state the obvious. Could he fix whatever this was?

"But, here, get out of the way . . . there's no reverse, is there? You can't drive this thing today . . . maybe never again. It's the transmission, I'd say." Jack paused. "It's too expensive to fix a car this . . . this . . . old." He took out the suitcase and lunch bag, moved to the house like the old man that he was.

Rita froze for one minute, then swept by him to call Aunt Rose's only friend who drove, an odd duck named Jerry.

Jerry was happy to drive Rita to work. He was a religious nut who drove an old station wagon filled with newspapers and rusted tools. A St. Anthony medal hung from the rearview mirror. He said things like, "Praise be to God."

His empty chatter allowed Rita to think. Her first thought: don't panic. Her second thought: see when Bob could look at her car. Third thought: call Joe Leonard for a ride to his house after work to visit Teri and Noreen.

As the Ford sat resolutely in Rose's driveway, Rita was picked up at work at 4:30 that evening by Bob's brother Joe, stayed overnight in East Hartford, and was dropped back at work by 8:30. On her lunch break, Rita finally got in touch with Bob at his apartment.

"Where have you been? I've been calling you. The kids haven't heard from you . . . and . . . my car's not working. I'm begging for rides everywhere."

"Out of town, making money. Fran and I drove to Ohio to help an old lady move. We each got a couple of hundred, so I've got cash for you."

Rita spoke softly, so her crazy life couldn't be overheard by colleagues. "Good. Good. Thanks, uh, are you avoiding me?" Like she needed one more thing to worry about.

"Do you always have to be so direct? Yes. I am. Avoiding you. I'll be by Rose's tomorrow to look at the Ford. By the way, Joe told me about your job. Congrats, if that's what you want."

She lowered her voice, "What's the matter with you?"

"Seems like your life is rolling along fine, Rita. I'll check out your damn car tomorrow." Bob hung up.

On Saturday, a surly Bob confirmed it. The Fairlane was ready for the junk heap. She asked him to come by for mechanical advice, not to badger her, like on the phone.

She knew the transmission was blown, and maybe could have found money to fix one thing on her car. When Bob got on all fours to peer underneath, he called out. "Not looking good. The muffler is pitted with rust, and the alignment looks off."

"So, I don't have a car now? Can I fix this? I mean, not me, but you?"

Bob opened the hood and clanked around. "Ah, no. I'd say you don't have a car. I couldn't fix all that's wrong with this baby. And, since paying you child support, I don't have any money for repairs either." He slammed the hood.

She minutely shook her head, annoyed he thought child support was *paying* her.

Rita saved half of her first two paychecks for a deposit on an apartment she had yet to find. "No. This is not acceptable. I need a car." She grabbed the antennae and bent it as far as it could go before snapping, releasing it to whip back and forth. *Fwip, fwip, fwip, fwu, fwu, fwa.* It finally calmed down.

Bob watched her, wiping his hands on a rag. "I'll get this car towed to Whitey's for scrap metal, get a few bucks."

Rita scrunched her face. "That's it? That's all you can do?"

"Yeah, Rita. That's all I can do. Be your servant, drive you and the kids around, fix your car. What else do you want? Mow this lawn? Sweep the sidewalks? I'm getting *nothing* from this moronic arrangement."

"Oh, and I am?" Rita stepped back.

"You wanted it. You wanted to split up. You're the only one, Rita, not me, not the kids. What the hell? Here's your *child support*." Bob tossed a grease-smeared envelope onto the front seat of the car. He threw the oily rag in, too.

He sulked down the driveway, slapping his hat on his thigh, whistling mightily.

Rita turned her face to place the tune. Conway Twitty's "It's All Only Make Believe." Rita recalled the words, shielding her eyes as she watched Bob go. He was also hurt and lonely. Well, too bad, she thought. He couldn't possibly be lonelier than a mother without her children. This camel's back could not accept one more straw. Rita made her way into the kitchen, where Rose was frying ham steaks.

"Hard times come again no more . . . " Rita puffed out. She was wearing pedal pushers and a button-down blouse, standing with her two hands on her lower back, elbows jutting out like wings.

Rose held a spatula in the air. "What?"

"Enough of this . . . this . . . " She hesitated.

Rose laughed, "Go on, you can say *shit*."

Rita pulled her hair back, gray strands now mingled with brown, and considered her upcoming week. Shawn, Carol, and Kitty were in South Windsor. Rob Davin picked Rita up on Monday night. On Thursdays, Joe Leonard drove. Mr. Mavis worked later, so his schedule determined when Rita got to Somers, Tuesdays, or Wednesdays. Kevin was the only one alone, making Rita anxious to get to him on time.

Each day, then each week, Rita was getting smaller, lonelier, and needier. "Shit." Yeah, that word worked, "SHIT."

Weeks later, while Rita waited for a ride after work, it started to rain. It was Joe's turn. If he drove the fire chief's truck, it was to quickly run her to his home on his break, then get back to work. She took refuge on the front porch, sitting in a blue chair, scanning the newspaper's automotive section. She looked up to see Mrs. Hatch, her boss, leaning against a pillar, having a cigarette. Rain gurgled from a gutter.

"Oh, hi. I didn't see you there," Rita admitted.

"Rita, do you ever rest?" Mrs. Hatch smiled and lifted her chin, exhaling.

"I'm sorry, what?"

Mrs. Hatch crushed her cigarette in a metal ashtray she held, then walked it and herself to sit near Rita. "You're always busy. Even when we eat lunch, you straighten up a little. Your coffee area is neat, your switchboard organized. People don't wait long for you to acknowledge them when they walk in."

Rita froze. Was it too much? Was she being obnoxious? She gave a small shoulder shrug.

"Mrs. Hatch, I . . . " Rita began, but to say what?

"Please call me Elizabeth. I'm impressed with your work ethic. You seem to be a kind of, I don't know, kind of a bright spot."

Rita's cheeks warmed. Her actions so far were good, her heart racing now was for the right reason. "Thank you. But what would you like me to work on, Elizabeth?"

"Well, your handwriting is horrible." Elizabeth dropped her mouth open in mock surprise.

Rita's face got hotter.

"Rita, I'm kidding. Well, not really, but as long as you type everything, you're fine. You're doing a wonderful job and we're glad we hired you."

"Thanks again. I'm enjoying the work. Are you waiting for a ride?" Rita moved the focus off herself.

"Yes. My son took my car for an appointment, saying he'll be on time, but he's always late. He's a *liar.*" Elizabeth gave a harrumph sound. She stood to look at the driveway.

Rita did a mental flipflop. Did Elizabeth suspect that Rita was a liar too? Guilt crept in on little mouse feet.

"Ah. My kid, he's a spoiled brat, but I love him. And I can assure you that he did *not* put gas . . . "

Rita was suddenly red, sitting in her blue chair.

"Rita? What is it? Are you sick?"

"I have something to tell you." She shifted, paused. How could she be honest, and hope to keep this very necessary job?

"All right," Elizabeth sat back down.

"I'm just going to say it. I don't live in a nice house in West Hartford. I don't have a husband, I mean, I do, but we are legally separated, I mean, we are working on that."

Rita stopped, ready to explain, but Elizabeth started laughing. Laughing. "Please tell me you have those six children, because that is a huge number to make up."

Rita's eyebrows shot up. "Oh, they are all real, there's Carol, and Kitty, and Kevin . . . "

"And you don't live under a bridge, I assume . . ." Elizabeth sobered.

"No, no I'm staying with my aunt."

"Then please tell me, for Pete's sake, why is it that a different man picks you up each evening, and drops you off in the morning?" Elizabeth was intrigued.

Rita's mouth opened, imagining what this looked like. Like a negligent parent. Or a cheat. Or a hooker. Heat gathered on her cheeks again. She gasped, then hurried to explain, "They are our friends, and my brother-in-law, sometimes my husband, ah, uh, *former* husband who drive me. I don't have a car because the transmission went the week after I got this job. I'm living at my aunt's house until I save enough money to get an apartment for me and my children."

Rita paused to breathe, to finish this. "When my husband and I parted, we split our children up because we were losing our home. I visit one or two of my children every night, stay over, and come back with the dads in the morning, to work. It's the only way for me to hold them, to eat with them . . . Please . . . I'm sorry . . . I . . . I . . . need this job." There. It was out. Rita grasped her hands in her lap, twisted her tiny diamond ring around, as if it, too, were a lie.

At that moment, Joe sped into the long driveway, in the chief's truck, honking the horn. She had to finish this conversation, yet Joe had just fifteen minutes. Rita waved to him, standing up.

"Oh, my word, Rita. I had no idea. How much you're doing, how you present yourself. Please, please rest assured about your work here. I am delighted that your family is . . . what? Disrupted . . . no, that's not what I mean. Together, but apart? We were wondering, a couple of the others, why, here you were the mother of so many children, and you never talked about them, making a meal, or running errands for them," Elizabeth inhaled air like a long-distance runner. Her mouth turned up, as she dabbed her eyes with a tissue she pulled from the sleeve of her cardigan.

Rita gathered her things. "I'm sorry I lied, Elizabeth."

Another car splashed to a stop behind the gleaming truck. Elizabeth smeared her mascara with the damp tissue. "Oh, look, perfect timing, my idiot son. Please, I'm the one who's sorry. Let us help you here, Rita, whenever we can. It's what we do."

Elizabeth's son gave a quick toot, and yelled, "Come on, Mom."

Joe rolled down his window. "Let's go, Rita."

"Well," Elizabeth joked, "let's not keep our men waiting. Sheesh."

Both women ran down the steps through the rain.

"Sorry, sorry, to be late, Joe." Rita shook rain from her hair.

Joe gave Rita a grin. "You made me late, Rita, now I gotta use this." Joe switched on the emergency siren, then blasted through Hartford traffic, careened over the Bulkeley Bridge, and zipped to his East Hartford home.

The rain tapered off, and a spectacular late-day sun made little jewels on the leaves of two newly planted trees in Joe's yard.

It would be a great evening to look for dandelions with her girls.

39

AMBITION

R ita sat on her sagging cot after lunch, hands idle. Rose huffed up the stairs with a pile of towels and poked her head into the porch-bedroom. "What are you doing there, sitting like the devil *hisself*?"

"Without a car, I have nothing to do and nowhere to go."

"Achh. You. Get up and put these towels about. Then, go for a nice long walk without that puss on your face. You can work with me at the club tonight."

"A walk? To where?" Rita hung the towels in the bathroom.

She had to buy a car, but no bank would give a single woman a loan. She needed courage to ask the one person who could help. Her father. She'd walk to his house, giving herself time to think.

Rita put on a cotton dress to show her father she was serious, and white socks and sneakers, to be practical. She passed Whitey's Garage, where a 1960 Rambler American was for sale. She cupped her hands on the windows to see if her kids could fit in this small car. They could, but only with a seating plan. Maybe Whitey would finance it.

Whitey came out wiping his hands on a rag. "Go on, try it out. Drive around the block if you want. The key's in the ashtray, the guy never smoked."

Rita took the Rambler for a spin. Back at the garage, when she asked Whitey to finance it for her, he just laughed. She then asked for a pen and paper to do the math. The car cost $1,475.00, as scribbled on the windshield in soap. She made $54 per week, $2,592 a year. Bob promised close to $4,000 a year in child support. Her paychecks could cover the loan, around $60 a month for 24 months. Bouncing pencil on paper, she felt a positive charge. This was a huge step, these facts to present to her father.

She'd never dropped by Daddy's house unannounced before. Her pulse quickened. Taking the two steps to his front porch, Rita raised her fist to knock. It took a few minutes before the door swung open. Her father wore slippers, gray pants, and suspenders over a white tee shirt. He held a newspaper in one hand and a cold cigar stub hung out of his mouth.

"*Reeta*? Did you walk here?" He stepped back and Rita ducked into her parents' home.

"Hi Daddy." Rita moved into the living room, then hesitated. She couldn't remember the last time they were alone. Was she crazy to ask him for money? "Whew, it's hot out. How about some water? I'll get it."

In the kitchen, she filled two glasses, then cracked the lever on the metal tray to add ice. Rita carried them to the living room, where Daddy was sitting on the couch, still holding his paper. She sat opposite.

Nervous, she spoke fast, "Daddy. I've come to ask for a loan. My car broke down and was towed for scrap, but I need to get back and forth to work, visit my children, and look for an apartment." Whoosh.

"What would you buy, Reeta?"

Her father hadn't yelled. He was calm, as if he had been waiting for her to ask for help.

"I saw a Rambler. Three-speed shift on the column. The interior looks nice, and there's no rust. I asked the mechanic who owns the garage to look at the engine. I have $50 and Bob will give me $100."

At Bob's name, Kieran pointedly spit out a tab of tobacco stuck to his tongue.

"So, I'd need $1,325, at most. But I could bargain, right?"

He hesitated, pursing his lips, and furrowing his brow. "Let's work out a payment plan, on paper. I don't trust you." Here, he smiled and winked, the only bone he would throw her. Daddy gave Rita a blank check, with advice to bargain hard. Rita stepped onto the porch, and Kieran stood in the doorway. He pulled six one-dollar bills from his pants pockets, "For the children."

She hugged him to say thank you. He pretended to groan, "Ah, go on with you, now." He slippered back into his dark house.

Rita haggled $25 off the price. Whitey filled out the sales agreement wrong, but she gently corrected him. He rubbed his mouth, "Sorry. Aren't you Bob's wife?"

"I used to be 'Mrs. Robert F. Leonard.' Now I'm 'Mrs. Rita H. Leonard.'"

"Oh. Ohhhh. Will do. You women, today, I don't know." He scratched his head.

She smiled, shaking his greasy hand. "That's right, Whitey, you don't know women today."

40

APARTMENT

Rita sat at the switchboard during lunch to call about apartments. It was the end of the pay period. Out of food and money, Rita polished off six Ritz crackers with peanut butter, washed them down with water, and began dialing.

"Hello. I'm calling about renting your apartment. I see it's two bedrooms—"

She was interrupted. "Do you have kids?"

"Six. But—"

Click. Rita jerked back, chastised, but, still, dialed the next number in the newspaper. Did she need a parking space? Her yes answer got another click. What did her husband do for work? No husband, click. She blinked rapidly, truly surprised. Rita was learning just how unfair this whole rental thing was for women. Telling the truth was not going to get an apartment. Did landlords want perfection? She'd give them perfect. She pulled together her liar's lines in seconds.

"Hello. I'm calling about your apartment. We have three kids, no pets, do not need a parking space, and my husband travels for business." Rita held her breath. No click. The landlord was still on the line.

"I see that rent is $95 a month, including heat and hot water. Three bedrooms? No? But there's a dining room? Security deposit is one month's rent? That's fine. When can I see this apartment?"

She drove her Rambler to a three-family house. Sonya Santos, the landlord's wife, brought her to the second floor. Rita grew up around the corner, where her father still lived, which felt nostalgic. The old kitchen had no counter space, and three appliances were spread out like distant cousins at a family reunion, making Rita laugh, including someone else's old wringer washer.

Sonya smiled. "I know it's ugly, but it works, and your clothesline is right off the back porch. You said you had three children?"

Rita mumbled, "Uh-huh," as she busied herself peering into the pantry. Rita pushed compliments to Mrs. Santos. "This is all so clean. And it smells good. Pine-Sol? That's what I use, too."

While showing the bedrooms, Sonya spoke of her husband. "He works nights, so he likes quiet so he can sleep during the day. And he likes things neat. I have a three-year-old boy, Charlie. Sometimes it's hard to be neat and quiet," Sonya mused as she yanked up the Venetian blind, revealing a swing set in the yard. Rita hoped Shawn, also three, could play there with Charlie.

Rita needed this apartment, so mentioned her husband's false travels again. Sonya suggested the ladies sign the lease now, and have their husbands sign later. Rita plucked a check from her and Bob's joint checking account, dated it August 1, 1964, and signed it. She wrote on the memo line: *Security Deposit on 22 West Beacon Street.*

Rita shivered on the ride home. How was she going to sneak six kids into a home leased for three? And a quiet one at that? How could she afford this? She'd have to cut back on groceries and think of something to sell.

The next day, Bob and Rita looked like a couple getting out of his truck. Using his limited acting ability, Bob signed the lease and shook Mr. Santos' hand. Driving Rita back to Rose's, he commented on her new car in the driveway. "Kinda tiny. Can the kids even fit in it? The apartment's small, too. But it's good they'll all be together."

Rita swallowed. "Yes, everything is too small. That's one reason I've decided to bring the three oldest kids home first, and plan for the rest after that."

Bob looked quizzically at Rita. "Jesus. I can never figure you out. I hope you know what you're doing. What's the other reason?"

Rita gave a crooked smile. "I don't know how to make six kids appear to be three kids."

Kevin stood on the front steps of his hosts' house, swinging a pillowcase stuffed with clothes and toys. He couldn't wait to be home with his sisters and brother and mother, wherever that might be.

No one seemed upset at his leaving, but they'd miss him when it was time to rake out the fake barn. He smirked and looked over the woods that had comforted him while he awaited new adventures with old buddies.

Kevin whooped as Dad's truck pulled into the driveway. He threw his bags in and said, "Let's go."

Dad whistled, "Slow down there, partner. Let's get the rest of your gear and say thank you. The Mavises took real good care of you."

Kevin turned his sunburned face to the steps, where they all gawked, then back at his dad. "You do it."

"Wow, Kevin. That bad, eh? Well, alright."

Dad got out and made nice comments as he loaded Kevin's bed parts and small dresser. He shook hands and came back to the truck, looking ready to scram, too. Kevin wasn't close to his father, but appreciated being busted out of jail.

They headed over to South Windsor for the big girls, where Kevin and Dad got a warm welcome and a confusion of emotion. Carol was all pressed and polished, ready to get home, but sad to leave this family. Kitty was torn between holding Shawn close to her and reuniting with Mommy. The girls hugged every member of the Davis family, with Kitty and Carol sniffling while getting into the truck.

When Rita heard Bob pull to the curb with precious cargo, she gave herself a quick pep talk, her heart thudding. You can do this alone. You have a job. You've worked out the rent. She ran down the stairs, holding onto both railings to keep from falling.

Rita and the big kids crashed in a hug.

They unloaded their gear, with Bob and Rita jostling the heavy stuff. Carol and Kitty were a little shy with Kevin. The five of them hustled clothes, toys, and furniture.

Eating pizza for lunch, Kitty looked at three empty chairs against the wall. "I know Shawn isn't coming yet, but what about Teri and Noreen? Aren't they coming today?"

"Uh . . . it's just you guys, for now." Rita sat rigidly.

Kevin vee'd his eyebrows. "No, Mom, you got to get everybody. Just three of us here? That was the whole point, that we'd all be together. You told me to trust you."

Bob was on his knees, screwing the legs into the overturned table, hearing and seeing everything.

Rita whined to Bob, "What was I thinking? I can't do this."

"What? This apartment?" He waved the screwdriver around, encouraged.

Her breath caught in her throat. "No. I need all my children. I can't be half a mother."

"Oh, but I can be half a father," he blurted, immediately annoyed at her callousness.

"I'm getting them back. Tomorrow. Bob, can you make one more sweep and bring Teri, Noreen, and Shawn here? I'll find a way to manage this." The other kids cheered. "Shh, keep it down," Rita warned.

That Sunday morning, Rita swooned as Bob came in piggybacking Shawn, leading Noreen by the hand, with Teri bouncing behind. Rita knelt on the floor and cupped their faces and kissed their necks. Rita was so glad when Bob said a hasty goodbye. The rest of the kids came from the bedrooms and joined the party.

Shawn smiled looking at Carol, Kevin, Kitty, Teri, and Noreen, then yelled out, "Here are all the kids!"

41

HIDING

Rita went to work on Monday, and the big kids cared for the little kids. Kevin moved stealthily into Kitty and Carol's room, acting like Vic Morrow from *Combat!* on television, his hands making a gun. Kitty was under her bed, trying to extract a flip-flop with a wire hanger.

It was easy to get by her, but Carol was sewing a button on a blouse, listening to her transistor radio. "What do you want, Kevin?"

"To get by the enemy and save all the ladies from getting captured."

"I'm pretty sure we're safe, you dolt. What's up?"

"Ma just got home from work and we hafta leave for swim team now. It's five o'clock. We'll be a little late from all this babysitting, so let's go."

Kitty got up quickly. "Mom, we're leaving."

Kevin led them to Kennedy Park on their bikes, riding on sidewalks, streets, and neighbors' yards. He and his sisters talked excitedly about the swim team, even though it was August and other kids had been competing all summer. At the park, Kevin skidded to an abrupt stop at the bike rack.

"Carol, tell Kitty to shut her trap. She's going to tell Ma about my towel. We don't tell Ma nothing."

"I only told her you stole it. What's the big deal?" Carol asked.

Kevin smacked his forehead. "Have you heard of telegraph, telephone, and tele*Kitty*?"

"We don't tell Ma anything. Not 'nothing' Kevin." Carol ramped her Sears Bluebird into the bike rack. From her metal baskets, she took out two ratty rolled-up towels and a newer red one. She then pulled out fourteen inches of black gimp.

"That's what I said." Kevin shoved his junker into the slot next to Carol's.

Worry scrunched Kitty's face as she wedged her bike next to Kevin's. "I'm telling Ma because you *stole* a towel."

Carol tied their front tires together with gimp. It wouldn't stop a thief, but it would slow one down.

Kevin knuckled her head. "Oh. I *took* a towel. It's from 'Lost and Found.' Someone lost it, and I found it. Tough noogies. Your towel looks like it died last year. Besides, she'd worry more. You want Ma to worry *more?*"

Kitty squawked, "That's dishonest, like the crackers you eat when no one's looking. You're going to have to hide the towel. And since when did we start calling Mommy 'Ma'?"

"Since we are no longer the babies, but the baby*sitters.* Time to grow up, Kitten." Kevin took off and called out to Jimmy Beattie to wait up.

Lifeguard Doug coached the team, forty kids, weekdays, from 5 to 6 p.m. Doug made them swim lap after lap, freestyle, backstroke, breaststroke, and, for the really coordinated, butterfly. The coach spat out encouragement, corrections, insults, and always, "Do it again." He'd *tweeeet* on his whistle, march the pool's edges, clapping, and shouting. Kevin studied the kids on the team. Some wore the Kennedy pool swimsuit: a navy blue, slim fitting, ugly one piece for the girls, and an equally *cornball*, but much tinier version for the boys. Ma bought Carol a new suit, but told the twins they would have to wait a year for theirs. Kevin wasn't going to wear a Speedo, ever.

"The way Carol is growing, she might burst out of that suit soon. Then I'll get it." Kitty clasped her hands together in a minor prayer, standing with Kevin on the pool deck, both shivering, waiting for a swim lane.

They got home for supper by 6:15 each night with bloodshot eyes, stringy hair, and growling stomachs.

"Ma, I hope we have spaghetti or rice, or, I don't care, potatoes, 'cause we're starving."

Kevin perked up because there were sausages in the spaghetti sauce. Bread and butter, salad. Noreen never ate sausage, so he'd snag hers when Ma turned to the stove, then wink at a grateful Noreen. He was always hungry.

Ma thought every pie, pound of cheese, or can of beans needed to be divided by sixths, or worse, sevenths. She didn't realize that as the oldest son, and the most physically active kid, he needed more. More milk, more bread, more meat. Ma was smart, and knew they needed daily vitamin C, protein, and fruit, so rationed everything.

He could relieve Shawn and Noreen of stuff they hated, but not the cookies or cereals they liked.

He didn't mind being poor, but he wasn't gonna go hungry, or go begging for stuff. He'd take what he needed, and not just at home.

The following Wednesday, Kitty called Teri into her room. "Look what I found. A Kennedy bathing suit rolled in a towel, right under my pillow."

"So? That's Carol's. Kevin must've hid it."

Kitty shook her head. "Moochie Gatchi Gu. Look." A note held on with an old diaper pin directed: "Put this in lawndry furst." Kitty knew Kevin got it for her: stolen, found, or traded. She smiled at his kindness and wasn't telling Ma. She made Teri promise, too.

That evening, Rita counted out fifty cents for Kitty and Teri to take to the corner store for a half gallon of milk. The girls were drooling at the glass-fronted candy counter, flip-flops hanging off their feet as they knelt down.

Doug the lifeguard sauntered in, tanned and chlorinated, twirling his whistle. He brought a Coke to the cashier. Next to it, he slid six Devil Dog cakes. Teri and Kitty secretly elbowed each other.

He held out a small paper bag. "Ta-daaa. For your brothers and sisters. See ya tomorrow at the pool." He zoomed off in his VW bug.

Standing on the sidewalk, with dusk falling, Kitty whispered, "We're eating these before we get home."

"All right." Teri was still hungry after a supper of canned Beefaroni.

Teri and Kitty minced toward home the long way, careful not to break the glass bottle of milk. They stopped at the corner, set the milk down, climbed on a U.S. mailbox, and each ate one Devil Dog.

"Let's eat them all. How will anyone ever know?" Teri boldly asked. The girls faced each other, poked tongues into creamy white filling and chomped all the dry chocolate cakes, while praising Devil Dogs, and Doug, in their secret language.

Thursday, Teri was climbing out of the pool, and overheard Doug ask Carol how she liked her surprise. She didn't get a surprise. Doug asked Kevin if he liked his snack. What snack?

Doug blew his whistle at Kitty, who was doing bad swan dives in the low end. He spied Teri and crooked his finger: C'mere. Teri's heart pounded, approaching the lifeguard's highchair. Kitty skinny-shivered slowly toward Doug. He yelled at them because he thought they knew how to share, kicked them out of the day session, and he told Kitty to skip swim team tonight.

"I am *that* angry." Doug barked.

They'd disappointed a good guy, giving Teri a lump in her stomach. Plus, Carol and Kevin were mad at them. Teri's lip quivered, but she forced herself not to cry.

Kitty, too, teared up. "We were jerks."

Teri agreed, "Yeah. Now we gotta tell Ma."

"No. We keep our mouths shut. We lied. And we kinda stole what wasn't ours. Worse than having to go to confession is how I feel. The only silver lining," Kitty explained, "is that no one will tell Ma."

Now she understood the code, and Teri did too.

That night, Mr. Santos expected rent money. Rita brought an envelope and knocked on his door. No one was home. Darn it, she thought, now he'd come upstairs for the check. Rita returned to her door, and said, "Big kids, meet in the back bedroom." She had a new plan.

Kevin sat on one twin bed, between Kitty and Carol, and Rita sat on the other. "Good. You're lined up. Listen here. You know Mr. Santos thinks we have three kids."

"Doubt it." Carol said. She folded her arms and stuck her bare feet straight out on the wood floor.

"What? Why?" Rita was sure he didn't know they were harboring three fugitives.

Kevin scratched a mosquito bite on his shoulder. "Uh, we tramp the stairs two times a day."

Carol and Rita, laughing, said in unison, "Four times."

"Listen, whether Mr. Santos does or does not believe we have three extra chickadees here in this nest, we're going to act as if we don't. If anyone comes to the front door, or rings the bell below, I answer it. Or one of you, if I'm not home. Get that?"

The girls said yes.

Ma raised her eyebrows. "Mr. Santos will be here sometime tonight."

"Is he bad? Is he a 'danger to society' like on *The Perry Mason Show*?" Kitty wanted to know.

"No, Kitty. You're watching too much television. No, he's not bad, he's pretty good actually, but doesn't like a lot of noise. Kevin, if Kitty is playing Barbies with Teri, she will take Teri and Noreen to this closet and sit quietly with them until the visitor goes."

Kevin tilted his head. "What does Carol do during this *espanash*?" He sat back on the bed, pulled his sneaker soles together to create a diamond shape of his legs.

Kitty pushed his leg out of her space and said, "Cut it out."

He hissed, "Make me."

Kitty sniped back, "You're already made and what a mess."

"Hey, Tweedledum and Tweedledee. It's 'espionage.'" Carol pulled her plastic hairband off, pushed her pool-bleached hair back, then returned it to its job. "We switch on and off. Answer the door, but only if we know them, Ma, right?"

Confirmed, she went on, "Three go into the closet, three children hang around looking innocent, I guess?" Carol glanced at her mother. "And then try to get rid of the creep at the door, whoever it is."

Rita got up, put her hands in her apron pockets. "Thanks, guys. I'll gather the little kids for supper. Oh. I found your team suit in the laundry, Carol. Hand wash that, it could get ruined in the wringer washer."

Carol spit out, "I didn't put—" but was jammed by Kitty and Kevin's shoulders. "Oh . . . ohhh. I'll hand wash it. Thanks, Ma."

"You kids do your chores now. Set the table and take out the trash." Rita left the room, pleased with both her message and delivery. Operation Hideout went well when Santos knocked. She let the big kids watch TV with her until 10 p.m., celebrating their new maturity.

42

BIKES

After four summer days of the kids being together, Rita got a call at work from Kitty. "We ran out of peanut butter and jelly. And Kevin forgot to make the Kool-Aid."

Rita looked around her office, lowering her voice. "That's not an emergency. You tell them to quiet down. Pack bologna and cheese sandwiches and get to the park. Don't call me at work unless it's important."

The bigger kids shouldered more responsibilities than they could handle. Rita knew it, and they knew it. She'd lined up Karen, their former tenant from Park Street, for autumn, babysitting Shawn only. The other kids would take care of Teri, eight, Noreen, almost six, and Shawn, three, until the end of the summer. The kid-watching, kitchen-sweeping, lunch-making, garbage-toting details fell to Carol, Kitty, and Kevin. They needed to make their beds every day, except for Shawn. He was toilet trained before he stayed with relatives but came back a bed wetter. The children ran out of clean sheets. They ran out of milk. They learned how to make do, eat burnt toast, and make siblings stop whining.

Rita knew they fought about everything: towels, flip-flops, the time to leave for the park. She overheard their morning conversations. *Who made you boss? Who stole my colored pencils? Stop being a jerk. How can I be the jerk when you are? I didn't say you said I was a jerk.* If they couldn't solve it with words, then pushing and shoving ensued and escalated to slapping and scratching. Once issues were settled, they left for Kennedy Park. Like dew on summer grass, post-fight grudges quickly evaporated.

Rita took her hands off the typewriter to rub her temples, "Please God, keep them safe." She pictured Carol putting her towel on her bike's fender and plunking Shawn there, his feet secure in the metal cages. Noreen perched on a seat as Kevin or Kitty stood to pedal the whole way. Teri's rusty little bike threatened to fall apart daily.

Rita had an especially trying Friday. It was not payday, and the ever-present shadows of poverty and loneliness slithered in. She needed a good cry.

At home, she greeted everyone, then changed into a housedress and sneakers. Rita cut onions. Peel, cut, chop, mince. The tears flowed, and she lifted a tissue to her eyes.

Kitty touched her arm, "Are you okay, Mommy?" Not "Ma," not now.

"Yes, yes, Kitty, it's those darn onions. Gets me every time." Rita pulled on a small smile and started banging pots and pans around for real.

Kitty slipped through the apartment telling her siblings to be quiet, clean up, and stop fighting. "Ma is sad." They obeyed Kitty.

Rita mulled over her life. She was organized and practical, but it was still so, so hard. They all grocery shopped at Motts' every second Monday. No leftovers were left long but were turned into a stew or salad or a loaf. Rita bought gas on Wednesdays. If it rained, and they couldn't use the clothesline, they went to the laundromat on Thursday nights. Rita did not drink, buy herself a coffee, dye her gray hair, or heed entreaties for candy or soda in a store. Rita did not dole out band-aids or baby aspirin randomly and did not own a thermometer. The family had breakfast, lunch, and supper at home. The routines, she thought, stabilized their world when everything else was a crapshoot.

Rita was sorting mail at work when she received a call from Teri she could not understand.

This was what Rita dreaded: one of her children was hurt due to her negligence.

Kitty and Carol double-rode the youngest kids on their bikes home from the park. Kevin and Teri went through the woods and came out near the convent. Kevin was trick riding, jumping off his moving bike, then leaping on, while gripping the handlebars. He and Teri crossed Park Road onto a side street. Kevin pedaled hard for a few turns and then stood on his seat until the bike wobbled and he dropped down, his butt landing on the saddle, his legs widened over the pedals.

"You try it." He taunted Teri on her tiny bike.

Teri pedaled, and kneeled on the seat, then bravely tried to stand on it. She hit a rock and flew over the handlebars, crashed onto asphalt, face first, breaking off her left front tooth, and tearing open her mouth from the inside, which gushed blood. Her knees skimmed and bounced on the street, and syrupy tar stuck to her shredded legs, gravel embedded in her palms.

"Holy shit." Kevin threw his bike down and ran to his sister. She was lying still on the road, face down, so he knelt to turn her over. Her face crumpled when she saw his blanched, wide-eyed fear.

Teri let out an animal shriek, "Yeeow."

Her hands flew to her face, and her tongue explored the gap. Teri's tooth was a jagged mess. She cried as Kevin pulled her gently to the side of the street.

Kevin looked around, but there was no one to help. Snot and tears and blood mingled on her cheeks and chin. He yanked his towel from his clamped fender rack and wiped some of Teri's goo away. When she pulled back, he gripped her arms tighter.

"Teri? Teri." He called out, noticing her hamburger knees. "Can you walk? Move your legs."

Teri sat on the curb and slowly bent each leg.

Kevin had no idea what to do. "I'll help you walk home. You can lean on me." He pushed his bike into bushes. "Teri. Watch this."

Kevin hoisted her wreck of a bike and two-handedly threw it into an empty lot.

Teri laughed, but her messed-up mouth made it too painful. She went back to weeping, so Kevin kept telling stories on their journey. A Japanese beetle got caught in his ear, the buzzing driving him crazy until the doctor dug it out with tweezers. Once, he cut his foot on a jagged-edged can and needed a tetanus shot. Then there was that time when his top bunk collapsed and he thought he killed Shawn, but Shawn was not in bed yet. Kevin paused when she stopped crying.

"Two things, Teri. One, I didn't swear back there. Two, no one made you ride like that. Got it?"

Teri nodded. She started hurting in earnest by the time they climbed the back stairs to their kitchen. Carol dabbed at Teri's cuts with a cool washcloth. Kitty held her hand while Teri called their mother at work.

"Mah . . . I ah . . . fehl off my vike . . . " Teri started.

Ma was listening, "What, Teri? What did you say?"

"Fehl off of my vike. I shplit my lif and broke my toof." Teri sucked up tears in three pulls.

"Are you hurt? Wait a minute . . . you broke your front tooth? Oh, Teri . . . " Ma's disappointment, her pain, came through the line, twisting Teri's insides, alarmed at her mother's alarm.

"What's so bad? I've losh teef before."

Ma sighed. "Those were baby teeth, Teri. This one will never grow back. And we don't have dental insurance. I don't know where I'll find the money."

Teri, feeling guilty at needing Ma's money, whispered, "I'm *thorry*." She handed the phone to Kitty, then went to her bed, and cried herself to sleep, thinking how ugly and needy she was.

Ma's gentle cupping of Teri's chin to assess the damage woke her up. The tooth was cut off in a sharp diagonal line, her upper lip a bubble of swollen tissue. Ma did not hug Teri. Hugs were coming less often these days. She did, however, get a crushed baby aspirin.

Rita got busy on the phone with her dentist, who suggested The Hartford Dental Dispensary, where students learned their skills, so it was cheap.

Kitty consoled her in Mootchi Gatchi Gu, but the only hug Teri got was from her life-sized ragdoll, Susan. She had straps under her feet, so Teri could dream of them waltzing again once her knee scabs had healed.

Rita needed Bob to take Teri to the dentist and pay for some of this. When Kitty cut her forehead, years earlier, they had wanted the best care for their child's face. Now they couldn't afford the best. Not even close.

Carol came into the kitchen, and asked her mother, "Where's my desk?"

Rita was confirming the time and place to Bob for the appointment. "Not now."

But Carol said, "Is that Dad? Can I talk to him?" Rita handed Carol the phone.

"Dad. You know my desk, that I write at every day? Do you know where it is?"

Rita tapped Carol, who held the receiver to her shoulder, to stare at her mother.

"I sold it." Rita spoke quickly. "I needed the money to buy your swimsuit and pay for—"

Carol got loud, so her father could hear, "You *sold* it? It was *mine*. It was my sanctuary, like *your* desk. I wrote there and read there . . . it was my only private spot in this dump of an apartment. God, I hate this place. Dad. Daddy? Can I live with you?"

Rita stepped forward, "You're being dramatic, Carol. What's more important? Furniture or, or swim team? Let me talk to your father."

Carol held the phone, not yielding to Rita, "Dad? Did you hear me?"

Rita overheard Bob answer, "Yes. I hear you, Carol. I don't have any room, you know that. But I'll come get you, take you for a ride, give you a break."

"Yes." Carol hung up the phone, claiming some tiny piece of power.

Rita shouldn't have sold Carol's desk. She tried to soften herself by asking, "Is he coming? What about supper?"

Carol twirled out of the phone's cord, walked to her bedroom, and said, "What about it? Who cares?"

Rita blinked several times.

Carol had asked to live with Bob.

Rita, rattled, held the phone, not to call Bob back, but to touch the warm spot Carol last held. Carol belligerently trotted down the front staircase to get outside.

Sixty minutes later, Rita let them in. Bob stood on the porch as Carol slipped by to run to her room.

Bob shifted his footing. "I took her to Friendly's. She had a cheeseburger, fries, and a milkshake. Then she railed against you for twenty minutes. Rita, she's angry. The swimsuit, the desk, her taking care of all the kids. You ask too much, and I agree with her. I'm going to put my feelings in a letter. I don't speak as fast or as well as our daughter does, but you need to hear us."

"She's not living with you."

"See, Rita, that's not what I mean. I never offered that. Just read it."

It was a miserable week for Carol and Rita, circling like sharks. Teri's face was still a wreck.

Perfectly timed, Rita's workplace gave her seven tickets to the circus. She had saved coins in a coffee can along with the six dollars from her father. She decided the children could spend it as they wished, a huge trust. At the state Armory, the Leonards popped out of the Rambler, their own clown car. They were excited by the crowds and the smells of sawdust and cotton candy. They marveled at the lions, the elephants, and the cranking of cool motorcyclists in a metal sphere. During intermission, they scattered to spend their dough on souvenirs.

Kitty unknowingly purchased a one-eyed goldfish, and Kevin bought a chameleon in a plastic bag full of chirping crickets, its food. He secretly used bottle money to buy a jackknife. The circus was a big hit.

Rita drove along Farmington Avenue, and peered into her rearview mirror at four squished, tired children, and glanced at Kitty and Carol, in the front, bopping to the radio. Their cheesy purchases made the children happy for a while.

She smiled, thinking about the dangers and usefulness of immediate gratification.

43

CONSTRUCTION

Kevin came home from the park dripping. It was dark and raining this August day, but not cold. He shook his head like a dog, spraying everyone at the kitchen table. Noreen and Shawn were smushing Play-Doh around and Teri was reading *Pippi Longstocking*.

"Stop it," Noreen complained, "you're getting my stuff wet."

Kevin ignored her, burped, and announced, "There's no swim team. It's canceled."

Carol yelled out, "Well, duh. It's dark at four o'clock and it's going to thunder and lightning."

Teri was glad she wouldn't be stuck playing with Noreen and Shawn again. The big kids did more fun stuff. But Teri knew six kids into two groups meant three and three and she couldn't change her place in the family.

Kitty stopped Kevin from moving around. "You're soaking. Go change."

"Nah. I'm already wet. Want to go adventuring? It's soda bottle time. I saw a bunch down the street. We'll get money for good food, like Snowballs."

Teri offered to go.

Kevin frowned. "You? You're a punk, but, Kitty, come on, you're good at bottles." Kevin opened the bread box, took a heel, and stuffed it in his mouth.

Kitty stretched herself into a better mood. "I'm coming only if Teri comes."

Kevin led his sisters to the construction site one block away. "Without a brook or woods, this neighborhood stinks, but this place is worth exploring. And it has mud."

The kids, hair plastered to heads, shirts pressed to skin, stayed outside the fence. The newly dug site had one steam shovel operator left. The construction guy slid off his seat, grabbing his black lunch box and plaid thermos. Teri watched the scene, wondering what Kevin and Kitty were waiting for, what they were going to do.

"Good. He's the last one to leave for the day. Too wet to build. We won't have to wait long." Kevin whispered, his arm swinging behind to keep the girls out of sight.

The worker skirted the pile of earth he'd created, jostling a set of keys. He started wrapping a clanging, wet chain around the metal gate to secure the dig. Just then a skunk, probably confused by the day/night light ratio, waddled up near his feet. Kevin tamped his sisters' shoulders. "Get down," he murmured.

This is what Teri wanted, to be outside with Kitty and Kevin and sneak around and have adventures. Kevin always turned them into stories at suppertime, with sound effects and dashing escapes. She wanted the stories too, but she would write them.

They watched from the wet-cement-scented sidewalk as the skinny man screamed, recoiled, and pirouetted into the truck end of his El Camino. Like a snake, he slithered into the open driver-side window onto the seat. Too late for the rain and stench, he rolled up the window and peeled away, fishtailing.

Kevin burst out laughing, "What a weenie. Running from a skunk."

Kitty and Teri giggled and jeered at the disappearing truck.

The rain sucked their sounds into the air, but Teri could see Kevin and Kitty's amused faces. She shrank back when the skunk waddled toward her. Even without spraying them, it emanated a pungent, oily smell.

Kitty twisted Teri's arm in fear, but Kevin raised his hands into monster claws, stomped, and snarled at it. The skunk hum-de-dummed away, like a cartoon.

Kevin grabbed both girls' hands, "C'mon. We're in like Flynn. Or is it Flint?"

He ran to the closed gate and unwound the slippery links enough to creak it back a foot. "That's all we need, fatsos. Let's go." He pointed to a painted sign advertising the new apartment building. "That's what I hate. They destroy perfectly good woods to build more stuff. The animals have nowhere to go."

Kitty sympathetically agreed, "And neither do you."

He heaved a rock at the sign, making a black mark above the word "NEW!"

Teri followed the twins to the back of the lot, mud speckling their legs.

The pit was cut sharp into the earth, about a ten-foot drop. Teri quivered looking over the edge at the jumble of wires and flats of bricks on the clay bottom. A dump truck and a tractor lurked on the upper edges, adding rust to their yellow armor. Hay was strewn around the dig's perimeter, the rim slick.

"There. And there." Kevin pointed to piles of debris. "The real treasure, bottles."

Each Coke or Canada Dry bottle would bring two cents.

Teri felt the thrill of the jackpot, seeing the green and brown glass. She was ready to move, but saw no way to get down. Kevin must have a plan, she thought.

He traipsed through muck, one gloppy foot at a time, toward a nailed-together construction ladder that was lying on the side of the hole. He pulled his left foot up, but his sneaker stayed stuck. He balanced, like a stork, pulled the now-brown shoe out, and forced it on his waiting foot.

Kevin called to his sisters, "Help me. Let's lower it down."

Teri and Kitty did as commanded. Kevin pushed wet hair off his forehead, stepped backward onto the ladder, and scurried down.

Kitty yelled, hands megaphoning, "Is it safe?"

"Not really." He called up. "Watch for slivers. And nails. Get going."

Teri, feeling brave, went second, and coaxed Kitty to follow.

She did, but worried out loud, "What if we fall? Why is it so wet? Where'd that skunk go?"

Kevin and Kitty ran around the mud pools and stomped in puddles. Kevin bent to scoop ammo and threw a lumpy patty at Teri's gut.

"Oof!" She coughed out, surprised. "Hey, Quickdraw McGraw, watch out." Teri patted a sloppy mess and tried to cream her brother, who pulled Kitty in as his shield.

"Dog fight!" Kitty screamed, gathering her own soupy mixture. They spun and slipped in the mud and laughed their heads off.

"We gotta get to work. Truce. Truce." Kevin yelled.

Kitty lobbed one more at him, but Teri dropped her two bombs into the puddles. Plop, plop. She wasn't going to risk not being asked again. Chocolate pudding and chocolate milk dribbled off them as Teri, Kitty, and Kevin collected a dozen glass bottles and six cans. Kevin took off his shirt and made a bag of it by tying a knot at the bottom, then led the climb up the ladder into the deepening dusk.

Kitty went up. "I don't want any slivers. Kevin, you hear me?"

Teri, not afraid of heights, climbed quickly until she banged into Kitty's butt. They stopped moving.

At the top, Kevin threw the shirt bag to a junk pile, sprang from the ladder, and soldier-rolled behind a dump truck, shushing those behind him.

The construction guy was back. "Hey."

He must have seen movement while trying to maneuver the slick gate. "Hey. Who's there?" He sounded closer even with the rain pelting the site.

Kevin crawled to the edge of the hole, to warn the underlings below. He stage-whispered, "Get up and move to the back fence. Stay low. Follow me." Grabbing the loot bag, he took off.

Kitty followed, scrambling to the chain-link fence where Kevin climbed slow enough to get over without breaking the glass bottles. She paced back and forth in a five-foot line, whimpering, "How do I get out? How do I get over?"

Teri, last up, took a hiding spot behind the tractor. "Go, Kitty," she prayed. Teri's wet skin, hair, clothes, and fear started her shaking. She rubbed her arms for warmth.

"Hey. You kids. Come here. Get over here you little . . . dammit . . . I'm calling the cops." The guy tumbled, and yelled out from the muck, "You're gonna regret this."

Teri saw Kevin spider back over the top of the fence, jumping down to Kitty. "Shut up. Step on this." He laced two hands together and boosted her up. "Stick your toes into the holes. Climb."

Teri saw Kevin searching for her. Shoot. He wouldn't leave her there, would he? The construction guy was laboring toward Kitty and Kevin, about 20 feet away.

Kitty got over the fence while Kevin stood in the shadows. Then he hurled a big rock at the dump truck far behind Teri. The clanging caused the construction guy to turn toward the pit side. Kevin had created the distraction to run back to take her arm. At the fence, he yanked up a section until the bottom bent, forming an escape hatch. "Crawl," he commanded.

Teri rolled under, grazing her shoulder on four twisted prongs. Kitty and Teri met up, both breathing heavily. Kevin looked through the fence at their checkered faces, bent his arm at the elbow, and jacked his thumb, *get going*. He sprinted off, covering half the site's perimeter leading to the construction guy, who lacked the agility or stamina to catch Kevin.

Angry, he challenged, "And don't come back, you little thief. Next time, I'll bring my guard dog."

Kevin wolf-howled at him, laughing, and running.

Kitty clutched their loot and clasped Teri's hand as they ran to meet him at the corner.

Huffing, Kevin paused to grab the shirt-bag, "Let's go."

They ran a block before he skidded to a stop, panting, "We . . . need . . . a story." He lowered the cache to the sidewalk, breathing hard, his bare muddy torso glistening and heaving.

The girls stood with their hands on their knees.

"Why? What's wrong?" Teri asked.

Kitty, puffing hard, dramatically put her hands on Teri's shoulders. "We have to give Ma a reason why we're late, like we were walking along, and . . . and a skunk crossed our path. We all walked backward and tripped over a log. Into mud."

"That's it?" Kevin protested, "That's lame. We're filthy. Our clothes are *brown*, Kitty. Covered in mud. How about, then we got into a mud fight? Ma would believe that cuz we're good, but not perfect. And the skunk will be our alibi."

"Al-i-bye?"

Kevin got dead serious. "Yes, Teri. With *a* alibi, and *a* exit, you can go anywhere. *Anywhere.*"

Rita arrived home to half of her children. Noreen and Shawn ran for a hello hug.

Carol sauntered out carrying her book, *The Kon-Tiki Expedition*. She greeted Ma by saying Kevin, Kitty, and Teri were outside somewhere.

"Hmm. It's raining pretty hard." Rita shed her shoes and raincoat. "I hope they come in soon."

Her children milled about while Rita started making Chun King chicken chow mein, with hot white rice on this stormy night. Rita searched the street below. They all loved a good storm, snow or rain, but with three kids still out after 6 p.m., she was nervous.

Shawn stopped revving his truck. "Kids are coming."

Kevin, Kitty, and Teri clumped up the twisting back stairway. They bobbled into each other when Rita yanked open the door. Rainwater dripped off her drowned rats. Blobs of mud were slithering off their skinny limbs and plopped onto the wooden steps, making "mwok" sounds.

Rita, trying not to laugh, pointed her wooden spoon at Kevin, the instigator. "Stop," she ordered, "and where is your shirt?"

Kevin rubbed bits of slime off pretend sleeves. "Well. Look at that . . . must've lost it." He pulled the bottle bag from behind him. "Ta-daaa. Bottles, for deposit money. We went into the construction site and . . . neatened it up for all the guys."

"But why no shirt? Oh, I see, it's your shopping bag. Stay here and I'll bring towels. Take turns for showers, then wipe up this hall, then you eat."

"But, Ma, we're hungry," Kevin objected.

"Good. You'll be ready for Chinese."

Before they dried off and stripped down to underwear, Kevin snagged the first towel. He was still more modest than the girls. Kevin asked if there were hot dogs.

"No. Go shower." Rita put Shawn in his seat and poured six small glasses of milk.

Kitty asked if there were biscuits.

"No. Clean yourselves up."

"String beans?" Teri inquired, rubbing her scraped shoulder.

"No. Plenty of rice. We're starting without you. Hurry up."

When the girls joined the table, Kitty told some tale about tripping over a log and a skunk. Rita held her hand to stop her. "Oh, you all fell over one log?"

Kitty and Teri nodded in earnest unity.

Rita laughed, "No, you didn't."

"Uh-huh," Kitty pushed back, wide-eyed.

"No, Kitty, you didn't. You three have never stood still long enough or close enough to fall over the same log. How was the mud fight?" Laughing, she took a bite, "I bet you had fun."

"They showed promise, Ma, they showed some really good mud skills," Kevin slid into his seat and dug into the steaming food.

That night, Rita went to bed at 11:00 on her pull-out couch, knowing she wasn't keeping close enough tabs on her children. She woke with a little snore and glanced at her watch. It was 11:05. "Well, we're all home together, eating together, playing together. It's . . . almost peaceful," she whispered.

44

TAXI

The midnight trilling of the phone jostled her awake. Rita leapt up before anyone else awoke. There was never good news at this time of night. "Hello?"

"*Didja* read my letter?" Bob asked. "It's *unpolite*, impolite not to, not to respond. Responday a voo. And all that crap."

"Yes, I did." She shivered in the night air, listening to Bob dig himself an ever-bigger hole. "You sound drunk, Bob, and it's late. We can talk when you're sober. And not in the middle of the night."

"I'm *drinkin'* vodka *alone* in the dark," he said, "'*cause* of you."

She hung up, annoyed at being woken, saddened at his admission, but determined to fall back asleep. Sitting at the table the next evening, Rita was working on getting Teri and Noreen registered at Whiting Lane School, and Carol, Kitty, and Kevin enrolled at St. Brigid School, when the phone rang.

"Hi, uh, Rita." Bob sounded . . . timid. He probably wanted to apologize for his late call.

"Bob, how are we ever going to resolve anything if you're still drinking?"

"That's not why I'm calling." He coughed. "There's something else."

Rita choked when Bob said he'd lost his job at the store. "Why? How did you lose your job?" God, he should have bent over backward to keep that. It was all he had left of the good Bob. Pain seeped into her temples.

"There's not much work there," Bob mumbled.

"You can't . . . you can't be without a job." Rita's voice rose into the wall phone.

When Kitty came into the kitchen to see why Ma was panicking, she turned her body.

Kevin nudged Kitty. "What's going on?"

They stood still as Rita escalated, "You need a job. I can't tell you how close to the bone we are, eating lettuce sandwiches, brushing our teeth with baking soda, drinking powdered milk."

"I've got a job. Driving a cab. Night shift to start."

"What? You're *driving* a cab? A taxi . . . you're a *taxicab driver*? What kind of crazy job is that?"

"It pays good, Rita."

"I don't care how *good* it pays. Will you be able to give me money on time now?"

Bob raised his voice, "Just shut up, Rita. Why is nothing I do enough for you? So, I got a new job, big deal."

"Don't tell me to shut up, I'm losing my mind here."

Bob got belligerent. "Rita, calm the hell down. I'll have more cash, not waiting for a paycheck. Can you tell the children? Can you do that little thing for me?"

"*Little thing*? Why don't you tell them yourself? And why do they have to know?"

"I'll pick them up in the cab, sometimes, when I have to drive them, like a doctor's appointment."

"Why do I have to do your dirty work? I've already crawled to your creditors. Put kids' shoes on layaway. Made payment plans at the drugstore for baby aspirin."

Bob was silent. She heard him crack his knuckles. A clock clicked somewhere. She knew he had nothing left to say, or to give.

"Wait, wait. When I'm calm, yes, I'll tell them. Jeez. Yes, but I'm in shock. But are you still coming to babysit tomorrow evening? Remember, I'm taking the older ones downtown for school uniforms?" Rita needed him because the store was rarely open late.

He could, because his job wouldn't start for two days.

"Don't drink Bob, not before, and not while you're here." Rita slammed the phone. "What a horse's ass. That jerk. A taxi driver. I have no idea how to handle that man losing his job."

Kitty was sad for Ma. "I'll tell the others."

Rita blinked, wondering if Kitty should tell everyone. She should. "Go ahead." There was no way Rita could be generous explaining their father's new job.

Kitty went to perform her two roles: town crier and Ma's protector.

Kevin crossed to the table, sat in his chair, and tipped back, asking, "What's the matter with that? It's a job, Ma."

"A *taxicab* driver? It's tacky. It's trashy. You want to see your father driving around town in a Yellow Cab? He's gone from owner to employee to being kicked out of his own business. You want Dad getting you from school in a taxi?" Rita was so humiliated, so distraught, that she was telling Kevin stuff that she would never share, never tell a ten-year-old, but he was here in the kitchen, as she paced around.

"Why?" Kevin asked as he palmed an orange from the mostly empty fruit bowl.

"Why what? That he lost his job? Because he . . . he drinks too much," Rita got quieter. "You know that." She sat down at the table, crossed her legs and arms, then swirled her foot angrily.

"Yeah. He was a jerk to me when he was drunk. Member him when I fell out of the tree? Or broke something by mistake? Or when Bruno ran away? Dad took his . . . his drunk out on me. Can I eat this orange?"

"I think I knew that. You'd be amazed at what I hid from myself." Rita nodded about the orange, which he peeled in one long coil. "But I didn't want to believe it."

She put her elbows on the table, balled her hands into soft fists, and bumped them against her lips. "Did I wait too long to kick him out?" She cringed at what Kevin might say.

"Nah. It's better without him here. But. I'm gonna kick his butt someday, like when I weigh more than 70 pounds," he raised his eyebrows and flexed his muscles, "like Popeye the Sailor Man, and get help from my guy Bluto." Kevin laughed.

And finally, so did she. She laughed in solidarity, relieved that Kevin didn't blame her like Carol did.

"How does your father *babysit*?" Carol snickered hearing why Dad was coming over.

They were taking a bus adventure to G. Fox in Hartford to get their St. Brigid uniforms: green, gray, and mandatory. Rita had to borrow money from Aunt Rose. If Bob was any kind of father, provider, man, she would've asked him. She was glad the uniforms would eventually save time, laundry, and money. Rita was taking Father McBride's free tuition, which he bribed her with when demanding she stay married.

Well, she'd called his bluff.

Dad used the front stairs to the second-floor apartment, the first time to come inside since he helped them move in three weeks ago.

He held the door open as Kevin sprinted by. "Hi, Dad, 'bye Dad."

Carol and Kitty did the same.

But Teri noticed Ma was not smiling when she gave Dad instructions about bedtimes, like to a real babysitter, before she left.

Shawn and Noreen rushed to Dad, hugged his legs, and reached for the bag hidden behind his back. Teri greeted him too, but much more calmly, holding her Susan doll: someone to hang on to.

Dad smiled at his children. "I brought gifts."

He pulled out a giant Troll doll for Noreen. For Shawn, he growled a stuffed tiger out, and for Teri, a plastic Palomino horse, with removable saddle and reins. Dad slapped his knees, then left the room, calling out, "You kids play with your new toys."

Teri noticed what he hadn't. None of the toys could be played together.

She sat on the couch, brushed her horse's mane, and listened as her dad spoke on the kitchen phone.

"Yeah, but later tonight, I'm with my kids. I can meet you, but don't have all the money. Hey, doing the best I can. My wife, uh, my ex-wife, she's taking all my dough, you know? Out shopping." Dad snorted and fake-laughed.

Small bells went off in Teri's eight-year-old mind. First of all, her father bought gifts, when he owed Ma food money, and he owed someone else money, too. Who would get the money if he didn't have "all of it"? Her stomach churned, wondering who was more important than his children. They never had enough, not enough food, not enough warm clothes, no extra nothing, especially toys.

Secondly, Kitty told her Dad said "Shut up" to Ma on the phone when he lost his job. Her stomach squeezed randomly because she didn't trust her father. Teri turned a corner that night, setting her allegiance to her mother. It was a new, concrete feeling that was more than love. It was a trust, a sense of reliance that her mother would take care of them, even if their father wouldn't. If anything happened to Ma, Teri would untie from this earth and float ever so slowly away from all that was right and good. She needed to matter to her mother, to belong.

Ma never said it, but Teri felt her mother's love.

Rita returned at nine o'clock with three children resigned to show Dad ugly plaid items that turned them into Catholic school kids.

He said things like, "nice" and "sharp," then pocketed his keys to hurry to his engagement, whatever that meant.

Teri was in the bedroom next to the living room, on alert. When she heard Dad leave, and Ma locked the door, she allowed herself to fall asleep. Her family was home.

The first day of school was chaotic. Ma set out seven bowls, tiny orange juice glasses, spoons, a pitcher of bluish powdered milk, and cornflakes. Rita pushed Shawn's chair in and poured his cereal, then filled five thermoses with milk and laid out the cheese, turkey, and bread. "Make your own lunches. Take a piece of fruit."

"That's it? That's the choice for breakfast?" Carol asked. She had on a white blouse, pleated skirt, and green knee socks.

"Carol. Can you wake the twins? Oh! You look grown up. Where's the blazer?"

"I'll put it on at school. It's going to be a hot bike ride today. Kitty is already awake. Come on, Kev. We've got to ride together."

Rita tidied the kitchen while prepping her younger daughters, "Teri, you walk Noreen to school. It's a fifteen-minute walk, like we practiced. Noreen, honey, don't stop to pet caterpillars. Hold Teri's hand to cross the streets."

Later, Rita was anxious to hear about her children's new schools during supper.

Teri was eager to share. "Do you want the good news or the bad news first?"

Rita laughed, "That sounds like a tough start. I hope you all have good news."

"Well, I met a nice girl with freckles. But Mrs. Cave was mean because I didn't know all my times tables. She only called on the girls wearing pink or purple dresses."

"Oh, I don't believe that. You have something yellow or blue you can wear tomorrow. See what happens."

Noreen's little ponytail had wisped out of its elastic. Her nice teacher had given her a box of fat crayons.

"I'm in the *exact* same classroom as Kitty. I looked around at all the dumb-bells." Kevin cracked up.

Carol had a question for her mother, but it could wait until Sunday night, after the little ones went to bed.

The children fell asleep easily after that first day of school.

Rita wished she could too, but Bob's job weighed heavy on her mind.

45

BURNING

Ma fished a sliver out of Kevin's palm with a needle. She picked away while addressing Teri, "You have a dentist appointment tomorrow to fix your broken tooth. It's in Hartford and Daddy will get you from school at 2:30. I wrote a note. I ironed that brown dress with the lace collar."

Teri walked to the office, wearing the hated dress that made her look like a Pilgrim. She was nervous about the new dentist. Dad's outstretched hand and smile didn't help, until he promised they'd go to Petersen's for ice cream after. Now she had something to look forward to.

They waited in an echoey hall filled with people on rickety chairs. Stuffy heat waved out of radiators. A sign on the wall read: "Cash Only. One Cavity = One Dollar."

This place was for poor people, Teri thought, as she noted the children's shoes, *pat* and *leather*, like Kitty told her. Kids ran wild, like her family would act outside. Dad read a beat-up magazine. Teri sat on her hands, swinging her legs. She wasn't great at telling time, but the sun was going down, and the waiting room darkened.

Coming here was punishment for falling off her bike, for being eight. Saliva gathered in Teri's mouth and her stomach churned. Occasionally, she'd get a sharp pain of panic in her heart. Tears welled as she ran her tongue over the wrecked tooth for the hundredth time. Teri could live with a broken tooth.

She whispered, "Can you take me home? I don't like it here."

Dad knuckled her arm, saying, "It will be alright. I'll go in with you. Get rid of those monster teeth."

A tall, mean-looking lady marched in, perused a chart, and cranked out: "Teri, Linda, Jose, Denzel."

Dad stood to take Teri's quivering hand.

"Oh no, not you, sir. Just the patients. There are seven dentists and four chairs in that room." Mean Lady did not smile or say hello to Teri or listen to Dad, who cleared his throat to speak. She marched ahead of the children, expecting them to follow. Awaiting instructions, Teri stood rigid at the door to the next room.

"As I called you. Teri. Chair one. Linda. Chair two. And so on." She spit their names out, seemingly annoyed at children who had teeth.

Sitting in the big green chair, Teri rattled from head to feet, and tears rolled down her cheeks as she glanced at a tray of sharp, shiny tools. A pick, a hook, a knife, and a mirror, little weapons to attack her very tender mouth. Sweat ran from her armpits to her waist. An acned dental student clipped a beaded chain to an adult-sized paper bib and hung it around Teri's scrawny neck. No one spoke to her.

The kid in chair four started screaming, "Stop it, stop it."

The room was made of big blocks of brownstone, so the cries were amplified.

Teri gripped the vinyl chair arms, carving tiny moons with her fingernails. One novice dentist, then the next, looked into her mouth and talked about Teri as if she weren't there, trying to recreate the accident. She could have told them, she wasn't an idiot, but they were busy blowing painful shots of air on the raw cuts in her mouth, making her wince and pull her left shoulder back.

A busty lady in a white uniform squirted the jagged tooth edge with cold water, with her big breasts pushing against Teri's arm, to scrape away bits of her gums with those sharp tools. Shutting her eyes, Teri heard her brown leather shoes knock against each other. Even if the workers couldn't see her, couldn't they hear Teri rattle in pain and fear?

She squeezed her eyelids tight to pray the Hail Mary, which was answered when the adults stopped working to confer about her tooth.

On her return visit, they'd drill a hole in the shard of tooth left, insert some nail or spike, and hope for a good color match.

When the bib came off, Teri was as limp as her ragdoll Susan. She was upset by those meanies, all of them, with their hands in her mouth. The room smelled of blood and burnt teeth.

When she came out alone, in her wrinkled brown dress, her face was awash in tears. Daddy pulled her in for a big hug, and she hugged him back.

He whispered, "I'm sorry."

She whispered back, "I'm *thorry*, too."

He guided his sad little daughter to the truck. When Dad asked if she wanted a milkshake, Teri faced the window and shook her head no.

The last thing she wanted was something cold in her mouth.

Rita met them in the upper hall, where Teri slid by her at Kitty's beckoning. Teri's slumped shoulders and her tight latch on Kitty told Rita she should have been there.

Bob stood against the wall, crossing his arms.

"Is this the best . . . you can do? I mean . . . we can do? That place was a torture chamber. Did you see her face? This is what I'm talking about, Rita. How can you do this alone? No one was watching her on that bike. I have some ideas that I wrote down in a letter . . . let me help raise the kids. Please? Just read it."

What now? What wonderful solutions would Bob come up with? I wouldn't be doing this alone if he were sober and provided a steady income.

Watching him drive away, Rita thought, I don't need his ideas on how to raise my kids. He had twelve years to come up with ideas.

In Kitty's room, Teri knew she could talk and cry, and Kitty would just ask a million questions, but she interrupted with an excited, "Mootchie Gatchi Gu."

"What?" Teri asked.

"Mrs. Klune, who took care of Noreen last spring, remember her? Well, she works at Mattel, and gave us three bendable-knee Barbies with clothes and a doll case. Look." Kitty pulled her to the dresser. Each could be a stewardess, a teacher, or a nurse. Perfect jobs for young women. Teri would like to be a stewardess because her teacher was such a meanie.

Ma came in, glancing at Teri's mouth. "How do you like the new Barbies?"

"I *lofe* them." Teri put the TWA uniform on Barbie and forced the navy-blue stiletto heels onto her truncated feet. Then, she pinned on Barbie's little hat. "Look Ma. *Thee* even *hath* a hat."

Teri's mouth was swollen and streaked with dried saliva. Glad that she was distracted by the Barbies, Rita left to get a warm washcloth. She'd call the clinic to give them a piece of her mind and *would* go into the exam room with Teri the next visit.

She checked on the boys. Shawn was crashing some Lego buildings with oversized Tonka trucks.

Kevin, beating a life-sized ragdoll, snarked, "Take that, you dirty rat."

He had strapped her elasticized feet to his, so that when he knocked the doll over, he'd catch her before she hit the floor, to do it again.

"Kevin." Rita caught his arm.

He was short of breath from the altercation. "What?"

"That's Susan, Teri's favorite doll." Rita bent to free the doll's feet.

"So?"

"Well, you're hitting a . . . a girl, sort of, and it's Teri's. She's had a tough day. Go give it to her, please."

Rita pointed his way out.

Kevin sprang from his doorway, holding Susan, to a chair in the living room, then leapt to the couch, to Carol and Kitty's bedroom, hopping onto the nearest bed. The impact skewed the slats off the frame and the mattress dislodged with a crash.

Rita was haunted by Teri's experience, so she ignored Kevin's behavior. But the girls sprang from their Barbie convention on the floor and gaped at him.

Kevin quickly put the boards back. "Gotta fix this wagon train, little ladies, and oh, I saved this damsel in distress."

He had an infectious laugh, and the girls joined in, he was so TV-talk ridiculous. He offered Susan to Teri, who didn't care because she was dressing Barbie in a nurse's uniform.

Rita thought the kids were fine right now, playing together, and laughing. Teri was fine. Bob was just being judgmental. Or . . . was he right? She'd had enough of this day, and started bedtime routines, to rush it to its conclusion.

Rita got home from work the following day at her usual time, greeted her children, and dropped the mail left of the sink. The table had been set by Carol, Kitty had swept the floor, and Kevin was pedaling Carol's bike to Central Wheel, two miles away, for tubes for his flat tires. Rita and Kevin would fix them later that night. Who but Kevin flattens two tires at one time? Rita shook her head.

There were enough eggs, ham, and bits of cheese to make an omelet, and she'd deep fry potato slices. Rita took the bread-box-sized fryer from the pantry, plunked it on the one foot of counter space right of the sink, added oil, and turned it on high. Rita peeled the spuds, dropping the spirals onto the newspaper. A few splatters of oil singed her arm, causing her to hold it under running water. She looked around as it cooled. She missed her modern kitchen: this one didn't even have an exhaust fan. Another reminder of all she had given up. Rita tossed the salted slices into the mesh basket and lowered them into the sizzling vat. She returned to the stove to break the eggs.

Dinner done meant dishes to the sink. Because that area was so crowded, Rita put the deep fryer on the floor to cool and put its lid back on. Carol washed the pans, a few others lingered, and Shawn got down to walk around. He retrieved a Matchbox car on the floor and sat down on a nice silver seat to play.

"Yeeow! Yeeow!" An ear-splitting cry of pain made her jump up, knocking her chair over. Who was that? Rita scanned the room and looked down just as three-year-old Shawn tried to get off his hot fryer stool.

She had to rip him up, smelling his flesh burn, tearing his skin. She carried him . . . where? where? A few short steps, thinking, thinking, thinking what to do. Shawn was screaming in pain, twisting the fabric of her housecoat, and her skin underneath.

Holding onto his shorts and shirt, Rita pivoted. "Carol, get ice. Kevin, strip Shawn's bed. Put those things on the couch."

Kevin tore his brother's bed apart, put the sheets on the couch, and on top of that, the rubber pad.

Rita called for a pair of scissors, which Kitty got from the sewing basket. Rita now gently coaxed Shawn face down onto the covered couch, and carefully cut his shorts and underwear off, all that had seared his buttocks and legs.

Carol brought the ice and Rita placed bits of it over Shawn's red, welted legs. He continued to wail in pain.

Keep your head, Rita, slow your breathing. You can't cry now. "Kitty and Teri, go get ice from Mrs. Santos. Ask the neighbors upstairs for ice also. Carol, please bring me baby aspirin and washcloths, then call Dr. Saunders. What Noreen? Yes, honey, he will be fine. Kevin, take her out of here, play a game or something."

Carol was efficient in relaying the burn accident to the doctor and also with his reply: wrap the ice in cloth before cooling his skin and make Shawn drink water.

Rita gave all her attention, love, and hope to Shawn. She moved the ice around, cooed and patted his head, wiped his tears, even sang Kieran's song, "A Mother's Love is a Blessing." She cried while gently singing, and as each child came back from his or her job, they cried too. That night, Rita slept on the couch behind Shawn, her body a "C," protecting him with comfort, care, and convalescence.

They were in a puddle of urine and water the next morning. The rubber mat had formed a well. They smelled bad, but Shawn was better. The back of his little legs and bottom had red corduroy welts, but no blisters or oozing, which would have required a hospital visit. Rita laid her hand on his forehead for a fever check and kissed his cheeks.

Kitty watched Shawn while Rita showered. She dressed him in one of Kevin's big white tee shirts, then told Shawn a story—she was a creative storyteller, talking about Tee-Tee who lived underground and sucked on potatoes.

Shawn smiled his little-teeth smile.

Rita brought Shawn a bowl of Cheerios. Lying on his side, he whispered, "Thanks, Mommy."

Shawn was waited on, played with, read to, and ate food in the living room all day. Kevin watched cartoons with him and changed the channel whenever Shawn wanted.

That morning unfolded with Rita, like Carol, hating this apartment. Between Teri's tooth and Shawn's burns, and the fact that she hadn't fixed Kevin's bike, maybe she couldn't do this, raise these kids, on her own. Who did she think she was? Rita scrubbed the deep fryer with fierce, jamming motions, and then noticed the mail on the counter.

Bob's letter was among the bills.

Late that night, Rita sat at the table with a cup of tea, perusing its six pages. It had no salutation, no date.

Bob opened well: *"I feel as though I might be able to communicate with you by writing, rather than talking to you. Somehow your thinking is muddled. A few years ago, I told you that if God put you on this earth for any reason, it was to be a mother."*

Rita sipped her tea. Well, not this week.

"I think you are confused. You didn't really think about asking me to leave our home, what that would mean to the family. I had nowhere to go. I have no intention of not being a father to our six children. You think I don't know I have faults, but I do, and you do too, and I'm done apologizing."

Rita rested back in her chair. My faults? Oh, that I'm quick to judge others, or can be sarcastic? I know my faults, Bob, but mine don't destroy people.

"Stop making me out to be the only bad guy, 'the bastard,' based on what you tell our friends, who, by the way, were shocked when we split up, and were probably tired of helping you out."

Nobody would have needed to help me, Bob, if you had. You were dependable in one way: your unreliability. I couldn't rely on your sobriety, wages, or temper.

"I thought I was the luckiest guy in the world when we got married. Remember how we met? You were standing on your father's porch with your sisters. All I could see was you. We needed each other, two insecure teenagers. Then the babies started coming, and it wasn't easy, but it was good. Maybe we could find each other again, especially now that our children need both of us so much."

She rubbed her forehead at this fairy tale. Her life hadn't been good for a long, long time.

"When I left the house, I didn't know what to do or where to go or how to help myself. But I have had plenty of time to think. What is a family? It is a mother and a father raising their children, in God. Our children love us for who we are and what we stand for. Don't walk with false pride. As for myself, this life is horrible, I have never known such pain as bad as this heartache, which is with me constantly. I will always love you, Rita. I love Carol, Kevin, Kitty, Teri, Noreen, and Shawn. I long to be loved, and to express my love. Let me be here for you all, p lease. Bob"

Rita sat, glancing around the quiet, ugly kitchen. The stove light made it possible to see her pitiful reflection in the darkened window. She'd bartered Carol's much-loved desk for a swimsuit. Because Rita hired a babysitter for only one child, when she had six, Teri had ruined her teeth. Her baby, Shawn, had burned skin because Rita had been too careless with a hot appliance.

And that was just half of her children.

Rita lowered her forehead onto her open palms, twined her fingers into her hair, and her shoulders quaked. Rita was not being a good mother. She could not do this, raise these children alone.

46

VOICES

TWA stewardesses wore crisp blue uniforms emblazoned with golden wings right above the heart, hats perched just so. Rita worked demurely in the galley. A light flashed on, telling her to see what a passenger needed. The stewardesses were trained to remain calm at all times, but also to use their voices effectively and their bodies efficiently. It was the guy in Row 35, Seat B, again.

"Yes, sir, what can I get you?" She already knew: a Manhattan, two cherries; his third. She reached over the fellow in Seat A to retrieve Seat B's glass. 35 B grabbed her wrist as she reached.

"Please let me help you. Let me go home with you. I can help. You won't have to ask your friends for babysitting or rides or money." His brown eyes were pooling with tears, his bourbon breath warm on her face, but his grip was tightening, becoming painful. Rita quickly took his drink away with her right hand, to put a hold on his neck with her left.

"You're hurting me," 35 B sputtered, his eyes locked on hers.

"I don't mean to hurt you, sir," she tightened her grip, fingernails ready to puncture skin, "but you have to stop calling for me, you need to stop asking for things. There are other people on this plane who need me."

He loosened his grip on her wrist, dropping his hands to twist his wedding band.

The passenger in 35 A morphed into Aunt Rose. She patted his knee. "You need to go home now, Bobby, you go home. Leave Rita be. Ah, she can do this without you."

Rita woke from her crazy dream. "Why . . . why would I . . . choke someone?"

Her eyes darted around the room for answers, and slick with sweat, her heart galloped. Light was sniffing through the windows. She peeled off her covers, and as the corners of the room revealed themselves, furniture took shape. Her cotton nightgown was damp.

She'd had a nightmare, but why? This was her bed, the pull-out couch. Her room, the living room. Her apartment. Her children.

Rita checked on each of them. Carol snored gently. Noreen slept with a Troll doll. Teri had climbed into bed with Kitty, scared of the night, their Barbies with them. Something nagged at Rita. Kevin, in the top bunk, had kicked his blanket off. Shawn, as usual, had wet the bed. His bedwetting had started when the kids had been split up, but revisiting that would be a bad dream for another time. Rita gently persuaded the sleepy toddler into the bathroom. She changed his pajamas as he swayed, then led him to her bed, where he could finish his night.

Somebody needed something in the dream. She took a shower, careful not to dampen the hairnet that held curlers in place. Resting near Shawn, she rubbed circles on his back, mostly to calm herself.

In Bob's letter, he'd asked to come back to help raise the children. Maybe she couldn't raise all these kids alone. She wasn't doing so well. Trying to get back to sleep, Rita turned the idea over and over, like a stone, retracing her life to look for the cracks.

Bob had good qualities. She used to love draping her legs over his on the couch on a Friday night or eating fried clams at the beach as their children played in the sand. Bringing him an iced tea when he mowed the lawn. Laughing at his stories, which were told with exaggerations, accents, eyebrows, imitations, and sound effects. When he hugged, kissed, and whispered in her ear, even last spring, she knew that he loved her.

Now, Bob asked for Rita to take him back, let them lean on each other again. Raise the children together. When Rita realized that Bob wasn't a good enough father, that was the biggest problem. And that was fueled by alcohol. She started to build her tough, outer layers then, because her core, her heart and soul, deeply scarred, couldn't do the hard work of letting him go alone. She wouldn't have ended their marriage if he had stopped drinking. He'd choked her, scared her, threatened her, which he would never do if he had stopped drinking. He'd squandered all of their money, which wouldn't have happened if he had stopped drinking.

Rita was not going to take Bob back.

She'd ask less of friends and more of her kids. They would meld and flourish. Although her dreams were dashed, her children could craft their own relationships with their dad. She'd use the church for her children's benefit and keep some of its useful traditions.

Rita chided herself for thinking she hadn't gotten far in the last six months. Since May, Rita found a job, bought a car, rented an apartment, gathered her children back, and kept ownership of their home on Exeter Avenue, into which one day they would move back.

Cuddling Shawn, Rita felt small, young, alone, poor, and guilty about her children being unsupervised, and bicycle tires that were left unfixed. Rita had to postpone healing her own broken heart. She had work to do, to care for her children and get out of debt to reclaim their home. And finally, to raise good people.

Aunt Rose said something important in the dream, about telling Bob to go home and let Rita do this without him. That was the message. God, you put me here to be a mother. Let me do this without him.

47

SCHOOL

Rita liked Sunday nights. Church and their day trip with Bob were over. They ate spaghetti with homemade sauce. She let the big kids watch TV later because they needed more of her time.

Carol had held a question since the first day of school, two weeks earlier. During a commercial, she remembered it.

Pulling her legs beneath her on the couch. She asked, "Ma, what does 'fuck' mean?"

Rita stopped ironing clothes and slapped her face. "Never say that. That's a sin."

Carol, stunned, rubbed her cheek. "What? What did I say?"

Kevin whipped around. "What did I miss?"

Kitty went wide-eyed. "Ma! Mommy, don't hit her for asking a question. Kids swear at that school."

Rita banged the iron around Kevin's shirt collar. She had never used that term. To hear it in her own home was . . . what? Embarrassing? Alarming? They needed to talk about . . . stuff. Rita unplugged the iron.

"Move over." She sat between Carol and Kitty.

Kevin lolled in the rocking chair, but he was looking at her. "Kevin, turn the TV off. Carol, what made you ask that?"

"On the first day of school, I was the new girl, and I thought, 'I'm looking good.' I rolled my waistband to shorten my hemline, like the other girls." Carol peeked at Rita.

"Go on."

"So, I was kind of happy in the cafeteria, for what I thought was a compliment. Three guys did some low whistling and hand gestures while leaning against a wall. One of them said, 'I'd like to fuck that.'"

"Who said that?" Kevin wanted to know.

Rita frowned at him.

"His buddy laughed like an idiot and told him he's full of shit and he'd be happy to hump a bra."

Kevin and Kitty hooted.

"I know," Carol smiled at them, "I thought it was funny, too. I just walked out, with my new friend, Roxanne."

"This is in sixth grade? Where were the nuns?" Rita asked.

"I don't know. Around. So, what does it mean?"

Rita went into a long explanation of love, longing, sexual desire, marriage, intercourse, and sometimes, the miracle of a baby. But, also how a baby can be a disaster for young people who engage in sex without knowing about birth control, which was not discussed in the Catholic Church.

Rita thought back to her own teenage pregnancy. The big kids had lots of questions. Rita answered them all, really stressing the waiting part. Carol asked if she and Dad had done this before they were married. Rita wasn't going to lie. "Yes, but we were *getting* married."

Kitty wanted to know how many times? Was it six?

No, many times. Rita answered.

Kevin wanted to know why, why have sex?

Rita let a nice memory wash over her. "It can be lovely. Very gentle, two people, very close . . . alone together . . . for a short while."

Carol asked, "But is it fun?"

Rita reined in a smile. "Yes."

Just then, Teri walked in from her bedroom, faking a yawn, and sat on a stool.

Rita cleared her throat, having been very explicit. "Did you hear all of this? How long have you been awake?"

"Since you turned the TV off."

Her siblings choked down their guffaws, waiting for Rita's response.

She shrugged. "Teri, you just became a big kid."

Kevin, Carol, and Kitty rode their bikes three miles to school each day. Kevin brought up their recent subject. "It's good we know about sex and stuff. St. Brigid's is a tougher school, and the kids are cooler."

Carol nodded. "Their parents picked Catholic school, but kids don't want to be seen as goody-two-shoes, so they act tough."

At the light, Kitty agreed, "Yeah, we gotta be cooler to fit in. I saw Roxanne in Go-Go boots at church."

"That's what I'm talking about." Kevin took off, trying to jump a curb with his fixed tires, but his bike was too heavy.

Kevin got in fights with . . . well . . . everyone. Then he became friends with his victims, especially if they clobbered him like Steve Langan or Billy Rhodes did.

Almost every student, even the poorer ones, had cash and bought hot lunches. The Leonards had to make their sandwiches and reuse their baggies and twist-ties. After eating, Kevin, embarrassed, folded his collection of junk tight enough to fit in his back pocket. He hid his thermos under the stairs to get later.

One fine fall day, fourth graders Kevin and Billy were clearing out their table when two sixth graders abruptly sat down.

"Hey. Cheapskate." The chubby kid's neck was pinched by his clip-on tie. He elbowed his buddy, one of the Fucci brothers, who laughed, but was busy arranging his hot dog, Hostess fruit pie, and milk on his tray. Fucci told Kevin to move. "Yeah, yeah, penny pincher fourth grader with a bad haircut. Shove off."

All the boys glanced at each other before Kevin grabbed the pie and ran for the exit. Fucci sprang up to chase Kevin, who blew by the door, twirled around the support pole, verbally screeching his brakes. He took a bite of pie. For his parting move, Kevin stood stock still, put a visual bead on his opponent, and hurled that dripping dessert right at Fucci's white shirt. Kids were standing and clapping, "Fight, Fight."

Kevin and Billy strode the stairs two at a time. Billy escaped to the asphalt recess area.

Kevin bolted to the second level and sprinted down the hall, but Fucci was right on him, their ties flagging behind them.

Sister Monica swished out of her classroom and clapped her hands, as if that would stop them.

Kevin yelled out, "Sorry, Sister."

He was getting a little scared and winded as he headed down a level, where Mother Superior and beefy Sister Agnes made a roadblock by holding hands.

Kevin skidded to a stop in his Hush Puppies, and Fucci crashed into him. The nun guided Kevin by his neck to the cinderblock wall and Mother Superior moved Fucci across. Both boys were sweaty and breathing hard. Panting, they eyed each other, chins up. Sister Agnes suggested that two fellows with their speed might consider playing football or baseball, but tussling was not allowed. Kevin and Fucci held in laughs about 'tussling.'

Mother Superior hid her hands in deep pockets, clicking her rosary beads. "Convent, after school for detention. Bring your homework." She walked away with expected compliance.

Kevin looked up from his shoes with a sideways smile on his face.

"You're dead, kid," Fucci snarled, "and I got brothers."

This challenge was kinda fun, Kevin thought. "First, you gotta catch me, Pie-Boy."

48

SLEEPOVER

K evin was off the couch, zipping the five feet to answer the phone by the second ring. "Pete's Pizza Palace."

His dad laughed. "You turkey. What're you doing?"

"Nothing much. Homework about the first Thanksgiving. We're waiting for supper, but Ma's teaching Carol how to make a lemon *marangay* pie, with the fluffy spikes that get browned."

Bob chuckled. "Ah, I think it's called lemon *meringue*. Hey, do you want to sleep over Friday night?"

Kevin crinkled his eyes picturing Dad's tiny apartment, watching boring baseball on a TV the size of a cat door. "Nah, I'm going to my new friend's house. He's got a pool table. I'll get Ma."

Rita, measuring flour, heard Kevin turn Bob down. She knocked the white dust off her hands and rubbed them down her apron, taking the receiver from Kevin, who backed away.

As he did, he mouthed, "No, no, no."

"Hello, Bob."

Bob was cordial, "Are you making Carol into Betty Crocker? You always did make a good pie. Look, I thought Kevin could sleep here Friday night?"

Rita noticed Kevin boldly breaking a rule by straddling the arm of the couch. He made gagging sounds, sliced a finger across his throat, pantomimed tying a noose around his neck, and slid to the floor with a dramatic seizure.

She had to turn her back to keep from laughing, but managed to get out, "No, Bob. He's going to Billy Rhodes' house. They have all sorts of games in a TV room."

"Can't fault Kevin for that." He sounded disappointed. "How about Carol?"

Rita cradled the phone under her jaw, cranking open a can of Crisco shortening. "Bob, what's with this new idea of sleepovers?"

He snorted. "Um . . . when I wrote that letter, that I wanted to help? That I never intended to walk away from my kids . . . and you wrote back . . . nothing. Figured I'd do it, too. Be a parent, at my place. And I *do* have a job, even if it's not the *same* job."

"Oh, don't get all maudlin on me. We should talk soon. Hold on. Carol, get the big mixing bowl from the pantry. Then get Noreen out of the tub. Bob, if someone wants to go to your apartment Friday, they can. It's better if you take two of them, so they can play Barbies or Legos."

Bob lit a cigarette, exhaling into the phone. "Alright, how about Carol and Kitty?" Bob clicked his lighter open and shut, twice. The butane smell always calmed him.

Knowing an older child and a younger one would be better, Rita said, "How about Carol and Teri?" Carol nodded her head as she rolled out the pie crust. Before they hung up, Rita raised her voice to get his attention because he was sounding chipper again. "They'll need supper, and they can sleep on the extra daybed. And here's the big one . . . "

When Carol left the room to get Noreen, Rita became more forceful. "You can't drink. At all. Got it?"

"Don't insult me. I know that."

Rita dug in, "I mean it. And you were late with child support last week. I need it *all* this week, Saturday at the latest. I told you Shawn needs glasses."

When Rita hung up, Carol pulled the stopper out of the tub, and the water gurgled out noisily.

Rita drove to Bob's, where Carol slid out with her banged-up suitcase, and chirped, "Goodbye."

Teri gave an unenthusiastic "Mootchi Gatchi Gu" to Kitty.

Rita frowned, just now realizing Teri didn't want to spend time with her father.

Their evening started at Silver Lane Bowling. Bob jiggled his leg and slid a cigarette in and out of its pack as he kept score. He was embarrassed by his daughters' bouncing gutter balls, and those that stopped mid-lane. They looked disheveled, too. Couldn't Teri have brushed her hair? Were Carol's pants too short, or was that the fashion?

Bob had them practice while he went to the neon-blazed bar to get them ginger ales. Bob quaffed a rocks' glass of vodka, then ordered the sodas and two Schaefer beers, which he pounded down, because the sign said, "When You're Having More Than One." Bob carried the sodas to their vinyl bench and threw the girls packs of peanuts.

Teri and Carol exchanged glances. Carol touched her father's sleeve, "Let's go, Dad. We're hungry."

He felt calmer, in a better mood, "No, sit a minute, eat your peanuts . . . play a few more games, I'll show you how to . . . stand straight to start, Carol."

"I never liked peanuts. You go pay, Dad, and Teri and I will get our shoes."

Teri and Carol put on their sweaters.

Bob zipped his baseball jacket and put on his cap. On the way to pay, he snapped at the bartender and held two fingers, a signal for a double shot. Screw Rita. Telling him about not drinking. Shit, it was Friday night. He wanted to have fun with his daughters. While they tied their shoes, Bob drank the odorless vodka and left a good tip.

Bob drove to a grocery store and told the girls to get Swanson TV Dinners, Cocoa Puffs, and a quart of milk: stuff Rita never bought. Bob pushed Marlboros, Beechnut gum, and a six-pack of Budweiser onto the conveyor belt.

Carol glared at him, but he pretended not to notice.

At his apartment, Teri watched Dad walk upstairs like their badly thrown bowling balls, his shoulders hitting the walls, and stopping to fumble for his keys. Unease moved up Teri's spine.

The door opened to his living room, kitchenette, and bathroom. It was sparsely furnished, ugly, and smelled of cigarettes. Stumbling, Bob sat down hard on the daybed, "Whoosh, long day driving schmucks. Carol, start the *hoven*. Three-fifty, four *hunert*, takes a lock . . . a long time for them to bake. Oh, I forgot, you know all about baking, Miss Lemon-Meringue-Pie. Smarty pants."

"Don't be mean, Dad. I'm learning to bake from Ma," Carol answered. "And don't tell me what to do." Carol turned knobs and pulled foil trays from cardboard boxes.

Teri poked the top with a fork to uncover the cherry cobbler desserts.

Bob swished his hand in front of his face, "Don't mean nothin'. Teri, get me that ashtray by the sink. And matches." He pawed around the TV tray for a can opener and pulled a cold tallboy from the bag.

Teri wrinkled her nose at the overflowing ashtray. She dumped the butts into the trash and rinsed it before approaching Dad.

"Well, hello there, Terry and the Pirates. That's comic-strip talk, before your time." When he patted the seat next to him, she shook her head, retreating to the kitchen.

"What's, what's the matter, girls?" They stood as far from him as possible in the 400-foot space. He had difficulty lighting a cigarette, then waved the match out searching for the ashtray. He raised his eyebrows at them, as if still waiting, "Where's that ash . . . "

Carol looked out of the kitchenette pass-through, "Teri gave it to you, Dad, on the TV tray at your elbow."

Bob stood up, making his dark eyebrows into a V, but sat down when he saw the clean ashtray.

Carol rolled her eyes at Teri.

"Teri. Teri Rita, come sit by your old man."

Bob blew a series of smoke rings as Teri snailed her way into the room and sat across from him on a straight-backed chair against the far wall, clearly defying him. He was drunk.

Scared, Teri bit her lip, pressing her arms tight to her body.

Carol paused when she heard her father whining into the falling darkness, "Why don't you like me, Teri? I like you. Your mother says I'm a . . . no good. What does she say? She hates me. When her mother died, she lost her marbles, became all bossy and shit. I mean stuff."

He took a swig of beer and mashed out his cigarette. Dad's voice pitched higher as he began to cry. "Could you please . . . sit with me?"

Teri got up to stand against the wall, holding her breath.

Carol came out of the kitchen with a towel on her shoulder. "Daddy, leave her alone. She's afraid of you right now. And don't say bad things about Ma. She doesn't say bad stuff about you." Carol started across the room, with her palms up, "Besides, you still have me."

"No!" He shouted, "I don't want you. I want her." Teri jerked her head around to see Carol's response.

Carol double gasped. Stopped approaching. Clapped a hand over her mouth momentarily, then reasoned, "I'm your . . . Dad, since I was little. We're alike."

"So?" Dad coughed. "You're not . . . Teri, she's like her mom, cold, stuck up . . . aloop? Is that . . . is that a word?"

Teri blended into shadows, invisible. The blood pounded in her ears, as her eyes flitted from Dad to Carol. He rolled onto his back, then curled in, facing the wall, sniffling. Carol stood frozen in the middle of the room, until he breathed jagged breaths, then choppily snored.

She dropped her arms and head. "I'm leaving Dad where he is, not throwing a blanket over him, or clearing his ashtray, all the normal stuff. I wanted to show Dad that he and I are still a team, even if he is driving a Yellow Cab for a job."

"I'm sorry he yelled at you. But *I don't like him*," Teri moused out.

Carol led her to the microscopic kitchen to sit on rickety chairs. "Dad walked me to kindergarten and swung me around on the lawn, gave me quarters and candy. Now, he wants you to be his favorite."

"No. No. I don't want to be Dad's favorite. I don't even want him to notice me. I'm never coming here again."

In the kitchen, the sisters held shaking hands until their breathing returned to normal. Carol needed one hand to hold her chin, as a slow parade of tears rolled down her cheeks.

Teri sat quietly. Her queasy stomach was hungry.

Dad snorted and rolled over. When he settled, Teri poured big glasses of real, not powdered, milk. She whispered, "Do we call Ma? To come get us?"

Carol pressed her eyelids. "Oh, Teri, we can't call Ma."

"Because of our code not to worry her?"

Carol smiled a bit. "No, because the little kids are sleeping. I'll tell her tomorrow. He'll sleep like the dead. I wish he was . . . dead. You know what it's like to be the oldest, with a . . . a father like him? And a dictator mother?"

Teri was confused. "No?"

Carol wiped her hands on the dish towel, "You wouldn't because you're the fourth kid, Kitty and Kevin and me, we've already tested the rules. Ma doesn't ask us to do something, she *tells* us. I thought I was special to Dad, I protected him from Ma. But he's . . . a . . . drunk."

A few tears slid from Teri's eyes. "I'm sorry I didn't sit with him. For you."

Carol shut off the timer. "Don't be, he's not worth it." She took the trays out of the oven. All the meat was underdone, and the desserts were burnt. "This is such crap."

Teri scraped gray gravy off her steak. "What? This food?"

"Yeah . . . all of this. This crap apartment, this crap food . . . and our crap dad."

Teri told Carol she could swear. "Kevin does, when he's mad or hurt."

"Yeah, how about *asswipe*? Our father is an asswipe." Both girls snickered soundlessly, careful not to wake the sleeping gorilla. "You try it, Teri. Then we'll throw this *shit* in the garbage and eat Cocoa Puffs."

"Yeah, the *damn* . . . what's next? Oh, Uncle Mac says, 'Jesus Christ God damn.'"

Carol low-hooted behind her hand. "We can't say *that*, but it's a good one. Sh-sh."

They called Ma at first light, sure Dad was sleeping, with his eyes shut and mouth open. Teri packed a paper bag with everything they didn't eat. Carol threw in a can opener, a pack of matches, and three dollars she found in a jar.

The Rambler beeped outside, and they ran down the stairs, noisily and fast, as escaping children do, flicking bits of paint off the steps.

Rita stood on the tiny lawn with fisted hands. "Are you hurt? Because I will march right up there and use any pot or pan and smash—"

Carol responded, "Ma, we're fine. I'll tell you at home."

Teri slid into the back, shoving the little kids over. "Go, Ma. Before Dad wakes up."

Carol slumped against the door with her arms crossed.

Teri noticed Carol's face looked like Ma's when she was angry, not even fiddling with the radio until Lesley Gore sang "You Don't Own Me." Only then did Carol blast the volume and sing along in her clear, determined voice.

49

SCHISM

Rita made tea and toast for Teri and Carol after their sorry night. Teri ate fast to be with the others, to watch Saturday cartoons. Carol, visibly crushed by her father's repudiation, stirred sugar into her tea.

"Ma, I stole these things. I wanted to make his bad habits harder to do." Carol pulled the can opener, matches, and money from her dungarees' pockets. "Let him suffer. If you're gonna say stealing is a sin, I don't care, some of those 'sins' are ridiculous."

Carol hit his drinking, smoking, and gambling vices hard.

Rita liked that. "Sometimes sins are justified."

"Ma, he drank at the bowling alley, and he bought beers at the store. He scared us. Mostly Teri."

Bile built at the back of Rita's throat, at her daughters' distress. "I'm listening."

"I'm telling you this, Ma, because . . . don't let the other kids sleep there. He drinks too much and should only see us with you."

"What would make you feel better?"

Carol smeared a tear off her cheek. "A record player. I want to listen to The Beatles or Gladys Knight and the Pips alone in my room. I don't even know what a 'pip' is."

Rita tread lightly. "I think . . . a 'pip' is annoying, but likable, like Kevin. How can any of us ever be alone in these five rooms with seven people? What do you want that I can do? Today?"

Carol pulled her legs onto her chair. "Any money I get from Dad goes to everyone. He'll forget the things he said, so he'll still give me candy and money, and I'll share it."

"But what about this . . . stolen loot?" Rita pointed at the money and they both giggled.

Carol picked up the bills. "Today let's go to Howdy Beefburger. We've never been."

"Sure, and I'll add money from the kitty." Rita took the coffee can from a shelf, then raised her voice, "Kitty get the other kids to come in here, would you? You might have to turn off—"

The TV was cut off before Rita finished her request, and the family assembled. "Carol has some money, and we'll go to Howdy Beefburger for supper today."

They all whooped, and Kevin yelped, "Can we eat in the car? Can we go now?"

Carol, the oldest, most vocal, and the richest, had power. "No, we'll go for supper. Also, there's no more sleepovers at Dad's. Teri and I went, and it wasn't fun."

Rita mixed a stiff drink of baking soda and water to fight her nausea, awaiting Bob's call.

Bob telephoned when he swam out of his vodka-and-beer haze around noon. His daughters were gone, and his kitchen was neat. The phone rang and rang, rare with a family that large. He tried again at one. Finally, at around two o'clock, Rita answered the phone.

"Hello? Oh, it's you Bob. We've been outside, all together. What do you want? Oh, I bet you want me to pick up money, since I've already collected my daughters."

Bob ran a hand over his mouth and chin. He needed a shave. He was sitting in the spot where he passed out the night before, shoes thrown out in front of him, ashtray, and beer cans painful reminders of . . . what? He couldn't remember.

"Is she alright? I mean, are Carol and Teri alright?"

"In what sense, Bob? Are they safe? They have been since this morning. Teri was afraid last night, and Carol was angry. Is that 'alright'? You got drunk. You cried and carried—"

"Jesus Christ. You can be such a bitch. I made a mistake." Bob's temples pulsed, remembering the bowling alley. "Can you put Carol on the phone?"

His trashy words shouldn't surprise her anymore. "She's outside. I'll get her, but I'll be right here, listening."

Rita called down to the yard, "Dad's on the phone, Carol, for you . . . no? You sure?"

Carol didn't want to talk to him. Bob gasped, then got silent.

Rita took the lead. "Hey, Bob, yes, I can be a 'bitch' as you said, but I'd prefer a better word like, say, 'parent.' We'll stop by your apartment for child support money, cash, I hope, because the banks are closed now. I'll send Kitty and Kevin in. And lastly, there will be no more sleepovers. Are we clear?"

Bob coughed, found his voice, "You're not the only parent here, Rita. I can see the kids whenever I want . . . we agreed on that. And yes, I'll think of a new name for you, like 'shrew' or 'viper.' Will those do? Does that work? Sure, hell, send two or three more kids for me to poison."

When she didn't respond right away, Bob knew she was forming her vindictive response. He swallowed hard and flicked his cigarette ash. He'd screwed up badly this time.

Her breathing was the only sound until Rita spoke in a low, calm voice. "*I am* the legal custodial parent, Bob. *I do* decide where they'll sleep at night. So, let's be civil and keep child visits to daylight hours, or evenings in my presence. Or you take them to a place with no alcohol, like a movie or mini golf. Not a restaurant, not a bowling alley, not a dive bar with your friends."

"You are pissing me off, Rita." Bob growled, then hurled something across the room where it shattered, "That ashtray was your face smashing into a wall."

When Rita heard that projectile shatter, she visualized the black and brown confetti of loose tobacco drifting to the floor. She knew not to push against an angry Bob, because he got dangerous.

Well, she was angry, too. His term for her, viper, would be welcomed, because Rita could unleash the venomous vocabulary that coursed through her head and heart whenever he hurt one of them. Rita controlled her anger. Her emotions needed to be tamped down, her quick tongue, cruel plans for revenge, had to lie dormant.

"I don't mean to hurt you." She breathed in and out, remembering her dream, and tried to switch to a conciliatory tone. "I'm thinking of safety here, for the children's sake. I'll stop by later today, and give us both a chance to cool down. I'll beep and you watch for the twins."

Bob parried, "Anything else, my queen? Yes, I'll be here, it's cash. But don't you come up . . . I don't think I can stomach that. And let's leave it at this: you go to hell."

Rita burnt up anger that afternoon by taking apart her vacuum cleaner when it wheezed to a stop. She got on all fours, unscrewed the plate with a butter knife, and pulled its guts out. She knocked the bag against a metal garbage can in the backyard, to dump its matted collection of dust, hair, and dirt. With the bag reattached, it purred like a kitten.

At 4:30, Rita gathered the kids in the Rambler to get the money. Kitty and Kevin ran inside, while Teri and Carol ducked down in the back seat.

Then it was off to Howdy Beefburger for a festive supper. Rita ordered 14 cheeseburgers, at 18 cents each, seven bags of fries, three milkshakes to split, and one black coffee.

Kevin scarfed both his burgers, turned from the front seat, appealing to Noreen, who was scraping everything off her first one, making a mess. "Hey, Noreen, you gonna eat that other one? Cause I'll take it off your hands."

"Shove off, Kevin," Kitty interjected, pushing his hand away.

Noreen smooshed the white bun into the flat patty and stuffed part of it into her mouth, "Yeah, Kevin, you," she took another bite, "shove" one more chunk, "off."

Kevin turned back to the front seat, bucked his front teeth out, jammed two French fries up his nose, then swiveled around to ask Shawn the same question.

Just to be a pip.

50

SANTA

A t Christmastime Rita was broke and her children knew it. She couldn't shake her malaise, and the gray skies and dirty snow didn't help. The holiday aloneness got to her, and she was short-tempered. On December fifteenth, her boss Elizabeth personally handed Rita a paycheck. "Open it."

Rita had gotten a raise. She skipped a quick breath.

This was a joy, this show of confidence in her work. Twenty-five cents an hour increase, which totaled ten dollars a week, forty dollars a month. Enough for a gift for each child. After Christmas, it meant more food and putting a few dollars away.

"Did you do this?" Rita asked, giddy.

Elizabeth laughed, "No, *you* did it. I just put in the paperwork. Come to my office after lunch. I just got a great idea."

Rita sat as Elizabeth shut her door. "As you probably know, the community makes holiday donations to us, as the Children's Village is nonprofit. I don't want to be presumptuous, but if your children could use some of the items we have received, most are new . . . some gently used . . . would you like to . . . "

"I'm sure we could, but I don't want to take away from less fortunate children."

Elizabeth checked the ledger with Rita's new wages. "I know *exactly* how much money you make, remember? Believe me, you are well below our income level for assistance, and you wouldn't be harming our children here. There are tables full of donations. Say, three items for each of your kids?"

Rita closed her eyes, as if in prayer, for a second. "Yes."

"Wonderful. I'll have Art Keyser show you where we store items. Also, Rita, find a gift for yourself."

"I just did. You have no idea. Thank you."

During lunchtime, Art led Rita to the basement where tables were laden with gifts. Everything from Fisher Price eye-balled telephones to a BB gun, and piles of clothes. She chose ice skates for Carol and Kitty, and a Mouse Trap game for Kevin, a Penny Brite doll, in a carrying case, for Teri. Noreen would love the Chatty Cathy doll. For Shawn, a wooden box of miniature tools. She picked out Army-type boots for the boys, to replace their black-buckled leaking jobs. This feeling of not counting pennies was exhilarating.

"How about something for yourself?" Art stopped working to look at Rita.

Rita glanced around the room. "That seems kind of silly. Christmas is for children."

"You deserve a nice Christmas too."

She chose a hand-held Sunbeam mixer, still in its box. Harvest Gold.

Rita held out her hand to touch Art's forearm, "Thanks for your help."

Art looked where she touched his sleeve.

She called out, while heading to her office, "Thanks, Art, and call me Rita."

"Mrs. . . . I mean Rita, would you like to get a cup of coffee one of these days?"

Rita paused. "Oh. I never thought that . . . I don't know, I always have to get right home after work."

"A half-hour? How about one half-hour some afternoon?"

"Um. That's kind of you. I'll let you know."

Her heart pounded her chest as her feet pounded the stairs. Art was asking her on a date. A *date*? All afternoon she was distracted from her work. She decided to have coffee with him the following day to get it over with. She had no time for dating.

Her father dropped off a Christmas tree. The season was getting brighter every day. On December 24, the kids wrapped clay pots and drawings they made for each other and put them under the tree. Rita got everybody organized for the Christmas Eve party.

"Carol and Kitty, get out of the bathroom, and take your curlers with you." Rita hurried them, commenting on their nice hairdos, Carol's flip with bangs, Kitty's red yarn hair band matched her dress.

When they were all gussied up with teeth brushed, and tights and ties on straight, they walked in the winter night around the corner to their grandfather's house.

It was full of light and warmth, unlike its daytime façade. All the aunts, uncles, and cousins were there. Aunts made sure the Leonard children got wrapped baseball cards, books, or fuzzy mittens. Dinner was ham and scalloped potatoes, a green bean casserole, and a foamy red Jell-O mold. Rita's kids went back for seconds and then waited for desserts. Kieran gave each daughter an envelope. Rita thanked her father by kissing his cheek and whispering, "For the tree as well."

The children became reacquainted with same-age cousins. They paired off to play with new toys or eavesdrop on the adults, who got louder, friendlier, and funnier as the night wore on. Grandpa's tree had electric lights that bubbled. Rita stood watching them. Her first Christmas without Bob was different, and she felt unmoored.

"Hey, it's a holiday, little sister." Nancy, regal and commanding, pulled Rita into the kitchen, yelling over her shoulder. "Jack. Can you make me and Rita whiskey sours?"

She gently pushed Rita into a maple chair. "Your hair looks nice. But . . . you seem sad. Everything alright?"

Rita moved onion dip and crackers away, patting her self-styled French twist, glad to talk to an adult. "Actually, I'm feeling better. This Christmas was almost my unraveling. It's hard to do everything by myself. It's so . . . lonely."

Their two other sisters, beautifully dressed and beauty-parlor coiffed, breezed into the kitchen, to deliver the drinks. Mary Alice dropped into an empty seat and took a cigarette from Nancy's pack. Carolyn stood by the sink, arms crossed over her protruding belly, pregnant with her third child.

"Rita says that her life is hard and lonely. I think we all told you that . . . that it would be," Nancy looked concerned. "Didn't we? It's a man's world. None of us is brave enough to leave our husbands . . . even though they can be bastards, we know it's impossible—"

"It's not." Rita ate the maraschino cherry and dabbed the stem on a napkin. Rita was unsteady in her new life, but she did not envy her sisters' marriages, just bits and pieces of having a husband.

Mary Alice asked, "What's 'not'?" She blew a smoke ring away, dipped a cracker into the beige paste, then sipped her drink.

Rita swirled her glass, "It's tremendously difficult, living apart, but . . . not impossible. I need Bob to be consistent with child support money . . . but beyond the bills . . . it's the aloneness that is the worst. I mean, c'mon, no sex?"

"That's what you miss? *The sex*? Ugh, it's like a man sneezes inside of you. Ugh." Nancy raised a glass to her sisters. "Here's to no more sex."

They all clinked and drank.

Carolyn said, "Hear, hear. We all have more kids than we wanted anyway. Screw that."

They sipped more.

"Screw that and screw them." Mary Alice chimed in. The Horan sisters were laughing their Christmas laugh. They had been cheated on, lied to, physically bullied, or hit outright. But this was fun. Nancy came and sat on Rita's chair with her to keep the jokes coming. They were storytelling and over-talking.

Mike came into the kitchen.

"Ladies, what's up?"

"Not you, not tonight," Carolyn said under her breath, and they all sputtered.

"Need anything?" Mike eyeballed their empty glasses. "I'll get refills."

Aunt Rose toddled into the kitchen, beer in hand. "Well, Lord save us, here you all are. The children are running wild, upstairs, and outside, mind you. What are you doing in here?"

"Talking about ses . . . sex." Rita giggled, leaning into Nancy's shoulder.

"Well. My Walter was a fine man in that department." Rose did her closed-mouth laugh, "I know it's wrong to say, but fun to do."

"ROSE." Nancy whooped. "He's been dead for years. How do you remember that?"

"Ah . . . a woman never forgets her first lover," she sipped her beer, "or her third or fourth."

The sisters fell over laughing.

Nancy started to break up the kitchen party. "Hey, it's late, gather your children, ladies. It's 11:30, I've got to get my family to Midnight Mass."

"You do not. You never go to that," Rita challenged her.

"Well, what we do is drive by church *during* the service. I tell the kids to yell an Our Father, belt out "The First Noel" and then we're set to go home and play Santa." Nancy chortled as she went to dump the crusted-over pale white onion dip. "See Rita, this is all that you're missing. Ew."

"Nancy, you are disgusting. But I always liked that about you. And I'm in a much better mood. Go fake your way through church, like you probably do other things."

Rita and her kids walked home at midnight, as they would go to church in the morning. This was too short of a walk to get cold, and Shawn and Noreen skipped as they held Rita's hands. Kitty pointed to glittering stars in a velvet sky, and whispered, "Wow" as Kevin slid on the ice-glazed snow and almost crashed Kitty into a bank. He whirled his arms in time to catch her, "Sorry. Sorry, Kitty. Merry Christmas."

That was sweet of Kevin. He could really be quite kind, Rita thought. They all were when they weren't jockeying for her attention. This family had come far. She looked forward to the new year, with this active, funny, friendly bunch.

Christmas morning, Rita sat on the couch in a bathrobe, with a cup of coffee at her elbow, and opened her father's envelope. There was no money or check, but better, a note: "I *weel* pay your car *insuranse* for the *yeer*, Reeta." She smiled at this gift. Her father was accepting her, helping her, but Kieran still couldn't spell her name.

She watched her children gleefully rip paper from unexpected gifts.

"Ma, how does Santa get in?" Noreen asked. "There's no fireplace."

"Did you see this on TV?" Kevin held the Mouse-Trap game, smiling.

Teri shrieked when she saw Penny Brite, breaking open the doll's carrying case in her excitement.

Shawn was fake-sawing boxes.

Kitty whispered, "How did you know what we wanted, Ma? And how did you pay for it? Where did you hide stuff? You always solve our problems, like magic."

Rita cupped her hand near Kitty's ear. "This year, angels helped me."

51

SKATING

Rita had only weekends to clean their apartment.

It was a sparkly, blue January day.

Kitty draped herself over the back of the couch while Rita dusted the furniture. "Can we go skating? Carol and I want to try our new skates."

"No, I don't have time for skating. Is your bed stripped? Clothes sorted for the laundry? Are rooms dusted, floors swept? Toys put away?"

"Oh, Ma, yes. It's Teri who's the slob. And Noreen. Carol and I are sick of picking up after them."

Rita started pushing the Hoover around their only decent rug. She couldn't hear over this machine but saw Kitty sitting quietly. Sitting quietly was hard for Kitty.

Rita had always used vacuum noise to think. She hadn't been much fun before Christmas, but now was better with her raise, and her sisters' and father's help.

Her children wanted to play with her. Couldn't she scrub the bathroom later? Rita glanced out the windows. The thick frosting of white powder erased the dirt patches and tufts of crabgrass between apartment buildings. The sun shimmered. The raw beauty of the pristine day soared Rita's heart. Nature seconded Kitty's request.

She clicked off the vacuum to turn to Kitty. "Yes."

Kitty lit up. "What? Yes? Yes. I'll tell everyone, and I'll make sure, Ma, that their rooms are ready, even the boys. When, and where will we go?"

Rita became enamored in the freeing possibilities of the glittering day. "Right after lunch, we'll swing by Aunt Rose's to get everyone's skates. I'm thinking of Elizabeth Park."

The children stripped the beds in minutes, toys were put away, laundry sorted. Grilled cheese sandwiches and tomato soup were downed in record time.

"Be careful of the soup. It's hot." Rita knew they'd chance scalded tongues to get outside sooner.

She loved watching her kids skate by, or in Noreen's case, scrape around in tiny circles, on double blades. Shawn, in a snowsuit, held Rita's hand, shuffling along, giggling when either of them was at risk of falling. Shawn fell down, but being little and closer to the ground, he bounced.

"Mommy, whoa, whoa," he tittered.

Rita momentarily mourned the loss of being a housewife, when she played with her children, was spontaneous, knew their feelings, asked about their days.

She snapped back to the moment, because it was a beautiful one. Kevin was whipping around, not with great form, but with great speed. He crashed happily, repeatedly, into snowbanks, or skated crazily under the arched stone bridges that lead to tiny tributaries. Rita heard him challenge his friend Rodney, encouraging chases, zipping by his sisters.

Carol was smooth, could snap around and skate backward. Kitty, more cautious, and Teri, less skilled, scraped along holding each other up and toppling each other down. Kitty retied Teri's dangling laces to firm up her wobbly ankles.

Like any body of water, the pond, its expanse of freedom, its ability to amuse those fast and slow, careful and reckless, created a scene of nature's joy, with children laughing, and not just tolerating the cold air and hard ice, but truly enjoying the wonders of a New England winter.

This was what Rita wanted, her kids loving life, enjoying nature, playing with each other.

Rita waved Carol over, who slashed to a stop, carving a plume of shaved ice. Shawn watched her. "Carol, that is whoa, whoa."

"Shawn. I'll take you for a spin." She airplaned him around, circling back to Rita's feet.

"I'm taking the little kids to the car to warm up," Rita laughed, "we're turning blue. Are you cold?"

"No, we're sweating. Ma, why don't you take them home? You can come back in ... " Carol pointed to her watch, a birthday gift/bribe from Dad, "about two hours?"

Rita blinked at Carol, amazed, then spoke with disbelief, "Really? You'll be okay?"

"Ma, I'm twelve, remember? And there are rink guards here. See that teenage guy with the whistle? He's already called Kevin over twice. Anyway, he's supposed to keep the skaters safe."

"I'll put Shawn in for a nap, then we'll come back. You stay together." Rita carried a tired Shawn and guided a frozen Noreen. Rita didn't feel burdened, or anxious, or rushed, but felt something sweet break free, a teeny, tiny icicle of hope.

At their apartment, Shawn rested with a stuffed bulldog. Rita gave Noreen a teacup of hot cocoa and Saltines with peanut butter. Rita made coffee and pulled the crossword section from the *Courant*. She hadn't finished a puzzle in two years. A favorite song, "Scarlet Ribbons (For Her Hair)," was on the radio. Noreen looked sleepy. Rita pulled Chocolate Girl onto her lap to rest, and she happily juggled coffee, paper, and child.

Her heart and arms were full.

52

STEALING

Kevin longed to be outside on this brilliant March day, but was stuck in school. He scribbled a note to Billy Rhodes, *Hey snotrocket, the brook?* Folded tightly, he lobbed it two desks away as Sister Veronica erased the blackboard.

Billy scrawled something to Kevin, but the wadded note bounced off Kitty's desk, landing near her foot. She smirked at Kevin as she kicked the note out of reach.

Kevin coughed, "Dipshit."

Sister Veronica stacked her books. "All right boys and girls, line up for lunch."

As the students moved forward in their rows, Kevin kicked Kitty's chair over. She dragged her nails across his forearm.

"Everyone except Kathleen and Kevin Leonard, and William Rhodes."

Kitty blushed as their classmates happily whispered the "Oooh, you're in trouble" mantra.

"Oh, and Kevin, please fix your sister's chair." Kevin chucked the note into Steve Langan's desk.

Sister Veronica addressed the three. "All of you could have benefitted from my spelling lesson. I mean, *charity* spelled 'c-h-a-i-r-i-t-e-a', Mr. Rhodes? As if one is at a tea party?"

Billy hung his head, his hair hiding his smile.

"And you, Kevin. What was so important that you hurled missiles at another student?"

Kevin was stumped. "I didn't throw *missals* at anyone. Those are church books, right?"

Sister Veronica surprised Kevin by laughing. "Yes, well, I meant like a rocket, oh, just hand over the note. I'm dying of curiosity."

Kitty stood scratching one palm. "I think the note got kicked out of the room when the kids left," she hurried on, seeing her teacher arch an eyebrow, "Kevin was asking Billy if he was going . . . to . . . to be an Altar Boy . . . 'cause, 'cause, *he* is. I mean, Kevin wants to be an Altar Boy next year."

The nun rocked on her black shoes. "Is that so?"

Kevin was caught. Kitty was *such* a kiss-up. But . . . he could delay the sentence, so he could still get to the brook this day. He could beat up Kitty later.

"Yes." Kevin's tie seemed to tighten around his neck, as he tried to get Billy's attention to join him on the altar. He rubbed his sweaty palms on neatly pressed gray pants. He'd be doomed without a sidekick.

"William? What about you? Your parents would love—"

"Yes, I guess, Sister."

She clapped her hands. "Delightful, gentlemen. I'll be happy to report this to Father Mc Bride. Kathleen, thanks for the keen eye. Now, you all have lunch detention."

Billy, Kitty, and Kevin ate in the classroom, but nobody seemed to mind.

Kevin opened his hard roll sandwich. Inside was lettuce and mustard. He scowled at Kitty. "What's this crap? Did you make this? No meat? No cheese?"

She shrugged. "At least you got big bread. I got two heals."

After school, Billy traded a Coke for a ride on Kevin's bike to the Rhodes' gas station. There he rocked the vending machine, and watched an icy bottle roll out. He did it again, then snapped the caps off with a rusty opener that hung from a hook. He pulled two tiny bags of chips off a rack. They sat outside.

"Kev, you need a better bike, man. That's what, ten years old? A piece of shit."

Kevin punched Billy's arm. "You don't even ride to school. You get dropped off, like a pansy. What've you got?"

Billy snorted, "I *work* here after school. Yeah, well, I've got a Playboy bike, banana seat, monkey handlebars. All us guys do. We jump stumps, pop wheelies. Ride girls around." He double-raised his eyebrows.

"I can't get a bike like that . . . I don't have a . . . " What was he going to say? A dollar? A job? A father?

Billy lowered his voice, "Man, there are ways. We could make one . . . or we could steal one. Or steal the parts to make one. Robbie would help us weld a frame." He gestured toward his brother under a Camaro's hood.

As he rode home, Kevin stopped at the brook to throw rocks and see if crayfish were crawling out of their holes . . . and to think about Billy's suggestions. He took his shoes and socks off and stuffed them in his shirt.

Barefoot, Kevin carried and dragged his bike through the cold rippling brook, and up the craggy cliff. As he re-tied his shoes, Kevin thought about hurling his rusted bucket of bolts over. Instead, he pulled the sticks out of the chain and pushed his bike through the woods toward the streetlight, dusk quickly falling. Across the road, resting in a pool of streetlight, was a black-and-white dog, thumping her tail. Kevin laid his bike on the lawn and sat close. She sniffed him and licked his face once.

"Atta girl, hey there. What are you doing outside, all alone? It's almost nighttime." He patted her head, and she rolled onto her back.

Kevin dug into his pockets. What did he have to share? Two crumbled potato chips were left in the tiny bag. He shook the crumbs onto his hand. The dog nosed it but didn't take any.

"Here, like this, girl." He licked his palm and held out the remainders.

Crumbs were taken gently, and the dog yapped.

A door swung open, silhouetting a girl older than Kevin. She couldn't see them on the slope of the lawn.

"Queenie? Queenie, get in here you dumb mutt, or I'll kick your sorry ass."

Kevin stood up. "She's right here. She's fine. That's her name?"

"My name?" The girl misunderstood. "It's Debbie, and I'll kick your ass too if that dog's not here in two minutes. Come on, Queenie, you mongrel."

Queenie slinked into the house and the door slammed shut. Kevin rode up Exeter Avenue, past his old house. He saw a bunch of lights on and two nice cars in the driveway. This day was getting worse by the minute. He pedaled wearily, shoulders slumped, watching the ground crawl by. Something had to get better.

Soon he was at the Shell Station. He noticed a new machine that sold quarts of milk. Milk. There was never a drop left in anyone's glass or cereal bowl at home.

The gas station was closed, so he knew it was after six o'clock. Ma would be worried.

Kevin walked around the phone-booth-sized machine and rocked it. Nothing. He moved to the front and pushed a black button. Nothing. His anger and frustration made him stronger. He wrapped his arms around the whole thing. Kevin clenched his teeth and balled his fists and demanded all the muscles in his back and arms rock this monster back and forth.

A hearty *plop* let him know his prize was delivered. He did it again. Kevin wrapped the cold cartons in his jacket and rode home fast, single-handedly.

Finally, a win.

It was 6:20. Light spilled out of their apartment when Ma opened the door. He quickly stashed the milk on a stairstep.

"Where have you been? I'm a wreck waiting for you." Ma pulled him in to assess him. "You look alright. Kitty said you were going to the brook after school, but Kevin, this is too late."

Carol came out of her bedroom, cutting him off, "Yeah, yeah, home at last. We're waiting to eat."

Ma unwrapped a plate of doll food, tiny sandwiches with egg salad and tuna fish, speared with tasseled toothpicks. There was nut bread with cream cheese, and a green salad wilted with dressing.

Noreen gagged and Shawn said, "Ew." Kitty pushed shoulders to shut them up.

"What's this? This food?" Kevin hovered over the table. "You gotta be kidding me."

Kitty whispered to him as she settled Noreen. "Aunt Rose promised the Ladies' Luncheon leftovers when Ma gave her a ride this morning. We're out of food. Remember how bad lunch was today?"

Ma was pulling something heavenly from the oven. She set out a foil pan of macaroni and cheese, a leftover miracle, and all the children accepted big glops.

Then Kevin retrieved his prize from the stairs.

"What's that?" Kitty asked, picking a pimento off a crust.

"Ah, duh . . . milk," Kevin offered, "two quarts from a new milk machine, still cold. I figured someone forgot them."

He thought to himself, this white lie was like an alibi. Actually, it took a certain amount of brain power to be a good fibber.

The children dumped their water and held glasses for Kevin to fill with the real thing.

Ma didn't even question him, but asked, "Is that part of why you were late?"

Kevin stopped shoveling food in to explain where he'd been, "I started out by giving Billy a ride to his dad's gas station, then the brook." No one was listening, so he got louder, "I met a dog."

They stopped eating. Ma put her fork down. "We can't have a dog here, Kevin."

"Where?" Shawn asked. "Where did you find a dog?"

Kevin had his audience. "On Trout Brook Drive, after I hauled my bike *through* the water. The dog's name is Queenie, and she licked my face and ate my crumbs, thumping her tail while I patted her head. Then some mean old girl called her names and told me she'd kick her ass and mine, too—"

Rita chirped, "Kevin." She indicated the little kids.

"Well, she did. She was mean to that nice dog. I'm gonna go back tomorrow after school. It's right around the corner from Exeter Avenue. Where we gotta go live." He needed to get back to his friends, this dog, his brook. He was choking in this apartment.

"How was our house?" Kitty asked quietly.

"Sad. It was sad without us. It said, like a ghost, 'Keviiiin, come baaaack.' I think the ghost hates that family with two kids. They don't know how to climb or play or throw toys on the front lawn. I bet the ghost lives in our hatchway. He'd let us throw our bikes around, right, Teri?"

Teri smiled. "Yes."

Carol asked, "Does it look nice? Is the yard better?"

"Better? No, why would it be? But it's ours. All of our trees are still there. Yours, Carol, and mine, and Kitty's. So, when can we? Move back? Ma?"

All heads twirled toward her.

She returned their gazes. "Well, not yet . . . in the fall or winter . . . I've got some bills . . ."

Carol mused, "I miss the intercom, with the radio always on."

"Dancing in the basement." Teri snapped her fingers.

Kitty didn't want to keep pretending only three kids lived here. "Ma? How about you? What do you miss?"

"Well, I won't miss sleeping in the living room."

That evening, Carol came out of the steamy bathroom, with her hair wrapped in a towel, a sweater draped over her ratty pajamas.

Kevin was poking around an old cigar box from her bureau.

"What are you doing in my room? You break everything you touch. Get out." Carol untwirled her towel and brushed her hair, looking around for her curlers.

"Now, now, favorite sister, give me a minute. You looking for these?" He held her bag of curlers. "Noreen was stacking them by color. So, you're welcome. I saved your hairdo." Kevin lay full out on her bed.

"Get up, twerp. Really, what do you want?" Carol stood before her mirror, sectioning off strands to twirl on purple, blue, and green rollers, kept in place with bobby pins, briefly held in her teeth. She swayed to Petula Clark's "Downtown."

"I need your advice. I need stuff. A bike. A dog. A house. Gallons of milk, Cokes. I don't wanna be this poor. It's boring and . . . Ma's word, degrading."

"You need a job," Carol took the pins out to speak. "I started babysitting the neighborhood kids. Ma let me when I turned 12. I had experience with you brats."

She sat on the edge of her bed winding a kerchief around the curlers.

"What can I do? I won't be eleven until May. What job can I get?" Kevin walked to her dresser and picked up her comb, ran a thumb down its teeth to make it sing.

Carol talked to the mirror. "It's spring. Mow lawns. Start with Aunt Rose, and she'll pay you. Collect more bottles at the construction sites. As soon as you can, get a paper route. We're all gonna have to buy our own stuff from now on. Ma's saving every dime to get home."

Kevin eyed her reflection, his elfish grin returning, "You're a genius. I'll help Rodney with his paper route. It's a start."

Carol twisted his arm to spin him around, "Na-uh, punk. Put my watch back."

They laughed. He was caught again. Boy, she was good, he thought. As Kitty walked in for bed, Kevin slipped the watch into her robe pocket, then held up two empty hands. Carol watched the whole reverse pickpocket move.

"Hey, Artful Dodger, go hang out with that Queenie dog."

"If she's outside tomorrow after school, we're gonna go to the brook." Kevin pulled a crumpled napkin from his shirt pocket. "I'm going to reward her with these." He opened it to show three tiny triangular sandwiches of chopped liver, taken from supper.

Carol snickered, shutting their bedroom door. "Gross."

53

FALLING

"I don't know how we can last in that small apartment. I'm telling lies left and right when the landlord asks who these kids are in the yard. I say a friend, their cousins, anything I can think of," Rita confessed to her sister, Nancy, delivering Teri for a sleepover with cousin Cindy. Sipping coffee on Nancy's patio, they watched the girls swinging on a tree limb.

Cindy's clothes, haircut, and self-assurance outshone Teri's whole pasty demeanor, with her poorly fixed tooth. She looked like second best, a runner up. Rita did not give her kids self-confidence, as she didn't have any to give.

"You could accept welfare or get food stamps." Nancy plucked a leaf from a potted plant.

"Uh, let's not have this discussion again. I don't want to tear off stamps at the supermarket that shout, 'Look, I'm poor.' If we take government help, they'll put a lien on our house." She pulled her sweater tighter. "I'll find a way."

Nancy went in for a bag of clothes Cindy had outgrown. Returning, she assessed Rita. "Hey, why don't you Clairol your hair? You're too young to be gray. You could look like that divorcee, Mitzi."

"Oh, that tramp with jet-black hair, at her age? She looks ridiculous, sashaying around with her fat can in tight pants—"

Nancy burst out laughing. "My, my, jealous, are we? Hey, at least she gets dates."

Rita picked fuzz off her sweater. "I had a date."

"What? When? Why don't you tell me these things?"

"It was nothing, really. A guy at work. He asked me out, saying just coffee. I felt guilty getting home a half-hour late."

Cindy ran by, leading Teri, "We're going to dip Oreos in milk."

Rita and Teri shared a bemused glance. Rita's kids didn't *tell* her what they were going to eat, and certainly not cookies before lunch.

"Okay, girls, then go watch the color TV. Have a ball." Nancy always mentioned her latest acquisition.

"I've got to go."

"Oh, no you don't. This is getting good."

"Kevin is supposedly watching Shawn. The girls are—"

"Did you have another date?" Nancy lit a cigarette, cozying in for a long, gossipy discussion.

"No. I mean, yes." Rita waved away the smoke.

"For God's sake. Yes, or no?"

"I told him I can't date now. It wouldn't be fair to anyone. Smothered by poverty, I can't go gallivanting at night. I'm not divorced and won't be any time soon. I have a hostile ex-husband and I can't start—"

"Oh, for the love of Christ," Nancy butt in.

"Art took me and my six children to see *Mary Poppins*. I think the half dozen kids scared him off."

Nancy spewed out smoke, coughing. "That's not a date. You sabotaged it. Six kids, what were you thinking? Rita, Rita, Rita. Someday you'll think of yourself first. Meanwhile, I'll look around for a man for you, some strapping guy, with a lot of money. And he won't be Irish, that's for sure."

Rita laughed. "Don't bother. Or wait ten years, when Shawn's a teenager. I'll be ready by then."

On the drive to the apartment, Rita fleshed out an idea of how to get her family to Exeter Avenue by the fall. Once her children were home, she could relax a little, and have more fun with them. Rita walked into Noreen, Kitty, and Carol dancing to *American Bandstand*. She turned off the TV. "You should be outside. It's a beautiful day, and it's half over."

"Ma," Carol spoke up, "we've been out all morning, kicking a ball around this tacky neighborhood with no playgrounds. We're waiting for the boys to eat lunch. Could you ask us before you turn the TV off?"

"Where are your brothers?" Rita clicked the show back on, begrudgingly, turning to Kitty for an update.

"At the construction site to find bottles," Kitty jumped back to dancing.

Kevin usually wasn't late for a meal. After she turned on the oven and made a SPAM and peaches casserole, Rita called Bob with her idea. "I think the children and I can get back to the house. I have a plan. Can you clear your debts, at least on paper, so I can qualify at the bank to carry the mortgage?"

"Um. You think I keep two sets of books, like a criminal on some detective show? I'm not a gangster, Rita. Besides, both our names are on that deed. You can't do anything about the house without my permission."

She clamped the phone between her chin and shoulder to put lunch in the oven. "Oh, Bob, relax. I'm not trying to cheat you of anything, but you want your children to live in a nice house. I need you to clean up things, like bills on your apartment, or debts leftover from the business. I need some clean slates here. I need more credits than debits. Even if it's temporary."

Bob paused. *"I need?* What about what *I* need? *I need* better visitation rights if we're bargaining."

"Bargaining? Over our kids? Jeez, what happened to the 'let me help you' in your letter?"

Bob gave a low whistle on the phone. "You never stop pushing, do you, Rita? I'll work on debt *consolation* or whatever it's called."

"One more thing. Can you help us move the furniture back? From here and Rose's garage?"

"As to moving you yet again, the answer is no. Do it yourself. I'm sick of kissing your ass."

"Well, I guess you're not the only guy who can help me." She slammed the phone, heart pumping, then quickly prayed that he didn't drive over to choke her.

Kevin had flopped on the lower bunk that morning. "Shawn, you want an adventure? Ma took Teri somewhere. Let's ditch the girls. It's sunny outside."

Shawn looked up from crashing his toy car into the laundry basket. "Yes, where is the *venture*?" He blinked behind tiny glasses.

"At the construction site, the same apartment building. They're putting in stairs and floors. We'll get deposit money from bottles and cans. Good money. Here, throw on this sweatshirt." Kevin zipped Shawn up, then pulled on a holey gray sweater.

At the site, Kevin lifted the loose fence. Shawn crawled under. Kevin tossed a canvas *Hartford Times* newspaper bag over, then monkeyed up the links.

He yelled, "Watch this."

He vaulted from the spiky top, landed in a crouch, and retrieved the bag. Kevin scanned the skeletal building awaiting an outer layer of walls and windows. The guys weren't working on a weekend, but materials were neatly stacked, and machinery squatted all around.

Shawn was three, and Kevin was ten, seven years older. He was responsible for amusing Shawn, but also keeping him safe. Ma expected that.

Kevin raised an eyebrow, and dared, "Run."

His siblings knew Kevin had a challenge in mind when he said "Run."

"Keep going, I'm gaining on ya."

The little guy ran ten steps before his brother lobbed a dirt clod that broke into bits at his shoes. Shawn stopped, scooped some brown nuggets, then returned fire.

"Ya got me." Kevin clutched his heart, falling into a fake death kick. Shawn pelted him with lumps of soil until Kevin lay still. Shawn stood over him, giggling.

Kevin cracked one eye open. "Where's your glasses?"

Shawn squinted, touched his face, feeling for them. "Uh-oh."

Recovering from being dead, Kevin ran back to the spot under the fence. The glasses weren't shattered, just dirty. He rubbed them on his shirt, like he'd seen Ma do.

Shawn put the glasses on, shut his droopy eye, and looked up at his brother to say thanks.

"Ma would freak out. Besides, Dad paid for them. They'd both freak out. Don't lose them."

The building was a highway of boards, bolts, and pipes. Metal beams spanned each level, built to accept flooring, but now held a few criss-crossed wood planks, and platforms for supplies.

Looking at this site, Kevin wondered if he could build something like this one day, and boss people around. When he rode his bike home from school, Kevin watched them work, hooking his fingers through the fence. During their breaks, the guys sat on high beams, eating, dangling their legs, spitting, and whistling at girls passing by. They left wrappers and bottles strewn about and sent lit cigarettes glittering into the mud below. That was the life Kevin wanted.

Kevin and Shawn collected soda cans and bottles into the canvas bag. Shawn pointed to a corner spot at the second level with skids of concrete blocks. "How about up *dere?*"

"Paydirt. Bingo. Red light," Kevin answered, "but the only way is me carrying you piggyback. Can you hold on tight that long?"

"Yup."

Kevin knelt down. "Get on."

Shawn took the familiar perch on Kevin's back, wrapping his skinny arms and legs around Kevin's neck and waist. They crossed from the stairs to the corner on narrow boards.

Shawn looked down over Kevin's shoulder. "Where are all the workers today?"

"I heard the boss yell he wasn't paying for overtime on Saturday."

Kevin heard Shawn whisper in his ear, "Good money."

At the first landing, there was a pack of Twinkies, which they ate. Kevin tossed a gross sandwich into the trees, to Shawn's delight. After gathering more bottles at the next level, Kevin slung the bag across his chest and lifted Shawn on his back for the return trip across the boards.

"Shawn. I gotta take it slower with more glass. Steady." He slid his foot along the second-floor planking. Down below was mud, stacks of lumber, and bales of hay. Pick-up sticks of boards intersected the floor in between. Kevin looked up to keep from wobbling. The bottles clanked and threatened to break with each step.

Shawn mimicked, "Steady. Steady. I'm slipping a little . . . "

Kevin jolted to a stop to hoist him up, but the bag swung around, so he threw one arm out for balance, the other to grab Shawn.

The jarring stop made Shawn lose his grip on Kevin's neck, his fingers clawing for purchase. Sliding down his back in slow motion, Shawn slowly grasped at Kevin's sweater at his waist, the ripped dungarees at his knees, and lost contact at his muddy ankles.

Shawn plunged, yelling, "Aaaahhh!"

Kevin was windmilling his arms to regain balance, one foot in front of the other. His breathing was roaring in his ears, or was that his heartbeat? There was a "Wwhompff."

Kevin's stomach lurched as the bag stopped swinging. He regained his balance and looked down. Shawn's little body had landed below. There was silence amid a small billowing of dust and dirt.

Kevin flung the clattering bag of bottles onto the nearest landing, leapt across the abyss, powered by adrenaline, and pounded down the wooden slats two at a time.

Shawn lay splayed on a platform at the first level, but his glasses had clattered beyond, to the foundation. His pale eyelids were still.

Looking around, panting, Kevin had no saliva in his mouth, but swallowed anyway. Why wasn't there ever anyone to help him? Shawn can't be hurt, he's too little to be hurt.

Kevin edged out on the narrow platform, bent one knee to the board, his other knee at a 90-degree angle. Kevin slid his arms under Shawn's shoulders and butt, stood up wavering, his forearms straining, sweat breaking out on his forehead, while his little brother's head was lolling. There was no room to pivot, so he walked backward with his little brother in his arms. When Kevin could turn around, he did, and carried Shawn gingerly down the rickety steps, and laid him upon hay bales in the basement.

Ma could not handle this, Shawn being hurt or maimed or worse. Not after having lost his twin Kieran.

Kevin needed to *do* something. He listened for breathing but couldn't hear any. He noticed rhythmic bumping on Shawn's translucent temples. He was so fair that Kevin could see tiny blue veins working, so he probably wasn't dead. He stopped himself from vomiting as Shawn's eyes opened wide.

Shawn inhaled magnificently, heroically, seeming to gather all the air that had been walloped out of his lungs, "Ehhhhh-Ehhhhh-Ehhhhh." Then he started to cry. Kevin felt a rush of relief, a giddy, silly happiness.

Shawn wasn't dead, although he was scared and hurt. He was breathing and his eyes were open.

"Thank God. Oh my God." Kevin remembered it was Shawn he needed to comfort, not himself.

"It's all right, it's all right." Kevin crouched, wiped his hand over Shawn's sweaty forehead, patted his dirty corduroy pants, "You're all right. I've got you."

Shawn's eyes were wild, rolling around, looking at his brother for help or answers.

Kevin's eyes started to fill, so he dragged his sweater sleeve over them. "We don't gotta cry, Shawn, cuz we're okay. We are A-OK. You're like Superman. You flew through the air, man."

Shawn took jagged breaths and cried and cried with his eyes closed.

Kevin sat on the hay bale, gathering Shawn onto his lap, waiting for their breathing to calm.

Shawn opened his eyes, cried a few more tears, then rubbed his runny nose with the back of his hand. He pushed away from Kevin and said through trembling lips, "I'm telling Mommy."

Kevin smiled. "Yeah, I think you should, but let me tell her first. I don't want you to get in trouble. I'll get your glasses. And our good bottle money, we'll split the money."

Although his mouth was more a pout than a smile, Shawn said, "Yeah, good money."

Kevin was shaking all over, as he chastised himself. Jesus Christ, that was close. I'm such a dumbass, he's too little.

He went to get Shawn's glasses. They were in the mud, as mangled as Shawn could have been. The little nose pads were missing, one lens was cracked, and a plastic arm was broken.

He picked his way through the boards and beams, back to Shawn.

"You want a piggyback ride home?" Kevin hoped that Shawn wasn't mad at him.

"No. *Dat* would be stupid. You dropped me from up *dere*." He pointed to the spot. "I'm walking *next* to you." He reached out a hand.

Kevin smiled at how smart this kid was, retrieved the bag, and gratefully held Shawn's hand.

Now he just had to face their mother.

54

LANDLORD

The bag of bottles clanked to the floor. Kevin and Shawn were extra dirty. Muddy pants, a rip at Shawn's knee. Their fingernails were rimmed in black.

After coming through the back door, they stood still, something neither ever did.

"What? What happened?" Rita stopped playing Candyland with Noreen.

"I'm . . . I should have . . . not . . . taken better care of . . ." Kevin tripped over his words.

"Spit it out Kevin, for God's sake, what is it?" Rita stood, annoyed at his hesitancy.

"Shawn . . . fell off my piggyback when we were crossing . . . a plank, at the construction site. He fell off and landed one floor down. Got the wind knocked out of him. He wanted to tell you . . . but I wanted to tell you first, cause it's my fault . . . but he's fine. Right, Shawn?"

Rita sank to her knees, gripping his upper arms, running her fingers over Shawn's head and back and neck.

She tried to slow her breathing, "He *fell* one floor? How is he not hurt more?"

Noreen teased, "Uh-oh, Kevin, now you're gonna get it."

Kevin's voice cracked, and he choked back a sob. "He was on my back high up. There was no floor . . . . He slipped off me, like, in slow motion. I lost my balance, and Shawn fell from the second level to the first."

Shawn said, "I'm good. Look." He twirled his hands and picked up one foot at a time.

She placed an open hand on his chest, and nodded her head. "I see."

She stood to turn on Kevin, "Is he?" Rita smacked his arm, a measly, mis-directed hit, her teeth gritted together. "Is he okay, or is he going to have a concussion?"

She flat-palmed the side of his head, not to hurt him, like his father did, but to get his attention.

Rita noticed Kevin didn't duck this time, or deflect her, but took her small slaps full on. He was obviously sad that he hurt his brother, but she wanted to be very clear.

"Shawn could have died."

Kevin's face reddened, and he ran a hand across his wet eyes. "He could have. Died. I'm . . . sorry."

Rita and Kevin locked eyes, a rare solemn moment between them.

Noreen pointed to Shawn. "Did you forget to wear your glasses today?"

"Noreen, go play in the living room. Wait, where are his glasses? Shawn, where are your glasses?"

"Kevin found *dem*, Mommy. Kevin found my glasses two times and I was a little hurt." Shawn was defending Kevin, standing in his dirty and ripped clothes. She could tell he had cried earlier, but now was chipper.

Kevin held out the mangled pair.

Rita pressed them to her heart, then slipped the glasses into her skirt pocket. She lowered her voice to engage Kevin. He couldn't stand still much longer, but he had to know this, to learn this. "You can't . . . we can't. Kevin, we have no room for errors, for mistakes. I could not go on without him." A current of pain crumpled her face, thinking of earlier agony. "I can't lose any more of my children."

Rita rubbed the top of Shawn's head as he hugged her waist. She welled up. "The glasses I can replace, somehow. But when one of you gets hurt, we all take a step backward. It costs money to fix broken bones. If someone is sick or injured, I have to stay home from work. If you can't take care of each other . . .

I can't work. I have to work to keep you all together, Kevin." She squeezed her eyes shut. "Go help him take a bath and call me if you see any bruises."

In the pantry, hating the cracked linoleum countertop, she took down the Bisquick. Back in the kitchen, she wiped tears while making pancake batter, and aimlessly dropped splotches into the hot skillet. Rita's thoughts drifted. The children's accidents, their fights, were beating Rita down again. How dare she make plans for September?

Rita had been brave leaving Nancy's house this morning. *Pfft,* she scoffed, home by fall, a few months away. She thought money was her biggest hurdle. Now, it was keeping her children from killing themselves and each other. She and her children weren't going anywhere soon. Rita could hardly handle the children in this small apartment.

How could she manage a house, with them running loose in it?

"Ma." Kitty broke into Rita's thoughts, "You're burning these pancakes." Kitty softened her voice. "What's wrong?"

Rita turned the burner down. "What isn't wrong?"

"I'll make you a coffee, go sit. And I'll make supper." Kitty guided her to the couch, where Shawn slept soundly.

Rita sifted his flaxen hair.

After the teakettle whistled, Kitty wobbled a black coffee into her mother's hand.

Kitty snapped her fingers at Teri to follow her into the kitchen, where she handed her younger sister seven plates. The feeling in the apartment was unsettling to Teri, like when she had to go stay with Aunt Pat. Kitty usually knew how to fix feelings. Kevin was quiet in his room, Ma was sitting still on the couch, cradling Shawn.

Nothing was right. Fear or danger was hovering near. Teri's stomach was queasy.

"What's going on?" She asked Kitty.

"Set the table. I think Ma is mad at Kevin. He told me he was *guilty* hurting Shawn. Teri, can you make a salad of lettuce, tomato, and cucumber? Then start taking in the laundry off the line."

See, Kitty knew stuff, how to fix things. But this was too much for Teri to remember, never mind do. "How am I supposed to do three things? Where's Carol, why can't she help?"

"She's babysitting next door. Get the laundry first." Kitty was acting like a big boss. At least she could say "please" or "thank you."

Teri moved to their second-floor porch with a basket and stood on a stool to bring in white shirts, underwear, and sheets. Two clothespins fell off into the yard from their clothesline.

Teri opened the back door. "Kitty, help me reel these big sheets in."

Kitty helped Teri, who dropped the last clothespin, which hit the railing and sailed below to bonk someone on the head.

"Ow. Shit. That does it." It was Mr. Santos.

Teri and Kitty burst out laughing and scurried with their load inside.

In two minutes, the landlord was storming the back steps. Now Teri wasn't laughing. He knocked twice.

Kitty pushed Teri forward to open the door. Kitty was a busybody, but also a chicken.

Mr. Santos was a small, dark man, with a neat mustache, and well-ironed clothes. He was scary because he was a man, with some power over Ma.

"*Who* are *you*?" he hissed.

"Teri? I mean, I'm Teri." She started to shiver.

Her mother came slowly into the kitchen. Slow was not Ma's speed. She looked blotchy and small, not at all like herself.

Teri twisted her arms around herself to stop shaking.

Ma could usually protect them from whatever this was, but Ma didn't feel good right now.

"Mr. Santos. Hello. What can we do for you?" Rita unclasped her hands to wave her daughters behind her, ever the wall.

"Who is that one? *Teri,* never heard that name. What about the other skinny one? Rides a bike and is bossy?" He pointed at Kitty, who turned off the burner, but kept her eye on Mr. Santos.

Ma tilted her chin. "That's Kitty."

Kevin came out of his room, calmly saying, "Hello, Mr. Santos."

Santos went on, "I know Carol, because she's the oldest, most polite and babysits. And then there's Shawn who plays with my Charlie sometimes. Sonya likes him. Is that it? Anyone else I should know about?"

Ma went into the living room, then steered Noreen by the shoulders into the kitchen. "This is Noreen. She's quiet."

Teri's eyes went wide. She failed to hide Noreen and Shawn in a closet, her job as a big kid. Her heart thudded guiltily. It was hard to concentrate when her brain was jumping from what she didn't do, to Mr. Santos' anger now.

Mr. Santos yelled, "I don't *really* care what their *names* are, or what they're like. I'm *making a point.* Do you remember how many kids you said you had, Mrs. Leonard? I do. *Three.* Here I count five and one is out. When I asked about all the comings and goings, you said nieces and nephews were sleeping over. So how many children *do* you have?" His neck veins were bulging, and spittle clung to his lower lip.

"Six." Ma spoke quietly.

"*Six. Six?* And where is the traveling salesman husband who signed the lease?"

Ma's head popped up. "I signed the lease, too. We are separated, but he pays child support for food and bills. I'm never late with rent, bringing it to your door the first of the month."

Mr. Santos crossed his arms. "Now I know why, so I didn't see this orphanage full of kids. What did you do with them those times I had to come up?"

Ashamed, Ma glanced at the floor. "They hid in closets."

"Closets." Mr. Santos raised his voice, "You get out, you and your whole tribe needs to clear outta here before the first of June—"

"I have a lease, we are good for a year, until August."

"No ma'am, you don't. It's invalid because you lied about the number of occupants. Your kids rode their bikes through my flower beds, they traipsed mud inside—"

"The number of occupants wasn't on the lease. I read it, all of it. I'm saving money to get our house back. I could be ready by September first."

He squinted. "You have a house? Why in God's name are you here? So, go there. You are formally evicted."

Kitty stomped to the head of the pack, louder than him. "NO, YOU'RE NOT TALKING TO MY MOTHER LIKE THAT—"

Ma warned her, "Kitty, I'll handle this."

She wheeled on her mother. "NO, I WILL. You don't feel good."

Kitty stood tall. "She's smarter than you and nicer than you. Look at this place. Clean. No bugs, no garbage, no broken anything. You know why? Because she fixes stuff. With a screwdriver, this crappy old stove or those windows that slide down and want to chop our heads off. She fixed those ropes."

Mr. Santos surveyed the stove and kitchen windows, then stopped all movement except to ask, "How *old* are you?"

Kitty didn't skip a beat. "Ten. Ma drives to work and cooks and cleans and makes the little kids take a bath. She lets your spoiled brat come play with Shawn 'cause Charlie's lonely. Well, we're not. Not lonely. Don't you dare tell my mother when we're leaving." Kitty snapped her head around. "When do you want to leave Ma?"

Ma licked her lips. "September?"

"Mr. Santos. We'll leave some day in September." Kitty put her hands on her hips.

He knit his brows. There was a light knock on the door. He opened it to Carol. Ma was sitting on a chair, with four kids standing around her. Kevin crossed his arms. Then Kitty, Teri, and Noreen crossed theirs, too. Carol canvassed the assembled mass frozen in the room.

"What did I miss?"

Mr. Santos held the door open a few minutes longer, looking at all the characters.

"Your sister, *Kitty*, renegotiated your lease, so you will be . . . ah . . . allowed to stay through the summer. Good luck . . . I guess . . . but I don't think you need luck." He slipped down the staircase to his apartment.

Ma sat with her fingers cradling her forehead, then covered her eyes.

Teri watched her sisters and brother for a sign, a clue, about what to do.

Ma started to laugh, "Oh my God, Kitty. You have to be a lawyer someday. Oh my God, you were so brave. You saved the day, the whole summer, actually . . . your big mouth, Kitty. I *love* it."

Rita reviewed her children's responses to adversity on this day. Kevin's guilt over Shawn, Teri's worry about not hiding Noreen, Carol's industry, Kitty's bravery.

Weren't these qualities of people, family, taking care of each other?

"You were all wonderful."

55

HERE ARE ALL THE KIDS

S ummer was flying by.

When Rita thought of Exeter Avenue, her heart soared. Storm windows that stayed in their tracks, sheetrocked walls, a telephone on each floor.

And summer was dragging, too.

Her stomach lurched thinking about tenants not moving out, a broken pipe, a missing lawnmower. What if she didn't get her security deposit back on the apartment? Or if Bob continued to be short on child support? Worst ever, what if something happened to her?

Rita had five minutes left driving home from work, so she chose to be optimistic.

They packed up the apartment on the last Saturday of the summer. The kids piled boxes into the kitchen, where Rita labeled them with a Magic Marker.

On Sunday, their older cousins and uncles moved their furniture. That night, the kids and Rita camped out on blankets and pillows on the floor, having an adventure even before the adventure of starting school.

Shawn got into a free Head Start Program.

Noreen was returning to Charter Oak School, and Teri was starting fourth grade at St. Brigid's. She'd gotten a used Bendix bike for her June birthday, in case they had to ride to school a little longer.

On that first day, Kitty couldn't make the sandwiches fast enough. Nervous, she told her siblings what to do.

"Noreen, brush your teeth. Carol, get her a sweater. Teri, your socks are falling down. Kevin, fix Shawn's shoes, they're on the wrong feet."

"Whose feet do you want them on?" Kevin thought he was so funny.

Carol and Kitty said in tandem: "Shut up."

Rita took time off for the move.

That Monday, she tied her shoelaces tight, having no time for them to untie. "Listen, big kids, here's the plan. You ride your bikes to St. Brigid's. Little kids, I'll drive you today. Meanwhile, Mrs. Malm and I will get the house ready. Once I hear from the bank, I'll call the schools after lunchtime to say if we can move home today. I'll get Noreen and Shawn around three o'clock. If something goes wrong, we'll meet here, at the apartment, around four o'clock, and try again tomorrow."

Rita drove to Exeter Avenue with freshly ironed curtains, buckets with rags, and a light heart. Eleanor was waiting. The two friends cleaned bathrooms and washed floors. At noon, they ate sandwiches on Rita's long-stored plates.

At 12:20, Rita checked her watch, wiped her brow, and called the bank to check if the liens were satisfied, the taxes paid, the mortgage intact. Her eyes misted and she swallowed, twisting her friend's arm, yelling, "I got it!"

Resuming work, singing, Rita hung curtains.

Nearby in the front hall, Eleanor swept broken glass, and looked up to see a pane missing from the small chandelier. She picked up the pieces. It was a lightly etched lily of the valley. The stalk, leaves, and bells of the plant were broken apart.

Eleanor looked aghast. "Oh, only three panes are intact. One gone forever. Tragic. This is such a tragedy."

Rita carefully took the pieces from her friend's palm to drop into the dust-pan. "No, Eleanor, *this* is *not* a tragedy."

Eleanor whispered, "Let me get out of here. You make your calls and greet your children on your own. Welcome home, my friend."

Teri watched the clock from noon on. Tick. Tock. Tick. It was hard to concentrate during History. Sister Agnes took a phone call at 2 p.m. The rock in Teri's stomach grew into a bowling ball and she prayed not to barf.

The teacher chose Jimmy Beattie to read aloud. She stopped at Teri's desk, to whisper, "Your mother called. You may go home today."

Teri covered her eyes, trying not to cry. The nun rubbed her back a minute, then moved on. The bowling ball started to melt, and she could breathe. Her classroom was across the hall from the twins'.

Teri heard Kevin whoop and Kitty cheer as their classmates clapped. They were going home.

The three o'clock bell rang, and kids streamed across the blacktop to the bike rack. Kevin's new best friend, Queenie, was waiting for him. He rewarded her with a piece of saved ham.

Kitty questioned, "Whose dog?"

"Mine," he smirked, "right, girl? She can go home at night, but during the day, she's mine, exploring the wildlife of the brook." Kevin pulled his recently welded bike from the rack. It was a frame he found at the dump, a stolen banana seat, and "borrowed" handlebars: a Playboy bike, oh yeah.

Carol called out, "Because we're going home, this bazooka of a bike is going off the cliff into the brook, today. I'll walk to school the rest of my life but, Holy Jesus," she quickly looked around the Catholic school, "today, I'm free."

Kitty elbowed Teri, "Let's go tell the McGill twins we can walk with them tomorrow."

"You go ahead." Teri was eager to get home, to see if their house was real. She rode fast on sidewalks, turning onto Exeter, pedaling up the driveway and onto the grass. Without Dad here bossing her around, she dropped the bike on the lawn, skipped to the back steps and peered in the window. Their table and chairs. Their curtains. A coffee cup she knew.

A warm spark caused her to smile because Ma made this happen.

Ma had gotten them home, so Teri would not float away. With two hands on the brown wood, she kissed the side of their home, then waited for Kitty or Kevin or Carol to go in with her. It was too scary, and special, to do alone.

Kitty came first, also throwing her bike down. "Yay. Come on."

She flung the door open, then pushed Teri through. Kitty always made Teri go first these days.

The sisters stood in the kitchen. All their stuff was there, except for one chair at the head of the table.

Kitty and Teri looked out to see Kevin pedal up the driveway, riding Carol on the banana seat, with Queenie running beside them.

Kevin tore into the house.

They ran around, poking into rooms, with the dog yapping and sliding on the slick linoleum.

When Teri got to her room, she flopped onto the unmade bed, and gave Kitty a cheerful, "Mootchi Gatchi Gu!" They checked the attic, the basement, and the circuitous route of kitchen-to-hall-to-den-to-living room.

Carol switched buttons on the intercom to carry her voice throughout the house, "Carol, Kevin, Kitty, Teri, Noreen, and Shawn, time to get up. And get that dog out of the house, Kevin, before Ma gets here."

That evening, after supper, boxes and bags were thrown into the right rooms. Rita supervised making up the beds, and dismissed the little ones to the living room.

Shawn pushed his glasses up his nose. "Where's that?"

Carol unfurled a sheet and let it drift down before making crisp hospital corners, "The empty room, Shawn. The living room has no furniture, *and* we are not allowed in it, which makes no sense."

Ma laughed. "Um, yes, there is—my desk—and I want to keep that room special. If we ever get a new couch or a—"

"New TV?" Kevin hung out of his room.

"Probably not that. We'll meet downstairs. Go call us on the intercom."

Kevin started, "Testing-one-two-testing. This is *an* air raid. Take shelter in the emptiest room at twenty hundred. Big meeting for losers, meatballs, and pee-pee heads, aka bedwetters. If the Russians come, put your head between your knees to kiss—"

Rita said one word: "Kevin!"

He signed off and ambled to the gathering, where Noreen and Shawn were doing somersaults. Kevin upstaged them by walking on his hands from the hall to the fireplace.

More kids filed into the room and sat in a circle. A brass lamp gave a warm glow from atop Rita's desk. She noticed a praying mantis clung to the sheer curtain at the window, pivoting its eyes at these new people.

When Rita cleared her throat, Kitty knelt up, "Ssh. Ssh. Ma wants to speak."

"This is going to be hard . . . we can't really afford to be here. But we've managed to get back home."

The children clapped.

"We have freedom here but have to be careful. It's our biggest asset." She noticed puzzled children and went on, "It's the most valuable thing we have. We have to keep it clean, not rip wallpaper or scratch floors. No leaving lights on. We can't afford that. No leaving outside doors open."

She pointed to the thermostat, "Nobody touches that but me."

Someone groaned.

Teri asked, "What if it's too cold in here?"

"Bundle up. Wear a sweater. We can cut corners by you doing your part. Don't take food without asking me and eat all of the food I give you."

"Hogan's Heroes ate better," Kevin mumbled, "Yes, sir, my commandant."

Teri shot him a look, then saw the praying mantis, and tiptoed to the window. "This is good luck."

Kevin examined the roving eyes, the jointed forearms, "Good luck? They're creeps. The females kill their mates after sex."

Rita trilled a laugh. "They probably deserve it." Shawn crawled into her lap. "The Greeks believed the mantis could show you the way home. We *are* lucky to be home. Alright, Noreen and Shawn, let's get you to bed, big kids you can watch TV in the den."

She tucked in the little kids with their favorite songs. She could hear her older children, one floor below, still scrambling for seats and attention. Rita walked to her bedroom to make up the brass bed, using the long-stored wedding ring quilt, which had kept its beauty but lost its meaning.

Looking out her window, she noticed a truck at the end of Exeter Avenue. A hatted silhouette sat inside, a cigarette glowing occasionally. Rita took a quick breath. Why was he here? She stood back from the window, to watch. After his refusal to help them, she thought he didn't want any part of this move.

She asked her family for help, had gone to the bank alone, and phoned all the schools. Rita was too busy all day to think of Bob. What did he want? She mentally confirmed locking all the doors. Did he think he should come in? That was the last thing she wanted. To badger her or the children? Or worse, show his anger, hit her? There was no landlord downstairs, no tenant above.

It was just her and the children. She thought back to when he broke in, smashing the door. Rita eyed the telephone on her dresser, connected the day before. Rita could call the police. They could hide in the basement or drive away in her car.

No. No, damn it. This was her home. She kicked him out to protect their children. After that, he had spiraled downward, losing his business, his job, his dreams. Bob had ruined his life with alcohol, now living in one room and driving a taxi, because he couldn't or wouldn't get help. He had ruined vacations and picnics and pets and relationships and their love and, almost, their kids.

Rita turned off the lamp, then pulled down the shades. She leaned into the wallpaper, her balled fists gently bounced against her thighs, fear changing to resolve.

She crept down the stairs and out the door, her bare feet on the dewy lawn, avoiding the driveway.

He couldn't miss seeing her approach under the streetlight.

"What do you want, Bob?"

He chuckled and rubbed his chin as if this was some pleasant exchange. "Look at you, out in bare feet. W-What would the neighbors-s think?"

"As if I give two shits what the neighbors think anymore. What are you doing here?" Her jaw was set.

Bob slurred, "I just wanted to s-see, if you got s-settled into our . . . house."

Rita saw the pint bottle in a paper bag that was half-hidden between his legs. "No. No help necessary. I can do this alone." Rita nodded toward the house. "But I'm not alone. I have six children with me. We're home now, Bob, in *my* house."

Bob ran his hands along the arc of his steering wheel. "I don't . . . doubt it. I didn't come to offer help. I came to *apologize*. I never meant to hurt you or ours-s."

"You're drunk."

He lifted two shaking hands. "Working on it. I can't stop, Rita," he whispered. "I s-sold my soul and abandoned my God. I never meant to hurt you."

"I can't help you anymore, Bob. I tried. I really tried."

God. Damn. She wished he had tried and succeeded.

Bob gave a small smile. "I know. I *member* . . . How shy you were when we met. I *blieved* in you even then. And I think you toler . . . tolerated me . . . all these years because of our love . . . now broken in a thousand pieces, which is multiplied by s-six."

Rita didn't want to smile, didn't want to cry. She looked up and down Exeter Avenue. "I've got to go."

Bob sat straighter. "Wait. I just gotta tell you. You . . . your courage is like a *wind* . . . *storm* on the horizon, a lioness, so fierce, to raise our children."

Rita hoped one day to stop loving him. She stepped back from his truck. "You go home, Bob."

He pointed to 23 Exeter Avenue. "You go home, too, Rita."

As he drove off, Rita had about 40 steps to make it back inside, to wipe her eyes, to slow her heart, and breathe normally.

She pulled bills from the mailbox, her alibi for being outside.

"Hey, big kids, I bought ice cream to celebrate coming home."

The four of them were off the couch like cannon blasts. Rita thought of the youngest two. They hadn't known the bad Bob, although Shawn and Noreen lived through the fallout of his addictions.

Maybe when they were older, Bob would be a better person, a better man.

How did Rita think they were all going to make it? How would her children stay true to each other, help the underdog, contribute to society, embrace nature, become good people? Who would make that happen?

The answer was the same one that she had given Father McBride a few years back when he had asked who would guide her children.

I will. I will.

EPILOGUE

My dining room has three walls of windows. In one corner is the antique desk my father gave my mother 60 years ago. On it are pictures of my mother, my sisters, my brothers and me. I type at my cluttered table, using two or three notebooks at a time, and none is devoted to one task, topic, or idea. I must edit sentences for my book. The doctors' appointments are waiting to be posted on my wall calendar. Theaters and their show times are scribbled on mailing lists.

I am about to have my first book published, and I am getting overwhelmed by all that I have to do.

Over my neighbor's yard, I saw a bald eagle flying with some small mammal in its talons. It was plowing right toward my biggest window, so I jumped up and out of its way. It lifted up like a jet on a short runway, so I hustled to my back deck, hoping it had landed on my roof. The eagle was gone. I mentioned this to my friend Jimmy Beattie.

He said it was my mother's spirit animal, trying to get in touch. "Look it up," Jim said, "and see what she is trying to tell you."

Bald eagles are symbols of strength, courage, and freedom. They are fierce birds that can overcome any challenge. Other words used to describe these majestic animals include focus, tenacity, and embracing new beginnings.

I have been writing for four years about my mother's difficult split from my father, to keep their six children safe from his addictions that led to his violence. The poverty, loneliness, and grief that tortured her made her stronger.

And yes, my book will be completed soon. No, not soon. Today.

Thanks for flying by, Ma.

ACKNOWLEDGEMENTS

Thank you to Rita Horan Leonard who never made excuses. She maybe told lies, but not excuses.

These stories poured out of me because of my siblings' retellings. Today these funny, active, sensitive people are my good friends: Carol Parker, Kevin Leonard, Kitty Langan, Noreen Leonard, Shawn Leonard, and the one who couldn't stay, Kieran Leonard.

I want to thank kind educators Miss Rosetta and Principal Foley of Charter Oak School; Sister Agnes at St. Brigid's School; Mrs. Stanton at Talcott Junior High, and Ms. Frappier at Conard High School, who loved books, art, and writing as much as I. Thank you, Whiting Lane Book Club for your hearty encouragement.

To my beta readers who got handed phone books, which they whittled down by finding errors, redundancy, and nonsense, thank you. Kitty and Jeannie Leonard, Cheryl Duey, Mary-Ellen Beattie, Rachel Michaud, Melissa Thom, and Lora Ashcraft.

My historians were my aunts, Carol "Carolyn" Sinon, Alicia Von Schomberg, and my cousins Bill and Deb. My great Aunt Rose was our extended family's protector, humorist, and Irish cultural icon for three generations.

I started writing these essays under the guidance of my first coach, the lovely C. Flanagin Flynn, who passed away during the COVID-19 epidemic. In her honor, two of my classmates, Jes Wardwell and Char Wilkins, and I meet every month to jam our words in a wringer-washing machine to churn out better stuff. Suzy Vadori stepped in as my super stellar second coach.

I especially want to thank all the families who took six sad children under wing. The Sinons, Klunes, Malms, Zambrellos, Leahys; and the out-of-towners: (East Hartford) Leonards, McKeons, Davises, and Davins, who ended up with three extra kids, and a cool pool.

To Elizabeth Hill, my coach and publisher, and the whole team at Green Heart Living Press. You make me breathe better making this book a reality.

My two powerful, precious daughters, Shawna Kitzman and Ashley Rigby, gave me writing advice, and unwavering love. Thank you, Jeff Rigby, my technical guru, and David Kitzman, my well-read grammarian. My five beautiful grandchildren, Edie, Colette, Emmeline, Julian, and Miles, always ask me to tell them my stories. I'm so blessed.

Writing at the antique desk my father gave my mother half a century ago, and reading his letters, made me understand his struggles a little better. Thanks, Dad, especially for the six other people you helped create.

The people of my youth in Elmwood celebrated wins and mourned losses together. I hold fond memories of our always-outside-unsupervised-times.

To Gary, the love of my life, I read so little of this book to you, because I knew you'd cry. Love you.

Mootchie Gotchi Goo.

ABOUT THE AUTHOR

Teri Leonard Michaud is an author and teacher. After 30 years of teaching reading, she has retired to intermittently flip houses and camp across the country with her husband. Teri wrote for School House Rock (Grammar Rock CD), Jump Start Learning (Explorers CD), *The West Hartford News* and *CT Working Moms*. She was awarded a 2023 Josie Rubio Scholarship for her micro fiction, "Hitchhikers" from Gotham Writers Workshop in New York City. She has hosted author talks in her home to help raise funds for relocating refugees. Teri, a third-generation West Hartford, Connecticut resident, enjoys writing with her dog lying at her feet, hanging around the Mark Twain House, and driving her five grandchildren to sports and music lessons. This is her first book.

Made in United States
North Haven, CT
15 September 2024

57466090R00189